HIDDEN MICKEYS

And Hidden Surprises

A Field Guide to

Walt Disney World®'s

Best Kept Secrets

10th Edition

• • • • • • • • • • • • • • •

Steven M. Barrett

SMBBooks, Inc.

Hidden Mickeys
A Field Guide to Walt Disney World®'s Best Kept Secrets
10th edition

by Steven M. Barrett

Published by
SMBBooks
7025 CR 46A, Suite 1071
Lake Mary, FL 32746
www.HiddenMickeyGuy.com

Copyright ©2022 by Steven M. Barrett
Tenth Edition
Printed in the U.S.A.
Cover design by Foster & Foster
Interior Design by Starving Artist Design Studio
Maps by Kevin C. Riley - Updated
Library of Congress Control Number: 2019917110
ISBN-13: 978-1-7342652-3-1

All rights reserved. No part of this book may be reproduced or transmitted in any form or by any means, electronic or mechanical, including photocopying, recording, or by any information storage and retrieval system, without the express written permission of the publisher, except for the inclusion of brief quotations in a review.

Trademarks, Etc. · · · · · · · ·

This book makes reference to various Disney copyrighted characters, trademarks, marks, and registered marks owned by The Walt Disney Company and Disney Enterprises, Inc.

All references to these properties, and to The Twilight Zone®, a registered trademark of CBS, Inc., are made solely for editorial purposes. Neither the author nor the publisher makes any commercial claim to their use, and neither is affiliated with either The Walt Disney Company or CBS, Inc. in any way.

Also by Steven M. Barrett

Disneyland's Hidden Mickeys:
A Field Guide to *Disneyland*® *Resort's Best Kept Secrets*

Hidden Mickeys Go To Sea:
A Field Guide to the *Disney Cruise Line*®*'s Best Kept Secrets*

Hidden Mickeys books also available as ebooks (with links to *YouTube* Hidden Mickeys videos)
www.Amazon.com

Author Steven M. Barrett paid his first visit to Walt Disney World in the late 1980s after attending a conference in Orlando. He immediately fell under its spell, visiting it twice yearly with family and friends for the next several years, offering touring advice to the less initiated, and reading almost everything written about the WDW theme parks. Barrett relocated to the Orlando area from Houston, Texas and began visiting the WDW parks every chance he got to enjoy the attractions, sample the restaurants, escort visiting friends and relatives, and find Hidden Mickeys! Over the years, he accumulated an extensive file of Hidden Mickey sightings which he organized into the Hidden Mickeys Field Guides to Walt Disney World, Disneyland, and the Disney Cruise Line. The books are organized as Hidden Mickey scavenger hunts arranged to help you spend the least possible time waiting in line as you hunt for the elusive Mouse.

Note: Since Mickey reserves the right to come and go as he—and Disney—pleases, these guides require periodic updates. You hold in your hand the Tenth Edition of *Hidden Mickeys: A Field Guide to Walt Disney World®'s Best Kept Secrets,* updated to include all the latest Mickey sightings all over Walt Disney World. Enjoy your hunts!

Dedication · · · · · · · · · · · ·

I dedicate this book to my wife Vickie and our son Steven, who willingly accompanied me on countless research visits to Walt Disney World and added invaluable insight to this book. Furthermore, updating this book would not be possible without the contributions of many wonderful Hidden Mickey fans I've met through my website and in the Disney parks.

*Thank You, My Fellow
Hidden Mickey Hunters*

Scores of dedicated Mickey sleuths have helped me find the elusive Mouse in WDW. Thanks to each and every one of you. You'll find your names in the Acknowledgements section.

* * * *

*Finding Mickey
Without Scavenger Hunting*

Want to look for Hidden Mickeys in an attraction, restaurant, shop, or resort without scavenger hunting? Turn to the Index! If Mickey is hiding there, the Index will direct you to the page(s) with the appropriate Clues. If the venue isn't listed, Mickey isn't hiding there. Or if he is, I haven't found him yet.

* * * *

Hidden Mickeys Are Elusive

New Hidden Mickeys appear from time to time, and old ones may disappear (see page 18, the paragraph above "My Selection Process"). So, if you can't find a Mickey—or if you're looking for just a few more—be sure to check out our website:

www.HiddenMickeyGuy.com

And our social media: "hiddenmickeyguy" on Twitter, Instagram, and YouTube - and "Hidden Mickey Guy" on Facebook.

Table of Contents · · · · ·

Read This First!	10
1. Hidden Mickey Mania	11
2. Magic Kingdom Scavenger Hunt	21
Hints begin	49
3. Epcot Scavenger Hunt	81
Hints begin	101
4. Disney's Hollywood Studios Scav. Hunt	123
Hints begin	145
5. Disney's Animal Kingdom Scav. Hunt	169
Hints begin	189
6. WDW Resort Hotel Scavenger Hunt	211
Hints begin	245
7. Hither, Thither & Yon Scavenger Hunt	281
(WDW Water Parks, Disney Springs & Beyond)	
Hints begin	295
8. Other Mickey Appearances	307
9. My Favorite Hidden Mickeys	309
My Top Ten	309
Ten Honorable Mentions	311
10. Don't Stop Now!	313
Acknowledgements	314
Index to Mickey's Hiding Places	328

Maps

Magic Kingdom®	22
Epcot	82
Disney's Hollywood Studios®	124
Disney's Animal Kingdom®	170
Walt Disney World® Resort	212, 282

Tip: To find a specific attraction, restaurant, shop, or resort, turn to the Index, page 328.

Read This First!

My guess is that you have visited Disney World before, perhaps many times. But if I've guessed wrong, and this is your first visit, then this note is for you.

Searching for Hidden Mickeys is lots of fun. But it's not a substitute for letting the magic of Disney sweep over you as you experience Walt Disney World (WDW) for the first time. For one thing, the scavenger hunts I present in this book do not include all the attractions in WDW. That's because some of them don't have Hidden Mickeys! For another, this book doesn't cover many things the first-time visitor should know and do to make that first trip to Disney World as magical as possible.

That doesn't mean you can't search for Hidden Mickeys, too. Just follow the suggestions in Chapter One of this book for "Finding Hidden Mickeys Without Scavenger Hunting." **Take note: the newest Hidden Mickeys are underlined in the book!**

Chapter 1

Hidden Mickey Mania

• • • • • •

Have you ever marveled at a "Hidden Mickey"? People in the know often shout with glee when they recognize one. Some folks are so involved with discovering them that Hidden Mickeys can be visualized where none actually exist. These outbreaks of Hidden Mickey mania are confusing to the unenlightened. So, let's get enlightened!

Here's the definition of an official Hidden Mickey: a partial or complete image of Mickey Mouse that has been hidden by Disney's Imagineers and artists in the designs of Disney attractions, hotels, restaurants, and other areas. These images are designed to blend into their surroundings. Sharp-eyed visitors have the fun of finding them.

The practice probably started as an inside joke among the Imagineers (the designers and builders of Disney attractions). According to Disney guru Jim Hill (JimHillMedia.com), Hidden Mickeys originated in the late 1970s or early 1980s, when Disney management wanted to restrict Disney characters like Mickey and Minnie to the Magic Kingdom. The Imagineers designing Epcot couldn't resist slipping Mickey into the new park, and thus "Hidden Mickeys" were born. Guests and "Cast Members" (Disney employees) started spotting them, and the concept took on a life of its own. Today, Hidden Mickeys are anticipated in any new construction at Walt Disney World, and Hidden Mickey fans can't wait to find them.

Walt Disney World's Hidden Mickeys

Hidden Mickeys come in all sizes and many forms. The most common is an outline of Mickey's head formed by three intersecting circles, one for Mickey's round head and two for his round ears. Among Hidden Mickey fans, this image is known as the "classic" Hidden Mickey, a term I will adopt in this book. Other Hidden Mickeys include a side or oblique (usually three-quarter) profile of Mickey's face and head, a side profile of his entire body, a full-length silhouette of his body seen from the front, a detailed picture of his face or body, or a three-dimensional Mickey Mouse. Sometimes just his gloves, handprints, shoes, or ears appear. Even his name or initials in unusual places may qualify as a Hidden Mickey.

And it's not just Mickeys that are hidden. The term "Hidden Mickey" also applies to hidden images of other popular characters. There are Hidden Minnies, Hidden Donald Ducks, Hidden Goofys, and other Hidden Characters in Disney World, and I include many of them in this book.

The sport of finding Hidden Mickeys has caught on and adds even more interest to an already fun-filled Walt Disney World vacation. This book is your "field guide" to more than 1,130 Hidden Mickeys in WDW. To add to the fun, instead of just describing them, I've organized them into six scavenger hunts, one for each of the major theme parks, one for the Walt Disney World Resort hotels, and one for all the rest of WDW: the water parks, Disney Springs, and beyond. The hunts are designed for maximum efficiency so that you can spend your time looking for Mickeys rather than cooling your heels in lines. Follow the Clues and you will find the best Hidden Mickeys WDW has to offer. If you have trouble spotting a particular Hidden Mickey (some are extraordinarily well-camouflaged!), you can turn to the Hints at the end of each scavenger hunt for a fuller description.

Chapter 1: Hidden Mickey Mania

Scavenger Hunting for Hidden Mickeys

To have the most fun and find the most Mickeys, follow these tips:

*
   If you want to spend the extra cash (usually $15.00 or more), use the current version of *Disney Genie+* and/or *Individual Lightning Lane* (you'll pay a separate cost for each one) to enter your chosen attraction's Lightning Lane and accelerate your hunts in the parks. You can access these extra services on the *My Disney Experience* app on your smart phone. On certain attractions, however, Hidden Mickeys can only be seen from the Standby (regular) queue. You'll miss them if you take the Lightning Lane route. Therefore, to speed up your hunts even more (if you choose to spend the money), I recommend reserving Lightning Lane (by purchasing the current version of *Disney Genie+* and/or *Individual Lightning Lane*) for the following:

- At Magic Kingdom: *Splash Mountain, Peter Pan's Flight, Ariel's Grotto,* and *Princess Fairytale Hall (left-side queue).*

- At Epcot: *Soarin' Around the World, Living with the Land,* and *Spaceship Earth.*

- At Disney's Hollywood Studios: *Voyage of The Little Mermaid, Disney Junior Play & Dance,* and *Fantasmic!*

- At Disney's Animal Kingdom: *Kilimanjaro Safaris, DINOSAUR,* and *Festival of the Lion King.*

If you don't opt for the Lightning Lane options, try to line up for headliner attractions during Early Entry or right after park opening.

*
   Arrive early for the theme park hunts, say 30 minutes before opening time (either opening time for Early Entry - if you qual-

ify - or "official" opening time). Pick up a Guidemap (and, if available, a Times Guide) and plot your course. Then look for Hidden Mickeys in the waiting area while you wait for the rope to drop. You'll find the Clues for those areas by checking the *Index to Mickey's Hiding Places* in the back of this book. Look under "Entrance areas." If you arrive later in the day, skip down a few Clues to try to stay ahead of the crowds.

*
"Clues" and "Hints"
Clues under each attraction will guide you to the Hidden Mickey(s). If you have trouble spotting them, you can turn to the Hints at the end of the hunt for a fuller description. The Clues and Hints are numbered consecutively, that is, Hint 1 goes with Clue 1, so it's easy to find the right Hint if you need it. In some cases (*Test Track* in Epcot is a good example), you may have to ride the attraction more than once to find all the Hidden Mickeys.

*
Scoring
All Hidden Mickeys are fun to find, but some are easier to spot than others. I assign point values to Hidden Mickeys, identifying them as easy to find (a value of 1 point) up to difficult to find the first time (5 points). I also consider the complexity and uniqueness of the image: the more complex or unique the Hidden Mickey, the higher the point value. For example, the brilliantly camouflaged Mickey hiding in The Garden Grill Restaurant mural at Epcot is a five-pointer.

*
Playing the game
You can hunt solo or with others, competitively or just for fun. There's room to tally your score in the guide. Families with young children may want to focus on one- and two-point Mickeys that the little ones will have no trouble spotting. (Of course, little ones tend to be sharp-eyed, so they may spot familiar shapes before you do in some of the more complex patterns.) Or you may want to split your party into teams and see who can

Chapter 1: Hidden Mickey Mania

rack up the most points (in which case, you'll probably want to have a Field Guide for each team).

Of course, you don't have to play the game at all. You can simply look for Hidden Mickeys in attractions as you come to them (see "Finding Hidden Mickeys Without Scavenger Hunting" below).

*
Following the Clues
The hunts often call for crisscrossing the parks. This may seem illogical at first, but trust me, it will tend to keep you ahead of the crowds. Besides, it adds to the fun of the hunt and, if you're playing competitively, keeps everyone on their toes. Warning: Many Hidden Mickeys are waiting to be found in the Disney Parks, and depending on the crowds and the park hours when you visit, you may not be able to complete the Scavenger Hunt in one day!

*
Waiting in line
Try not to waste time in lines. If the wait is longer than 20 minutes, consider the option of using the *My Disney Experience* app to purchase the current version of *Disney Genie+* and/or *Individual Lightning Lane* (you'll pay a separate cost for each one) to enter your chosen attraction's Lightning Lane at a later time, and then move on to the next attraction. The lines at popular attractions should not be too long if you start your scavenger hunt when the park opens and follow the hunt Clues as given. If you do encounter long lines, you can come back to the attraction later during a parade or in the hour before the park closes, or use the Single Rider queue if available (check your Guidemap for a big "S" symbol next to the attraction, or ask a Cast Member).

*
Playing fair
Be considerate of other guests. Many Hidden Mickeys are in restaurants and shops. Ask a Cast Member's permission before searching inside sit-down restaurants and avoid the

busy mealtime hours unless you are one of the diners. Tell the Cast Members and other guests who see you looking around what you're up to, so they can share in the fun. (Note: Some restaurants, such as the Coral Reef, do not welcome drop-in Hidden Mickey Hunters. I don't include these restaurants in the Hunts.)

Finding Hidden Mickeys Without Scavenger Hunting

If scavenger hunts don't appeal to you, you don't have to use them. You can find Hidden Mickeys in the specific rides and other attractions you visit by using the *Index to Mickey's Hiding Places* in the back of this book. To find Hidden Mickeys in the attraction, restaurant, hotel, or shop you are visiting, simply turn to the *Index,* locate the appropriate page, and follow the Clue(s) to find the Hidden Mickey(s).

Caution: You won't find every WDW attraction, restaurant, hotel, or shop in the Index. Only those with confirmed Hidden Mickeys are included in this guide.

Hidden Mickeys, "Gray Zone" Mickeys, Wishful Thinking

The classic (three-circle) Mickeys are the most controversial, for good reason. Much debate surrounds the gathering of circular forms throughout Walt Disney World. The sideways classic Mickey made of blue bubbles on the *Living with the Land* entrance-queue wall mural (Clue 90 in the Epcot Scavenger Hunt) is surely the work of a clever artist. However, three-circle configurations occur spontaneously in art and nature, as in collections of grapes, tomatoes, pumpkins, bubbles, oranges, cannonballs, and the like. Unlike the bubbles Hidden Mickey in Epcot, it may be difficult to attribute a random "classic Mickey" configuration of circles to a deliberate Imagineer design.

Chapter 1: Hidden Mickey Mania

So which groupings of three circles qualify as Hidden Mickeys as opposed to wishful thinking? (Keep in mind that no master list of actual or "Imagineer-approved" Hidden Mickeys exists). Purists demand that a true classic Hidden Mickey should have proper proportions and positioning. The round head must be larger than the ear circles (so that three equal circles in the proper alignment would not qualify as a Hidden Mickey). The head and ears must be touching and in perfect position for Mickey's head and ears.

On the other hand, Disney's mantra is: "If the guest thinks it's a Hidden Mickey, then by golly it is one!" Of course, I appreciate Disney's respect for their guests' opinions. However, when the subject is Hidden Mickeys, let's apply some guidelines. My own criteria are looser than the purists' but stricter than the "anything goes" Disney approach. I prefer to use a few sensible guidelines.

To be classified as a real classic Hidden Mickey, the three circles should satisfy the following criteria:

1. Purposeful (sometimes you can sense that the circles were placed on purpose).

2. Proportionate sizes (head larger than the ears and somewhat proportionate to the ears).

3. Round or at least "roundish."

4. The ears don't touch each other, and the ears are above the head (not beside the head).

5. The head and ears touch or are close to touching.

6. The grouping of circles is exceptional or unique in appearance.

7. The circles are hidden or somewhat hidden and not obviously intended to be part of the decor.

Having spelled out some ground rules, allow me to now bend the rules in one instance. Some Hidden Mickeys are sentimental favorites with Disney fans, even though they may actually represent "wishful thinking." (My neighbor, Lew Brooks, calls them "two-beer Mickeys.") Who am I to defy tradition? For example, the small circles in the tile floor along the Standby entrance of *Rock 'n' Roller Coaster* are all the same size. Nevertheless, although the image doesn't meet our classic Mickey criteria, many guests and Cast Members call the tile image a Hidden Mickey. So, I include the tile floor Mickey in the Disney's Hollywood Studios Scavenger Hunt (Chapter 4 - Clue 55).

Hidden Mickeys vs. Decorative Mickeys

Some Mickeys are truly hidden, not visible to the tourist. They may be located behind the scenes, accessible only to Cast Members. You won't find them in this field guide, as I only include Hidden Mickeys that are accessible to the guest. Other Mickeys are decorative; they were placed in plain sight to enhance the decor. For example, in a restaurant, I consider a pat of butter shaped like Mickey Mouse to be a decorative (aka decor) Mickey. Disney World is loaded with decorative Mickeys. You'll find obvious images of Mickey Mouse on items such as manhole covers, displays in shop windows, and restaurant menus. I do not include these ubiquitous and sometimes changing images in this book unless they are unique or hard to spot.

Hidden Mickeys Can Change with time

Hidden Mickeys can change or be accidentally removed over time, by the process of nature or by the continual cleaning and refurbishing that goes on at Disney World. For example, several great Hidden Mickeys in the gift shop at the exit of *Star Tours – The*

Chapter 1: Hidden Mickey Mania

Adventures Continue disappeared when the shop was remodeled. Moreover, Cast Members themselves sometimes create or remove Hidden Mickeys.

My Selection Process

I trust you've concluded by now that Hidden Mickey Science is a dynamic and ever-changing specialty. Which raises the question, how did I choose the Hidden Mickeys in the scavenger hunts in this guide?

I compiled my list of Hidden Mickeys from all resources to which I had access: my own sightings, friends, family, Cast Members, websites, and books. (Cast Members in each specific area usually—but not always!—know where some Hidden Mickeys are located.) Then I embarked on my own hunts, and I took along friends or family to verify my sightings. In this guide, I have included only those Hidden Mickeys I could verify.

Furthermore, some Hidden Mickeys are visible only intermittently or only from certain vantage points in ride vehicles. I don't generally include these Mickeys, unless I feel that adequate descriptions will allow anyone to find them. So, the scavenger hunts include only those images I believe to be recognizable as Hidden Mickeys and visible to the general touring guest. It is likely, though, that one or more of the Hidden Mickeys described in this book will disappear over time.

Take note: on the following pages, the newest Hidden Mickeys are underlined!

Chapter 2

Magic Kingdom Scavenger Hunt

• • • • • •

Before You Start

* Prior to your visit, try for Advance Lunch Reservations at **Be Our Guest Restaurant.** Otherwise, try to line up for lunch there as covered later in the Scavenger Hunt.

* Many great Hidden Mickeys are in Standby queues, and you might miss them if you take the Lightning Lanes. So, for optimal Hidden Mickey hunting, (if you choose to spend the money), I recommend reserving Lightning Lane (by purchasing, on the My Disney Experience app, the current version of Disney Genie+ and/or Individual Lightning Lane) for the following attractions: **Splash Mountain**, **Peter Pan's Flight**, **Ariel's Grotto**, and **Princess Fairytale Hall (left-side queue)**.

* Be sure to keep track of your Lightning Lane windows and return to those attractions at the appropriate times. In the Scavenger Hunt below, if you come to your Lightning Lane attraction and it's not time for it yet, you can skip to the next stop in the Hunt and return to the Lightning Lane attraction during your time window. If you don't opt for the Lightning Lane options, try to line up for headliner attractions during Early Entry or right after park opening.

* Some of the Hidden Mickeys in this park are in restaurants and shops. Be consider-

Walt Disney World's Hidden Mickeys

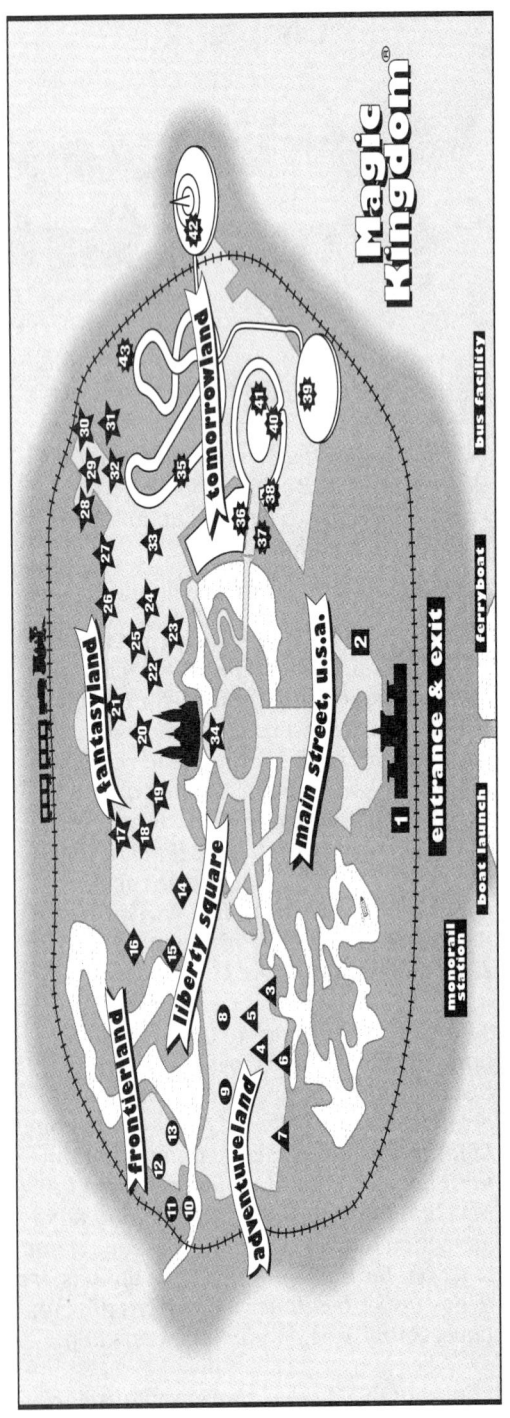

22

Chapter 2 : Magic Kingdom Scav. Hunt

main street, u.s.a
1. WDW Railroad
2. Mickey's Meet 'N Greet in Town Square Theater

adventureland
3. Swiss Family Treehouse
4. Walt Disney's Enchanted Tiki Room®
5. The Magic Carpets of Aladdin
6. Jungle Cruise
7. Pirates of the Caribbean®

frontierland
8. Frontierland Shootin' Arcade
9. Country Bear Jamboree
10. Splash Mountain®
11. WDW Railroad
12. Big Thunder Mountain Railroad®
13. Raft to Tom Sawyer Island

liberty square
14. The Hall of Presidents
15. Liberty Square Riverboat
16. Haunted Mansion®

fantasyland
17. "it's a small world"®
18. Peter Pan's Flight®
19. Mickey's PhilharMagic
20. Prince Charming Regal Carrousel
21. Enchanted Tales with Belle
22. Princess Fairytale Hall
23. Fairytale Garden
24. The Many Adventures of Winnie the Pooh
25. Seven Dwarfs Mine Train
26. Under the Sea ~ Journey of The Little Mermaid
27. Ariel's Grotto
28. Pete's Silly Sideshow
29. Casey Jr. Splash 'N' Soak Station
30. WDW Railroad
31. The Barnstormer
32. Dumbo the Flying Elephant®
33. Mad Tea Party
34. Castle Forecourt Stage

tomorrowland
35. Tomorrowland Speedway
36. Stitch's Great Escape!
37. Monsters, Inc. Laugh Floor
38. Buzz Lightyear's Space Ranger Spin
39. Walt Disney's Carousel of Progress
40. Tomorrowland Transit Authority PeopleMover
41. Astro Orbiter®
42. Space Mountain®
43. Tron Lightcycle Run

ate of fellow guests and Cast Members as you search. Tell them what you're looking for, so they can share in the fun. Avoid searching restaurants at busy mealtimes unless you are one of the diners.

* Each person has unique needs for sustenance. If I don't have specific suggestions for restaurants (related to Hidden Mickeys), then I leave it to you to decide when and where to break for snacks/meals.

*
Ride the *ferryboat* to and/or from the Magic Kingdom to the Transportation and Ticket Center (TTC).

Clue 1: During your walk onto or off of the ferry, look around for a classic Mickey.
4 points for one or more

Clue 2: If you happen to ride the *General Joe Potter ferryboat* to or from the Magic Kingdom, study the inside walls for a Hidden Mickey.
5 bonus points

Clue 3: Outside and not far from the Magic Kingdom entrance gates, look around for Mickey under your feet.
3 points

*
Check your Times Guide or *My Disney Experience* app for any morning, afternoon, and evening parades, shows, and fireworks. There are generally both decorative and Hidden Mickeys in the shows and on the floats, vehicles, and banners.

Clue 4: Once you are in the park, examine the scrollwork of the roof of the *Main Street Train Station*.
2 points

*
If the rest of the park is not open yet, you may want to hunt for Hidden Mickeys on *Main Street, U.S.A.* (See Clues 185 to 197.)

Chapter 2 : Magic Kingdom Scav. Hunt

*
Head for *Fantasyland* and **Seven Dwarfs Mine Train**.

Clue 5: Stay alert for a smiling Hidden Mickey above you in the first part of the outside Standby queue. (Tip: he's above a lantern).
5 points

Clue 6: Study the gems along the Standby entrance queue.
4 points for one or more images

Clue 7: On the ride, check out a Hidden Mickey next to Dopey.
5 points

Clue 8: Watch for Grumpy on your right side. Do you see a Hidden Mickey near him?
5 points

Clue 9: Don't miss Oswald the Lucky Rabbit on your left side. He's etched in wood on a beam.
5 points

Clue 10: Before your train rolls outside, squint up to your right for Mickey with an axe.
5 points

* Line up for **The Many Adventures of Winnie the Pooh**. Study Mr. Sanders' big tree.

Clue 11: Search for a Mickey made of rocks embedded inside the tree.
3 points

Clue 12: Look for a submarine image in the wood of the tree. (Note: This is a Hidden Tribute rather than a Hidden Mickey.)
4 points

Clue 13: Find a side profile of Mickey in the bark outside.
4 points

Clue 14: Locate Mickey on a wooden post by a window outside.
5 points

Clue 15: Next check out two Hidden Mickeys inside the entryway play area.
4 points for both

Now hop into your honey pot.

Clue 16: During the first part of the ride, study floating leaf shadows for a Hidden Mickey leaf!
5 points

Clue 17: Examine a flower-pot marker in Rabbit's Garden.
4 points

Clue 18: In Owl's house, find the picture of Mr. Toad and Owl.
3 points

Clue 19: Near the end of Owl's house, locate a picture of Mole with Winnie the Pooh.
3 points

*
 Walk to *Tomorrowland*.

Clue 20: Look for a shadow on the pavement near the **Tomorrowland Speedway** that's shaped like a classic Mickey.
3 points

Now queue up for **Space Mountain**. (You can enjoy the ride after walking through the entrance queue or exit the attraction just before boarding.)

Clue 21: Be alert for a Hidden Surprise (a reference to Disney) along the entrance queue.
3 points

Clue 22: Watch the instructional videos along the last part of the entrance queue for a Hidden Stitch and two sets of Hidden Mickey ears.
5 points for all

Chapter 2 : Magic Kingdom Scav. Hunt

Clue 23: Along the exit walkway, search for a Hidden Mickey formed of metallic orbs on the floor.
4 points

*

If you don't have Advance Reservations, amble over to the entrance area for **Be Our Guest Restaurant** at or after 10:30 a.m. and line up for lunch. Otherwise, go at your Reservations time.

Clue 24: As you enter *Be Our Guest Restaurant,* study the walls behind the suits of armor for some Hidden Mickeys.
3 points for one or more

Clue 25: Search the room to the right for a Hidden Mickey on a suit of armor.
5 points

Clue 26: In the food order room, spot two Hidden Mickeys on books.
4 points for both

Clue 27: Look for Mickey bubbles on a wall in the Rose Gallery seating area to the right (as you enter the restaurant) of the restaurant's Ballroom.
5 points

Clue 28: Find Mickey in fabric hanging in the West Wing seating area, located to the left of the Ballroom.
5 points

Clue 29: Pay attention as you exit the restaurant and walk along the bridge toward the rest of *Fantasyland.* Glance to your right before you reach the end of the bridge.
4 points

Clue 30: At the entrance walkway to *Be Our Guest Restaurant,* examine a short rock wall for a classic Mickey at the side of the check-in station.
5 points

*
Return to *Tomorrowland*.
Go to **Buzz Lightyear's Space Ranger Spin**.

Note: Some of the planets with Hidden Mickeys appear in several places along the entrance queue and on the ride.

Clue 31: Inside the building on the right wall, find the planet with a continent shaped like the side profile of Mickey Mouse.
3 points

Clue 32: Scan that same sector for a classic Hidden Mickey.
3 points

Clue 33: Look for the side-profile Mickey continent further along the entrance queue to the left.
2 points

Clue 34: Search for a Hidden Mickey in Sector 2 nearby.
3 points

Clue 35: Pay attention to the right wall in the very first interactive room on the ride for two tiny classic Mickeys in the stars. (They're close to one another but tough to spot!).
5 points for each

Clue 36: During the first part of the ride, spot another side profile of Mickey. Look to the left of your vehicle in the room with batteries.
3 points

Clue 37: Now quickly turn to the right side of your vehicle and stare at the star field to the right of the cone over Zurg to find a blue classic Mickey star.
5 points

Clue 38: Catch another view of the planet with a side-profile Mickey in the space video room.
3 points

Chapter 2 : Magic Kingdom Scav. Hunt

Clue 39: Just past the space video room, look straight ahead to spot that side-profile Mickey planet one more time.
2 points

Clue 40: Find a Hidden Mickey at the edge of a big blue galaxy.
3 points

*
  At your Lightning Lane time, cross over to *Frontierland* and ride **Splash Mountain.**

Clue 41: <u>Along the outside queue, locate a birdhouse with Hidden Mickey gems; they're below a window.</u>
4 points

Clue 42: Soon after you start the ride, search for barrels that form a classic Mickey.
3 points

Clue 43: Just as your boat goes outside, spot a tiny classic Mickey on a "moonshine" barrel!
5 points

Clue 44: Look for a rabbit with a broom and then try to catch a moving Hidden Mickey silhouette on a wall nearby.
5 points

Clue 45: Just past Brer Frog, find the fishing bobbers that form a Hidden Mickey.
4 points

Clue 46: In the room with jumping water, spot the hanging rope classic Mickey.
4 points

Clue 47: As your boat ascends toward the big drop, look toward the opening for a side profile of Mickey's face.
3 points

Clue 48: Along the exit walkway, look for the birdhouse with at least two acorn classic Mickeys.
3 points for two or more

Clue 49: Do you see a Hidden Mickey in the children's play area along the exit?
3 points

Clue 50: After the ride, take another look at the mountain from the outside viewing area to spot that Clue 47 side profile (again).
3 points

* Now get in line to ride **Big Thunder Mountain Railroad.**

Clue 51: During the first climb, search the cavern floor to the right of the coaster.
4 points

Clue 52: In the last part of the ride, look to the right of the train for a three-gear Hidden Mickey.
5 points

Clue 53: Study the reddish rock along the exit walkway for a Hidden Tinker Bell.
4 points

*
   Go to **Peter Pan's Flight** at your Lightning Lane time.

Clue 54: Study the overhead attraction sign at the entrance for two decent Mickey images.
5 points for spotting both

Clue 55: If you're lucky, you may spot Mickey on the rotating moon and earn yourself some bonus points.
5 bonus points

Clue 56: Search for a classic Mickey near mermaids.
3 points

Clue 57: Squint your eyes for two shadow Hidden Mickeys near two different sets of cannonballs.
5 points for each one

Chapter 2 : Magic Kingdom Scav. Hunt

* Head over to **Ariel's Grotto**. (You'll visit here again at your Lightning Lane time to spot a different Hidden Mickey in the Lightning Lane queue!)

Clue 58: Study the Standby entrance queue for a Hidden Mickey.
5 points

*
   From near *Big Thunder Mountain Railroad,* float on the *raft* over to **Tom Sawyer Island**.

Clue 59: Look across the river for a classic Mickey rock formation at the right end of the bridge in *Frontierland*. (Note: This Hidden Mickey is also visible from the *Liberty Square Riverboat*.)
4 points

Clue 60: Inside Harper's Mill, say hello to a resident of the Mill (a Hidden Surprise).
3 points

Clue 61: Search one of the caves for Goofy.
3 points

Clue 62: In *Fort Langhorn*, look around in the rear right Rifle Roost for a Mickey in wood.
4 points

Clue 63: Also inside the Fort, admire the display inside the Blacksmith's shop for a Hidden Mickey.
3 points

*
   Now pop over to **Jungle Cruise**.

Clue 64: Study the sign outside for a Hidden Mickey.
2 points

Clue 65: Along the Standby entrance queue, look for a map with a Hidden Mickey.
4 points

Clue 66: Stay alert for a Hidden Mickey on an airplane.
4 points

Clue 67: Coming out of the temple, look hard at the first undecorated column on the left for a chipped area of brick that forms part of a profile of Minnie Mouse's head and face. (This is a tough one!)
5 points

Clue 68: <u>Now be alert for a Hidden Mickey in a net near monkeys playing in a display.</u>
3 points

* Walk to ***Pirates of the Caribbean***.

Clue 69: Look near a faux fireplace along the queue for a Hidden Mickey. (This image is fading with time).
5 points

Clue 70: Now search for two classic Mickey locks in the left queue.
4 points for spotting both

Clue 71: From your boat, watch for a Hidden Mickey in front of a window to your left.
5 points

Clue 72: Try to spot the classic Mickey shadow above the drunken pirate's cat.
4 points

Clue 73: Near the end of the ride, look left at the recessed doors in the wall.
4 points

Clue 74: Don't miss an image to the right of the treasure room.
4 points

Clue 75: Now glance at the wall behind Jack Sparrow.
4 points

Clue 76: As you exit the ride, search for some coins and jewels.
5 points for both

Chapter 2 : Magic Kingdom Scav. Hunt

Clue 77: In the gift shop, spot a classic Mickey in a painting.
3 points

Clue 78: Outside the attraction entrance, look around for a Hidden Mickey on a cart.
3 points

*
  Stop by the **Frontierland Shootin' Arcade**.

Clue 79: Find a classic Mickey in front of the target area.
1 point

*
  Then turn right to *Liberty Square* and cross the street.

Clue 80: Find a classic Mickey near the **Liberty Square Riverboat** entrance.
1 point

* Head for **Haunted Mansion**.

Clue 81: Along the interactive "Scenic" left side entrance queue, search for a Mickey made of barnacles.
4 points

Clue 82: About halfway along the outside entrance queue, examine the pavement for a hidden finger ring (a Hidden Surprise).
5 points

Clue 83: In the first room inside the entrance, look for some classic Mickeys in the border design around a portrait.
3 points

Clue 84: During the ride, be alert for Donald Duck on two different chairs.
4 points each

Clue 85: Find the Mickey on the ghostly banquet table.
3 points

Clue 86: Spot plates on the floor in the attic.
4 points

Clue 87: Look closely (for a Hidden Mickey) to your far right at the "Grim Reaper" by the opera-singing lady.
5 points

Clue 88: <u>Along the covered exit walkway, study windows for a Hidden Mickey.</u>
4 points

Clue 89: Outside, as you exit, look for a classic Mickey next to a gate.
3 points

Clue 90: Find Mr. Toad along the exit walkway.
3 points

* Enter **Columbia Harbour House** restaurant and look for a classic Hidden Mickey. (Be considerate of the diners.)

Clue 91: Check the art on the downstairs walls.
2 points

*
   Go to **Ariel's Grotto** at your Lightning Lane time.

Clue 92: Examine the short rock wall along the Lightning Lane queue for a Hidden Mickey.
4 points

Get a Lightning Lane pass for the left queue of *Princess Fairytale Hall* on your mobile device's "My Disney Experience" app. (Ask a Cast Member or study the attraction yourself to find out which Princesses are greeting guests in the left queue).

* Walk to **Under the Sea - Journey of The Little Mermaid**. Spend some time in the Standby entrance queue to find all the great Hidden Mickeys here (let people walk by you in line if you need to).
(Note: Many collections of circular rock im-

Chapter 2 : Magic Kingdom Scav. Hunt

pressions in both the entrance and exit areas and inside this attraction suggest classic Hidden Mickeys. I include below my favorite images, which seem intentional.)

Clue 93: Spot a Hidden Mickey on a rock just outside the Standby entrance queue.
4 points

Clue 94: In the outside Standby queue, be alert for another Hidden Mickey on a rock in the lagoon near a waterfall.
5 points

Clue 95: Gaze way above and to the right of the rock in the lagoon to find another classic Hidden Mickey on the rock wall.
5 points

Clue 96: Look down over the right side of a bridge railing for a classic Hidden Mickey.
5 points

Clue 97: Now stare high above this railing for a small classic Hidden Mickey in the rock.
5 points

Clue 98: Also in the outside Standby queue, study the rock walls for a submarine image. (Not a Hidden Mickey, but an awesome Hidden Image!).
5 points

Clue 99: Just before you enter the inside portion of the queue, stop and look above and behind you for a three-circle Hidden Mickey impressed in the rock.
5 points

Clue 100: In the inside Standby entrance queue, at a large opening in the rock ceiling on your right and just past a carved wooden figure, stay alert for a classic Mickey in light on the lower wall to your left. This Hidden Mickey is designed to appear only on November 18 (Mickey's birthday) around noon, but it just might appear other times of the year as well!
10 bonus points

Clue 101: Along the inside Standby entrance queue, find a Hidden Mickey in the rock wall above some bottles on your left.
5 points

Clue 102: Search for Mickey on the ceiling just as you enter the room with Scuttle, the talking seagull.
5 points

Clue 103: On the ride, look up for a purple coral classic Mickey on your right.
5 points

Clue 104: Before you reach Ariel, stare hard down to your right for a three-coral Hidden Mickey on the wall.
5 points

Clue 105: Keep your eyes peeled and gaze to the left side to spot a green fish with a Hidden Mickey.
4 points

Clue 106: Don't miss the frogs with Hidden Mickeys!
4 points for one or more

Clue 107: Along the inside exit walkway, scan the walls for an upside-down Hidden Mickey.
4 points

Clue 108: Further along the inside exit walkway, study the wall near the floor for a collection of circles that make a Hidden Mickey (or two!).
4 points for one or more

Clue 109: Look through the large opening in the exit walkway's left wall for another classic Hidden Mickey.
4 points

Clue 110: Outside the cave exit, look around for Steamboat Willie!
5 points

Chapter 2 : Magic Kingdom Scav. Hunt

Clue 111: Scan the area near Steamboat Willie for a classic Mickey in the rock.
4 points

* Relax on *"it's a small world."*

Clue 112: In the Africa room, look up at the vine with purple leaves.
3 points

Clue 113: In the South Pacific Room, search for an animal classic Mickey.
3 points

* Walk over to the *"Tangled" Tower restroom area.*

Clue 114: Spot a Hidden Mickey on a wall poster.
3 points

Clue 115: Check out a wall of the women's restroom for a Hidden Mickey. (You can see this wall from outside the restroom).
4 points

* Head *toward* **Peter Pan's Flight**.

Clue 116: Find grapes arranged like a classic Mickey.
2 points

Enter **Pinocchio Village Haus** restaurant.

Clue 117: Look for a tiny, dark classic Mickey on the wall near the exit to the restrooms.
4 points

Clue 118: Locate a minuscule, white classic Mickey near the word "All."
4 points

Clue 119: Keep searching this wall for another tiny, white classic Mickey at the other side of the same mural.
5 points

Walk to **Sir Mickey's Store**.

Clue 120: Observe a classic Mickey outside the store.
1 point

Clue 121: Gaze inside a display window of the store to find more classic Mickeys.
3 points

Enter the **Castle Couture** shop.

Clue 122: Search high on a wall for a bronze frieze with a tiny classic Mickey on a bush.
5 points

Clue 123: Walk over and bow to Cinderella at her fountain for a Surprise effect!
4 points

*
Check the shields on the *Adventureland bridge to the Hub*. (The Hub is in front of Cinderella Castle.)

Clue 124: Find two Hidden Mickeys.
3 points for both

* Enjoy **Walt Disney's Enchanted Tiki Room**.

Clue 125: Analyze the roof support poles along the left side of the entrance queue for a Hidden Mickey.
4 points

Clue 126: Find classic Mickeys at the bottom of two bird perches. One is in the left corner as you enter, and you'll find the other in the right corner as you exit.
3 points each

Clue 127: Near the entrance to *Walt Disney's Enchanted Tiki Room*, look around for a Hidden Mickey on a statue.
3 points

Clue 128: Study the cement for a tiny classic Mickey between the Agrabah Bazaar shop and *The Magic Carpets of Aladdin* ride.
4 points

Chapter 2 : Magic Kingdom Scav. Hunt

*
At your Lightning Lane time, choose the left queue at **Princess Fairytale Hall**.

Clue 129: Keep your eyes peeled for a painting on a wall with a Hidden Mickey.
5 points

* Walk to **Mickey's PhilharMagic**.

Clue 130: In the first waiting area inside, squint at the wall mural.
4 points for two or more

Clue 131: Inside the main theater, examine the border of the video screen.
2 points

Clue 132: In the show, look for a shadow Mickey on a table.
4 points

Clue 133: Stare at Ariel's jewels for a classic Mickey in a ring.
5 points

Clue 134: In "The Lion King" segment, watch for round orange treetops that form classic Mickeys at times.
5 points

Clue 135: Keep alert for a classic Mickey during the magic carpet ride.
5 points

Clue 136: Stop in the gift shop at the exit and find a classic Mickey.
2 points

*
Now cross the park to *Tomorrowland* and go to **Tomorrowland Transit Authority PeopleMover**. Find a Hidden Mickey as you ride.

Clue 137: In the last part of the ride, observe the accessories of the woman getting her hair done.
3 points

Visit the **Merchant of Venus** shop.

Clue 138: Find Mickey's face on a classic Mickey.
2 points

Clue 139: Can you spot a Mickey hat?
2 points

Stroll toward *Space Mountain* and into the **Tomorrowland "Cool Scanner" Station**.

Clue 140: Look up for tiny Hidden Mickeys.
3 points for one or more

* Go to **Walt Disney's Carousel of Progress**.

Clue 141: Admire a classic Mickey on a mirror.
3 points

Clue 142: Search for Mickey's blue hat.
4 points

Clue 143: Observe a painting on the rear wall.
4 points

Clue 144: Find a Mickey nutcracker.
2 points

Clue 145: Spot a Mickey Mouse doll.
2 points

Clue 146: Search around for green Mickey ears.
3 points

Clue 147: Look fast for a classic Mickey on a spaceship.
5 points

Clue 148: View objects with Mickey ears in the kitchen.
3 points

Chapter 2 : Magic Kingdom Scav. Hunt

Walk to the far side of ***Astro Orbiter*** and search carefully for a small classic Mickey traced in the cement nearby.

Clue 149: Check the side facing *Space Mountain*.
5 points

* Go to ***Monsters, Inc. Laugh Floor***.

(After finding the Hidden Mickey, you can exit before the show or stick around and enjoy the humor.)

Clue 150: As you enter the waiting area, search for a classic Mickey in a window display.
4 points

*
   Head for *Fantasyland* and join the Standby queue for ***Enchanted Tales with Belle***.

Clue 151: In Maurice's cottage, study the window glass to the left. Can you see a Disney Character?
5 points

Clue 152: Look near the fireplace in the first room for two Hidden Mickeys.
5 points for both

Clue 153: Search below your feet in the Wardrobe Room for a Hidden Mickey.
3 points for one or more

Clue 154: Spot Hidden Mickeys on a book near the back wall of the Library.
5 points for both

*
   Stroll over to Town Square Theater on *Main Street, U.S.A.* and visit ***Meet Mickey***. (Hidden Mickeys in here change at times).

Clue 155: In the queue, look for some special mail.
2 points

Clue 156: In Mickey's Room, find a Hidden Mickey made of rings.
2 points

Clue 157: Spot another classic Mickey in Mickey's magic chest. (It's sometimes covered by a scarf.)
2 points

Clue 158: Don't miss Oswald the Lucky Rabbit!
4 points

Clue 159: Look around for Sorcerer Mickey.
4 points

Clue 160: In the gift shop at the exit, find Mickey hanging on a table and on a nearby tall display case.
3 points for both

Clue 161: In the gift shop, search for Mickey on a house.
3 points

* Check out **Fairytale Garden**.

Clue 162: Find a classic Mickey on a light pole.
3 points

Clues 163 and 164: Search for two Hidden Characters on the walls. One belongs to Mickey and the other to Merida.
5 points for both

* Walk to the *exit area* of the **Fantasyland Train Station** in *Storybook Circus*.

Clue 165: Check the walkway that stretches from near the train station exit to *Dumbo the Flying Elephant* for at least two Hidden Mickeys.
5 points for two or more

Chapter 2 : Magic Kingdom Scav. Hunt

Stand outside **Casey Jr. Splash 'N' Soak Station**.

Clue 166: Look over the boxcars in *Casey Jr. Splash 'N 'Soak* for a classic Mickey.
5 points

Clue 167: Spot some numbers (a Hidden Surprise) on one of the boxcars.
4 points

Cruise over to **The Barnstormer**.

Clue 168: Find a classic Mickey near a picture of Goofy outside *The Barnstormer*.
3 points

Clue 169: Study a large billboard outside *The Barnstormer* for a Hidden Mickey.
5 points

Walk back to **Pete's Silly Sideshow**.

Clue 170: Search for a classic Mickey on a poster outside *Pete's Silly Sideshow*.
5 points

Check out the large tent next to *Pete's Silly Sideshow*.

Clue 171: Locate tiny Mickey balloons.
5 points for finding eight balloons

Explore inside the **Big Top Souvenirs** store.

Clue 172: Spot Mickey on an animal on the wall.
5 points

Return to the area near **Dumbo the Flying Elephant**.

Clue 173: Look for a classic Mickey near the entrance to the *Dumbo* Lightning Lane queue.
3 points

Walt Disney World's Hidden Mickeys

Now, over by **Ariel's Grotto** ...

Clue 174: Find a Hidden Mickey at the Disney Vacation Club kiosk.
2 points

Clue 175: Search for a Hidden Mickey in the walkway near the Disney Vacation Club kiosk.
5 points

Locate **Gaston 's Statue**.
Clue 176: Study the statue for a Hidden Mickey.
5 points

Gaze around inside the **Bonjour Village Gifts** shop.
Clue 177: Donald Duck is in the shop!
3 points

Walk toward **Enchanted Tales with Belle**.

Clue 178: Before you reach the entrance walkway to *Be Our Guest Restaurant*, keep your eyes down for a horseshoe Hidden Mickey.
4 points

Clue 179: In the main walkway, not far from the entrance sign for *Enchanted Tales with Belle*, search for a pebble image of Oswald the Lucky Rabbit. (Psst: it's not in the side walkway to *Enchanted Tales with Belle*.)
5 points

*
  In *Liberty Square*, walk into the **Liberty Tree Tavern**.
Clue 180: Search for a classic Mickey in the waiting area.
3 points

Clue 181: Now look for a classic Mickey in a painting in one of the seating areas to the left of the waiting area. (Psst! You'll have to climb some stairs to find this Hidden Mickey.)
4 points

44

Chapter 2 : Magic Kingdom Scav. Hunt

*
 Enter the ***Frontier Trading Post*** in *Frontierland*.

Clue 182: Spot a cowboy with a Hidden Mickey.
3 points

Check out the inside of ***Pecos Bill Tall Tale Inn and Cafe***.

Clue 183: Squint for a classic Mickey on a plate that's sitting on a ledge.
4 points

Head for *Adventureland* and stop inside ***Tortuga Tavern***.

Clue 184: Search for a candle image.
3 points

*
 Cross the nearest bridge to ***Main Street, U.S.A.***

Clue 185: Look around the outside of The **Crystal Palace** restaurant.
3 points

Clue 186: As you enter the short side street off of *Main Street*, study the area near the bricks outside the entrance to the **Crystal Arts** store for a tiny classic Mickey.
5 points

Clue 187: Near the **Emporium** store outside, search for Hidden Mickeys on a door sign.
3 points for all

Clue 188: Find Mickey in stained-glass windows high on the *Emporium* exterior.
3 points

Clue 189: Look for a tiny Mickey on a building in an outside display window of the *Emporium* store.
5 points

Clue 190: Closely examine the ***Caffe Italiano coffee cart*** (present seasonally) near *Tony's Town Square Restaurant*.
2 bonus points

Clues 191 and 192: Just as you enter **Tony's Town Square Restaurant** dining area, study the left corner for two classic Hidden Mickeys:
- one is on a shelf
3 points
- one is on the floor near the left wall.
5 points

Clue 193: Look up for a classic Mickey as you exit *Tony's Restaurant*.
3 points

Clue 194: Smile at a Hidden Surprise in the cement outside of *Tony's Restaurant*.
5 points

Clue 195: Find Hidden Mickeys on *Main Street's* horse-drawn trolley.
2 points for one or more

Clue 196: Stand in Town Square Plaza and look for a classic Mickey on a ceiling.
2 points

*
You can often spot a classic Mickey in the sky during the ***evening fireworks*** show. If you see one, give yourself bonus points!
5 bonus points for spotting one or more

Keep your eyes peeled for another Hidden Mickey or two as you end your day in the park.

Clue 197: As you leave *Main Street* under the train station, search for Mickey on a gate.
2 points

Chapter 2 : Magic Kingdom Scav. Hunt

Now tally your score.

Total Points for Magic Kingdom =

_____

How'd you do?

Up to 298 points - Bronze
299 to 594 points - Silver
595 points and over - Gold
744 points - Perfect Score

If you earned bonus points in ***Under the Sea - Journey of the Little Mermaid***, ***Peter Pan's Flight***, on ***Main Street, U.S.A.***, at the ***fireworks***, and/or on the ***ferryboat***, you may have done even better.

Chapter 2 : Magic Kingdom Scav. Hunt

Ferryboats

Hint 1: Ropes coiled into classic Mickeys can often be spotted at the ferry loading docks at the Magic Kingdom and the Transportation and Ticket Center. Look next to a large post on either side as you walk onto or leave the boat at either loading dock. Cast Members usually maintain one or more of these rope images.

Hint 2: If you ride on the *General Joe Potter ferryboat* to or from the Magic Kingdom, look for this classic Hidden Mickey on the middle of an inside wall. It's on the port side between two doors and about 20 to 30 feet back from the front staircase (as your ferry approaches the Magic Kingdom).

Magic Kingdom Entrance

Hint 3: Classic Mickeys are formed in the bell clapper designs of some of the commemorative bricks in a few of the walkways near the Magic Kingdom.

Main Street, U.S.A. - Train Station

Hint 4: The periphery of the *Main Street Train Station* roof, second level, has scrollwork that repeats a classic Mickey motif.

Fantasyland

- *Seven Dwarfs Mine Train*

Hint 5: As you walk into the Standby entrance queue, check out the fourth lamppost on your left. A classic Mickey with eyes and a smile is impressed into the left side of a wooden crossbar. Look above you at the part of the crossbar that holds a lantern above your walkway.

Hint 6: Bright colored gems are in the interactive games along the Standby entrance queue. At times in these games, three gems come together to form a classic Hidden Mickey. One good image, made of a green gem for the "head" and two clear gems for the "ears," is at the top of the first barrel in the "Spin the Barrels" game.

Hint 7: On the right side of your train and to the right of Dopey's ears, a classic Hidden Mickey, tilted to the left, is formed by jewels. Find the larger red jewel for Mickey's head— the left ear is a smaller red jewel and the right ear, an amber diamond.

Hint 8: Along the ride on your right side, three gems (a purple "head" and one green and one light purple "ear') are stuck in the wall behind Grumpy's head. Grumpy is pulling on a rope.

Hint 9: After passing Doc going up the second lift, Oswald the Lucky Rabbit can be

Chapter 2 : Magic Kingdom Scav. Hunt

seen as a 3-D image on the left-hand side of the ride on a horizontal log. You can see his tiny legs, his belly pooching out, his round tan face with eyes and nose, and his right hand to the upper left of his face. His dark ears flop back from the top of his head and are less distinct. (This image is difficult to spot; you'll only get a fleeting glimpse.)

Hint 10: Just before you leave the inside of the dwarfs' mine, stare up to your right for a triangular block in a high corner of an arch support for the mine. Mickey Mouse, holding a pickaxe, is etched into the wood of the block.

- *The Many Adventures of Winnie the Pooh*

Hint 11: Inside the big tree, a classic Mickey, tilted to the left, is formed by embedded rocks above the frame of the smaller children's entrance.

Hint 12: Above the frame of the larger entrance to the inside of the big tree is a depression in the wood shaped like a submarine: a tribute to *20,000 Leagues Under the Sea* - the previous attraction near this location; thus, a Hidden Tribute rather than a Hidden Mickey.

Hint 13: On the outside of the big tree, in back, a side profile of Mickey is carved into the bark. It's at the upper left corner above the lower window.

Hint 14: Outside on the far side of the big tree, behind the fence, a classic Mickey is etched into the wood in the middle of a vertical brown post on the left side of a window.

Hint 15: Two Hidden Mickeys are in Rabbit's Garden along the entry area (accessed through the Standby queue):
A head of lettuce and two tomatoes form a classic Mickey.
Three watermelon drums are positioned to create a classic Mickey.

Hint 16: During the first part of the ride, keep your eyes peeled at the scene on your left. Near a drawing of a tree, Piglet is hanging on in the wind, and shadows of leaves drift and twist in front of him. The last leaf turns to simulate a classic Mickey wearing a small sorcerer's hat.

Hint 17: At the beginning of the ride, in Rabbit's Garden, the small marker with radishes (in the middle pot to the left of the "Letus" sign) has one radish shaped like a classic Hidden Mickey.

Hint 18: At the beginning of the left wall of Owl's house (the second room on the ride) is a picture of Mr. Toad handing the deed to the house over to Owl (a tribute to the previous attraction in this building, *Mr. Toad's Wild Ride*).

Hint 19: Near the end of this room, on the right side of the floor, is a picture of Mole standing with Winnie the Pooh.

Tomorrowland

Hint 20: A tall lamppost casts a classic Mickey shadow on the pavement outside *Tomorrowland Speedway*. It's best seen on a sunny day in the late morning or early afternoon.

- *Space Mountain*

Hint 21: On the left wall along the Standby entrance queue, "Disney's Hyperion Resort" (a Hidden Surprise) is located in the upper right corner of the second space sector map.

Hint 22: In the instructional videos along the queue, a figure wearing Mickey ears stands above the caption "Children Under 7 ...", and a Hidden Stitch and more Mickey ears are among the items shown above the caption "Remove All Loose Items" or "Stow Away All Space Cargo."

Chapter 2 : Magic Kingdom Scav. Hunt

Hint 23: On the right side, along the last part of the exit walkway, the floor of a deep pit is covered with round metallic orbs of varying sizes. At the middle of the left wall of the pit, three orbs form an upright classic Hidden Mickey; his right ear (the viewer's left) touches the wall. Other orbs in the pit come together to resemble classic Mickeys.

Fantasyland

- *Be Our Guest Restaurant*

Hint 24: Just inside the entrance to *Be Our Guest Restaurant*, in the room with the suits of armor, classic Hidden Mickeys are formed at times in the corners and intersections of the border design on the wall behind the suits of armor.

Hint 25: In the room with suits of armor, the ax blade at the end of the room on the right has a classic Hidden Mickey hole cut out of it.

Hint 26: At the right rear terminal as you enter the food order room, take a look at the stack of books. Two images form Hidden Mickeys; one is at each corner of the top book cover, and another is on the spine of the second book from the bottom.

Hint 27: On the left side of the rear wall of the Rose Gallery seating area (to the right of the restaurant's Ballroom dining room), look for a small painting of Mrs. Potts and Chip. Chip is playing in a dish filled with bubbles. Three of those bubbles form a classic Mickey.

Hint 28: Inside the *Be Our Guest Restaurant*, walk to the West Wing room and stand in front of the rose at the rear of the room. Now turn and look up to your right to spot a small Hidden Mickey hole in tattered fabric hanging from the ceiling.

Hint 29: Outside along the bridge, on your right as you exit toward the rest of *Fanta-*

syland, a classic Hidden Mickey is etched in stone. The Hidden Mickey, tilted left, is on the back of the partial wall behind the check-in station.

Hint 30: A faint classic Mickey in swirls is on top of a short rock wall to the left of the check-in station (as you face the station) at the beginning of the entrance walkway to *Be Our Guest Restaurant*. It's on top of the last flat rectangular stone before the wall ends.

Tomorrowland

- *Buzz Lightyear's Space Ranger Spin*

Hint 31: Just inside the building, in the entrance queue, the second poster on the right wall is called "Planets of the Galactic Alliance." In Sector 2, the central continent on the earth-like planet is shaped like a side profile of Mickey Mouse's head.

Hint 32: In this same poster, to the upper right of the side-profile Mickey, is a planet of green spheres, some of which group together as classic Mickeys. One such Mickey is at the lower middle of the planet.

Hint 33: The side-profile Mickey continent appears in the top left of a recessed wall farther along the entrance queue, just before the last right turn in the queue.

Hint 34: Sector 2 in this same mural contains a planet made of many spheres, some of which form classic Mickeys. One of them is an upside-down classic Mickey at the outer part of the planet at about the "ten o' clock" location.

Hint 35: On the ride, in the very first interactive room with targets, scan for two Hidden Mickeys. To see them, you have to rotate back and to the right in your vehicle as soon as you enter the room. First, a tiny classic Mickey with a green head and blue ears is on the first part of the lower right wall. This Hidden Mickey is below and between two

Chapter 2 : Magic Kingdom Scav. Hunt

five-point green stars. Another classic Mickey is a foot or so to the left and below the first one. It's made of circular markings on a tiny faint star.

Hint 36: You go through three different rooms during the first part of this ride. When you enter the room with lots of batteries, look to the left of the ride vehicle. You'll see a side profile of Mickey's head in the rear left under the words, "Initiate Battery Unload."

Hint 37: Also in the battery room, look to the right of your vehicle and high over Zurg's left (your right) shoulder to spot a tiny blue classic Mickey star, tilted to the left. It's above a round green star, in the star field to the right of the large blue and yellow cone suspended over Zurg.

Hint 38: As the ride vehicle moves through the space video room, the earth-like planet with continent Mickey flies by on the right wall.

Hint 39: Just past the space video room, in the final battle scene on the ride, the earth-like Mickey planet shows up yet again on a wall straight ahead and to the upper left.

Hint 40: Also in this room, look to the left of forward motion of your vehicle to view a large, spinning blue galaxy on the wall. At the upper left outer edge of the spinning circle, three round stars come together as a classic Mickey, sideways to the left.

Frontierland

- *Splash Mountain*

Hint 41: <u>Along the outside queue, search for this birdhouse, sitting in a tall wooden post below a fan, with an upright classic Mickey made of gems. The Hidden Mickey is just above the ledge and below the window, and it has a white "head" and white and brown "ears."</u>

Hint 42: As you ride halfway up the second crankhill, on the right side, three barrels in the lower right corner of a stack of barrels form a classic Mickey.

Hint 43: During the first part of the ride, when your boat is outside, look to your right for a barrel with "Muskrat Moonshine" painted on the side. A classic Mickey is formed by holes in the paint, above the "s" in "Muskrat."

Hint 44: On the right side of your boat and to the left of the rabbit sweeping a porch, small animal silhouettes run right to left along the top of a hill on the rear wall. Just before the last animal disappears, its head becomes a classic Mickey silhouette. These moving animal silhouettes repeat at regular intervals.

Hint 45: Look for a picnic basket up on a small ledge. You'll spot it just past Brer Frog, who is sitting on an alligator and fishing with his toe. Near the basket are three red-and-white-striped fishing bobbers in the shape of a classic Hidden Mickey.

Hint 46: On the right side of your boat, in the room with jumping water, a classic Mickey design in a rope is hanging halfway down from the ceiling. It's in the shadows behind a lantern and just past a turtle lying on a geyser.

Hint 47: The hole in the mountain at the top of the big drop is sculpted to form a side profile of Mickey's face. As you approach the big drop in your boat, Mickey's nose juts out from the left side of the hole. (You can also see this one from the outside viewing area; see Hint 50.)

Hint 48: As you pass the photo viewing area on your way out, look over to the entrance queue to spot two classic Mickeys formed by acorns on a birdhouse. One classic Mickey formation is above a door and below blue roof slats. The other is on the right side of

Chapter 2 : Magic Kingdom Scav. Hunt

the birdhouse and near the peanut-shell chimney, above the curve of the red handrail. (Other classic Mickey images are simulated elsewhere in the acorns).

Hint 49: Along the exit walkway, at the *Laughin' Place* children's play area, a sideways classic Mickey is formed by the ends of three logs stuck to the wall to the right of the "Laughin' Place" sign.

Hint 50: Walk in front of *Splash Mountain* after your ride. The hole in the mountain for the big drop forms a side profile of Mickey's face. From the outside, Mickey's nose juts out from the right side of the hole.

- *Big Thunder Mountain Railroad*

Hint 51: Three stalagmites in the cavern to your right at the beginning of the ride form a classic Mickey. Look down at the left side of the floor of the cavern to spot it.

Hint 52: Near the end of the ride, a classic Mickey made of three gears, facing sideways away from the train, lies next to the right side of the train track.

Hint 53: On the left side as you exit the ride (in the exit closest to the Standby line entrance), a cutout in the reddish rock resembles a side profile of Tinker Bell. She's behind the fence and between two metal carts, and she stands facing to your left.

Fantasyland

- *Peter Pan's Flight*

Hint 54: An incomplete classic cloud Mickey, tilted slightly to the right, sits at the lower right of the entrance sign cloud formation. It's just to the right of the "t" in "Flight." Peter Pan is standing on the sign between the ears of another Mickey, distorting it. You can see Mickey's ears and just the top of his head.

Hint 55: Bonus Points Hint - When the rotating moon is in just the right position, you can see a faint dark classic Mickey on the moon, above the silhouettes of the flying Peter Pan and his entourage. Unfortunately, since the moon rotates, you can't spot this Hidden Mickey on every ride through the attraction.

Hint 56: On the rocky edge of the mermaid lagoon, three flowers on the grass form a classic Mickey; the "head" is yellow, and the "ears" are light orange.

Hint 57: As you fly over one side of the ship with the fallen pirates and then back over the other, look down for two sets of cannonballs, one on each side of the ship. Shadows directly below the first pile of cannonballs form a classic Hidden Mickey. A more pronounced "shadow" classic Mickey is next to and apart from the second pile of cannonballs; this Hidden Mickey appears to be painted on the deck of the ship.

- *Ariel's Grotto*

Hint 58: As you make your last turn in the inside winding Standby queue, marvel at a side profile of Mickey etched on the rear wall near the floor. He's not far from an exit sign, and he's looking left.

Frontierland

- *Tom Sawyer Island*

Hint 59: Across the river from the island docks, look at the right end of the bridge in *Frontierland* for three rocks that form a classic Mickey. They're located halfway between the lost two vertical posts that support the handrail, about one foot down from the top of the rocks. The Hidden Mickey is in the second row of rocks from the top. (Note: This Hidden Mickey is also visible from the *Liberty Square Riverboat*.)

Chapter 2 : Magic Kingdom Scav. Hunt

Hint 60: To the right of the loading/unloading dock, a sign out front of Harper's Mill says "please don't scare the birds." Walk inside the mill and look for a chirping bluebird nesting in a horizontal rotating wheel (a Hidden Surprise).

Hint 61: Halfway through *Old Scratch's Mystery Mine*, bright shining gems embedded in the wall form a side profile of Goofy. He's looking to your right.

Hint 62: In *Fort Langhorn*, enter the Rifle Roost at the far right corner. To get there, climb up the stairs to your immediate right after you enter the fort and walk across the right upper walkway to the far right Rifle Roost. On top of the right handrail, about halfway up the steps to the top of the Rifle Roost, there is a Hidden Mickey created by: a wood knot, an additional mark, and an indentation in the wood.

Hint 63: Inside the *Blacksmith's shop*, an upside-down classic Mickey (slightly distorted) is impressed on the side of horse bridle gear, which is hanging about six feet high on a post to the right of a man standing with his back to us.

Adventureland

- Jungle Cruise

Hint 64: Check the big sign outside. On the side of the sign that faces the attraction, three barnacles under the "J" in "Jungle Cruise" form a classic Mickey.

Hint 65: About halfway along the Standby entrance queue, a classic Hidden Mickey made of dark circles and tilted to the right is at the lower left of a map of Africa in a display cabinet on a wall. The display cabinet is to the right of several masks on the wall.

Hint 66: After the waterfall, a wrecked silver plane sits to the right of the boat. Look back to spot three circles etched in the metal at the lower right of the visible section of fuselage. The circles are all the same size, but many folks and Cast Members consider them to be a Hidden Mickey. (Note: The image may be obscured at times by foliage).

Hint 67: The first undecorated column on the left wall (the third column from the end as you come out of the temple) has a chipped area of brick on the third block from the top. The chipped area forms part of a profile view of Minnie Mouse's head and face. Don't get discouraged if you have trouble spotting it; this one is tough to find—especially the first time.

Hint 68: <u>After you pass through the dark temple, watch left for a display of supplies for jungle explorers of the past. At the upper right of monkeys playing on an old gramophone is a hanging net with three colored glass balls that form a classic Mickey.</u>

- *Pirates of the Caribbean*

Hint 69: Along the left entrance queue is a room with a faux fireplace on the right side. A classic Mickey is in the plaster on the sloping area to the right and above the fireplace mantle. It's about seven feet up from the floor. (This image is fading with time.)

Hint 70: Tall gun cabinets stand on both sides of the left entrance queue. On two of the cabinets are classic Mickey-shaped locks (one on each side).

Hint 71: In the room with women chasing men in circles to the left of your boat, a black classic Mickey is suspended in front of the left side of an upper-story window.

Hint 72: About halfway through the ride and past the auction scene, a cat behind an intoxicated pirate casts a classic Hidden Mickey moving shadow on the corner of the wall above and behind it.

Chapter 2 : Magic Kingdom Scav. Hunt

Hint 73: As your boat approaches the last scene (the treasure room), a classic Mickey lock hangs on large wooden recessed doors to the left.

Hint 74: As the treasure room comes into view, a classic Mickey lock hangs on a wooden door on the right. A long key with a cord hanging from it juts out of the keyhole of the lock.

Hint 75: Classic Mickey locks hang on the cabinets behind Captain Jack Sparrow in the treasure room.

Hint 76: Just as you enter the gift shop after exiting your boat, several classic Mickeys are formed by coins and jewels in two hanging plates near the right wall. Look along the edges of the plates for some of the best images.

Hint 77: Inside the gift shop, turn left and find a painting at the lower right of a wall map on the shop's rear wall. In the painting, a lady in a multicolored gown has a classic Mickey, tilted slightly to the right, on her left shoulder.

Hint 78: Along a side pathway outside the entrance to the *Pirates of the Caribbean* attraction, the wheel of a cart forms a classic Mickey with two barrels above it. To spot it, walk to the side of the cart away from the main *Adventureland* path.

Frontierland

- Frontierland Shootin' Arcade

Hint 79: In the front center of the target area is a group of cactus plants. One near the middle, just below the gray tombstone, has three lobes forming a classic Hidden Mickey.

Walt Disney World's Hidden Mickeys

Liberty Square

- Stocks near the Liberty Square Riverboat entrance

Hint 80: Padlocks on the stocks near the entrance are shaped to resemble classic Hidden Mickeys (even though the "ears" are a bit small).

- Haunted Mansion

Hint 81: Along the interactive "Scenic Route," a classic Mickey made of barnacles is on a huge bathtub with the words "Here Floats Captain Culpepper Clyne." The classic Mickey is tilted right and is below and between the letters "R" and "C" in the name.

Hint 82: As you wind along the outside entrance queue, study the pavement for a Hidden Surprise. At one point, past a handrail on your right and not far from a wall, you can spot a ring embedded in a gray splotch in the cement. The story goes that it's a wedding ring that once belonged to the murderous bride you'll encounter on the ride. In the attic scene, the bride is standing on your left by her wedding cake.

Hint 83: Just inside the entrance to the first room, you'll find some small classic Mickeys in the oval border design around the portrait of the dressed-up aging man above the fireplace.

Hint 84: As you pass by the library room (at the beginning of the ride) and then the "endless hallway" on your right, check out the backs of two purple chairs for an abstract Donald Duck. Near the top of the chairs, you can see his cap, which sits above his distorted eyes, face, and bill. (Note that the chairs may change locations at times.)

Hint 85: A plate and two saucers on the ghostly banquet table are arranged to form a classic Mickey. They're usually at the bottom left corner of the table. (This image disappears at times.)

Chapter 2 : Magic Kingdom Scav. Hunt

Hint 86: In the first part of the attic area, on the floor to your left under a small table with shelves, plates form a classic Mickey. A large lower plate serves as the "head" and two smaller plates or dishes are the "ears."

Hint 87: To the right of the opera-singing lady (her left) is a ghost resembling the Grim Reaper. He is holding up his left arm. Hanging from his left hand is a cloth with dark markings at the top that form a classic Hidden Mickey.

Hint 88: <u>Along the covered exit walkway, in the third window from the end at your upper left, large classic Hidden Mickey holes are in the lower part of cobwebs.</u>

Hint 89: Outside, at the left end of the covered walkway, a classic Mickey metal latch holds a wrought-iron gate open.

Hint 90: In the middle of the pet cemetery on the left side of the outside exit walkway stands a Mr. Toad tombstone – a tribute to the previous *Mr. Toad's Wild Ride* attraction in *Fantasyland*.

Columbia Harbour House restaurant

Hint 91: In the downstairs table area, a wall across from the food-order counters is decorated with three small circular maps covered by a single piece of glass. (The central map is labeled "Charles V.") The three circles form a classic Mickey.

Fantasyland

- *Ariel's Grotto*

Hint 92: As you make the first left turn in the Lightning Lane queue of *Ariel's Grotto,* three round impressions at the top of the short rock wall to your left come together as a classic Mickey. The Hidden Mickey is near a group of tall, vertical green leaves.

- *Under the Sea - Journey of The Little Mermaid*

Hint 93: A classic Hidden Mickey made of three circular impressions in the rock is to the upper right of the sign at the Standby entrance to the attraction.

Hint 94: On the right side along the outside Standby entrance queue, a classic Mickey made of impressions is at the top right side of a rock that sits in the middle of the small lagoon in front of the waterfall.

Hint 95: Above the lagoon rock with the Hidden Mickey is another small classic Mickey made of impressions in the rock wall. Look for it on a flat sloping wall face just below the very top of the rock wall. The Hidden Mickey is above the right edge of the large opening in the wall; the waterfall spills over the left side of this opening.

Hint 96: Directly below the right side of a bridge with a rope-covered side rail is a classic Hidden Mickey made of impressions in the rock. You're facing a rock arch with a waterfall, and the Hidden Mickey is at the right side of the rock base of the stream below you. Water streaming over the Mickey blurs the image.

Hint 97: Now stare up at the higher part of the rock arch. To the right of the small waterfall, a tiny classic Mickey impression is in the rock in the upper middle of the arch.

Hint 98: At the left side of the outside Standby entrance queue, a Nautilus submarine impression is in a rock wall behind a small pond. When you reach a fence on your left strewn with ropes and nets, look back to your left and study the rear rock wall near the waterline. First spot the round porthole that resembles an eye; the nose of the submarine points to the left.
Note: "Nautilus" is the submarine, commanded by Captain Nemo, in Jules Verne's novel *Twenty Thousand Leagues Under the*

Chapter 2 : Magic Kingdom Scav. Hunt

Sea. It was the ride vehicle in the WDW ride of the same name, which closed in 1994.

Hint 99: Just before you enter the inside portion of the queue, look up high above and behind you for three circle depressions on a rock that is jutting out. The circle Hidden Mickey is tilted slightly to the left.

Hint 100: Each year on Mickey Mouse's birthday (November 18) the noontime sun shines through holes carved in the rockwork above you at just the right angle to form a classic Mickey on the wall of the inside part of the entrance queue. The Mickey-shaped light lasts for several minutes. The top of Mickey's head is formed by the carving in the inside rock, and the lower part of his head is formed by the carving in the rock higher and farther away from you. Stay alert, because the sunlight just might shine through both rock openings at other times of the year to form Mickey!

Hint 101: Along the left side of the inside Standby entrance queue, a classic Mickey tilted to the left is formed by holes in the rock above some bottles on a table.

Hint 102: A side profile of Mickey Mouse, looking left, is etched in the ceiling. He's at the beginning of the room with the talking Scuttle, high to your left as you enter and near a cubed light cover.

Hint 103: In the first part of the room where the song "Under the Sea" is playing, three oval purple corals clinging to a rock to the right of your ride vehicle form a classic Mickey. They're just past and behind the second singing chorus line of fish that are standing on their tails.

Hint 104: Before you reach Ariel, who is on your left, stare down to your right to the lower wall near you. Three round purple corals in a classic Mickey formation, sideways to the right, are stuck on the lower wall and are visible only for a second or two.

Hint 105: Just past Ariel in the "Under the Sea" room, a green fish with a purple seashell hat has a classic Hidden Mickey at the top of her earring. For the best vantage point, look back to the earring after you pass by the fish.

Hint 106: Toward the end of the ride, check the pond (to your right) for frogs with dark green spots on their backs that form sideways classic Mickeys. The frogs are perched on lily pads to the left of a boat with Ariel and Eric.

Hint 107: Along the left side of the exit walkway inside the cave, just as you curve left and can see outside light, you'll come across an upside-down classic Mickey made of impressions in the wall. It's about two feet up from the floor.

Hint 108: Further along the left side of the exit walkway inside the cave, spot a classic Hidden Mickey made of a large depression for the "head" and two smaller depressions for the "ears." This upright Hidden Mickey is just inches up from the floor and below a large opening in the left wall that looks into the exit path from *Ariel's Grotto*. This image is part of a collection of circles that form other potential sideways classic Mickeys.

Hint 109: Through the large opening mentioned above, you can see another Hidden Mickey: a classic Mickey formed of three impressions in the rock wall along the left side of the exit from *Ariel's Grotto*. This image is tilted to the left and it's about halfway up the wall and below a ceiling light. (Note: You'll probably find other rock impressions along the exit that resemble classic Mickeys.)

Hint 110: At the end of the exit walkway from *Under the Sea,* turn to your right to spot an amazing Hidden "Steamboat Willie" Mickey Mouse. The Imagineers sculpted this image on a series of rocks. His left leg and shoe are closest to you, then his right leg and

Chapter 2 : Magic Kingdom Scav. Hunt

shoe are on the next rock. Two holes in the rocks represent the buttons on his shorts. His whitish face is on a flat rock, and he's looking left. His tall hat is the last rock above his head. There's even a ship's wheel in the rock to the left of his face!

Hint 111: A classic Mickey made of three depressions in the rock is across the stream to the right of the Steamboat Willie image. This Hidden Mickey is below and to the left of a lantern that sits on top of the rock.

- *"it's a small world"*

Hint 112: Toward the end of the Africa room, vines on the right side of your boat above the giraffes and also on the left side of your boat have purple leaves shaped like classic Mickey heads.

Hint 113: Near the end of the South Pacific room, several koala bears hang on a tree. As you approach the bears on your left, the back of the blue bear's head forms a classic Mickey.

- *"Tangled" Restroom area*

Hint 114: On a wall poster outside the Ladies' Restroom near the "Tangled" Tower, a classic Hidden Mickey is on a Mime's lips. Smaller round, solid black circles form the "ears" just above the upper lip.

Hint 115: In the *Tangled area* women's restroom, three purple spots - a classic Mickey - are at the lower right corner of a mural painted on the left wall as you enter the restroom. (You can spot this wall from outside the restroom).

- *Near Peter Pan's Flight*
Hint 116: Between the entrance to *Peter Pan's Flight* and *Columbia Harbour House*, you'll find paintings of grape clusters on the walls. Three grapes at the lower right of the upper left cluster of grapes form a classic Mickey.

- Pinocchio Village Haus restaurant

Hint 117: As you head from the dining area to the restrooms, a tiny dark classic Mickey appears above the word "dreams" on the "When You Wish Upon A Star" mural. You'll find it on the left wall near the exit to the restrooms.

Hint 118: A tiny white classic Mickey is in this same area of the mural, below and left of the word "All."

Hint 119: On the left side of the same mural, a tiny white classic Mickey hides near a sparkling star. It's to the left of the Fairy - at her mid-thigh level - and her right thumb points to it.

- Sir Mickey's Store

Hint 120: You'll find a classic Mickey toward the top of the store's sign-shield. The shield is hanging under a vine, across from Castle Couture shop.

Hint 121: In a display window to the right of the main entrance to the store, classic Mickeys are along the border of the archer's collar in a painting on the rear wall of the display.

- Castle Couture shop

Hint 122: To find a tiny classic Mickey on the wall, walk through the entrance doors to the right of the Cinderella fountain. Then turn right and look up at the bronze horizontal frieze near the ceiling. You'll spot a series of arches over bushes with flowers. Walk forward to the far end of the frieze and count back six arches to a bush with three flowers at its upper left that form a classic Mickey. If you have trouble spotting it, ask a Cast Member to point it out for you. (You may also see a similar image repeated elsewhere in the frieze).

Chapter 2 : Magic Kingdom Scav. Hunt

- *Cinderella Fountain*

Hint 123: Check out this Hidden Surprise: if you bow or curtsy to Cinderella in front of her fountain, the crown on the wall behind her will fit perfectly on top of her head.

Adventureland

- *Adventureland bridge to the Hub*

Hint 124: Shields are propped at the sides of the bridge connecting *Adventureland* with the Hub in front of *Cinderella Castle.* Two classic Mickeys with smiley faces for "ears" appear on separate shields. One with white ears is at the bottom of one shield, while the other, an upside-down classic Mickey with blue ears, is at the top of a second shield.

- *Walt Disney's Enchanted Tiki Room*

Hint 125: Along the left side of the entrance queue, a classic Mickey is made of three depressions in the wood, about 5 and ½ feet up from the floor, on the third post before the beginning of the wall.

Hint 126: Upside-down classic Mickeys are camouflaged in the designs at the bottom of two bird perches. One perch is to the left as you enter the theater. The other is to the right of the exit doors.

Hint 127: To the right of the entrance to *Walt Disney's Enchanted Tiki Room,* a statue with several faces has classic Mickeys formed by beads in the middle of the forehead, above the nose.

- *Near The Magic Carpets of Aladdin*

Hint 128: A charm embedded in the cement between *The Magic Carpets of Aladdin* exit and the Agrabah Bazaar shop contains a tiny classic Mickey. It's near a shop pole that has blue paint above its base.

Fantasyland

- *Princess Fairytale Hall*

Hint 129: Mickey's profile is in a painting in *Princess Fairytale Hall*, left-side queue. The side view of Mickey's ghostly face looking in a second-floor window is in a painting of a cottage with a water wheel in front. Find the painting on the right wall at the end of the Lightning Lane queue. You can also spot this painting from the end of the Standby queue, just before entering to meet the Princesses.

- *Mickey's PhilharMagic*

Hint 130: In the first waiting area inside, the wall mural with musical instruments has several small white classic Mickeys.

Hint 131: On the right vertical border of the video screen in the main theater, a classic Mickey hides inside a French horn.

Hint 132: In the "Be Our Guest" portion of the movie, there is a point where you are watching Lumiere dancing on the table with other characters. The view goes to an overhead shot and there are shadows cast on the table from the candle hands of Lumiere. These shadows come together at times to form what appear to be Hidden Mickeys.

Hint 133: In "The Little Mermaid" segment, Ariel throws jewels out into the water in front of her. Focus on the gold ring to the right of Ariel. A dark classic Mickey is visible just as you first spot the open center of the ring as it starts rotating. The center hole in the ring becomes round—not Mickey-shaped—as the ring completes its rotation.

Hint 134: Stay alert for the orange dancing trees in "The Lion King" segment. At times, the circular tops of orange trees come together as classic Mickeys. One image is to the left of the sun which has an outer ring of triangles, and a blue zebra's tail is over the

Chapter 2 : Magic Kingdom Scav. Hunt

left (the viewer's right) ear of another orange tree classic Mickey.

Hint 135: Watch closely as Aladdin and Jasmine ride their magic carpet in the sky. Stare at the bottom left of the screen for a quick glimpse of three buildings on the ground. Their bright domes are clustered together as a classic Mickey, tilted left. The lower dome sits in a larger round dark circle to form the "head" of the Hidden Mickey.

Hint 136: Music stands shaped like classic Mickeys are on shelves along the walls and high up above the merchandise in Fantasy Faire at the exit of *Mickey's PhilharMagic*.

Tomorrowland

- Tomorrowland Transit Authority PeopleMover

Hint 137: The woman getting her hair done sports a belt buckle with a classic Hidden Mickey.

- Merchant of Venus

Hint 138: Find a mural on the wall with a depiction of *Tomorrowland*. In the foreground is one of Stitch's cousins holding a Mickey balloon. (Mickey's face is on the balloon.)

Hint 139: In the middle right of the same mural, another cousin of Stitch is wearing Mickey ears.

- Tomorrowland "Cool Scanner" Station

Hint 140: Several tiny, dark classic Mickeys are formed by holes underneath the overhead dome of the station.

- Walt Disney's Carousel of Progress

Hint 141: In the first scene, on the right side of the stage, where the daughter is getting ready for the evening (on Valentine's Day), a classic Mickey made of cloth decorates the top of her mirror.

Hint 142: In the third scene, Mickey's Sorcerer's Hat sits at the right side of the room, next to the girl in the shaker machine.

Hint 143: In the last scene, an abstract Mickey Mouse as the Sorcerer's apprentice from the film *Fantasia* is in a painting on the dining room wall. To spot it, look immediately to the left rear of the scene as it rotates into view. The painting is on the dining room's right rear wall.

Hint 144: On the left side of the room, a red nutcracker shaped like Mickey Mouse stands on the left side of the mantelpiece.

Hint 145: Under the Christmas tree, a plush Mickey Mouse is behind the wrapped presents.

Hint 146: On the last stage, one of the Christmas presents near the tree (near Grandfather's chair) is decorated with a large classic Mickey head cut out of green paper and glued to the side of the gift, which is sometimes partially hidden by another present, so you may only see the ears and part of the top of Mickey's head. The green Mickey ears are to the right of Grandpa's lower leg.

Hint 147: A classic Mickey appears (just for a few seconds) on the top of a spaceship in the middle of the television screen. Look for it just as the game starts on the TV, before Grandma starts playing.

Hint 148: Salt and pepper shakers on the kitchen counter have Mickey ears.

- *Astro Orbiter*
Hint 149: A small classic Mickey is traced in the cement close to a *Tomorrowland Transit Authority PeopleMover* support beam near *Astro Orbiter* on the side toward *Space Mountain,* between Cool Ship and The Lunching Pad.

Chapter 2 : Magic Kingdom Scav. Hunt

- *Monsters, Inc. Laugh Floor*

Hint 150: As you enter the attraction, look for a window display of a city on the rear of the right-hand wall just past the entrance doors to the second room. A classic Mickey is under the apex of the triangular roof segment on the building in the front center of the window display.

Fantasyland

- *Enchanted Tales with Belle*

Hint 151: Along the Standby entrance queue, in the window to your left as you enter the first room of Maurice's cottage, look at the lower left pane. An image of Donald Duck is in the glass swirls at the middle right side of the pane.

Hint 152: Inside the first room of Maurice's cottage, a stack of firewood stands to the left of the fireplace. An upright classic Mickey made of three logs is at the lower middle of the stack, and a sideways classic Mickey is at the upper middle left of the stack. Other combinations of logs also resemble classic Mickeys.

Hint 153: The red carpet in the Wardrobe Room has a number of small Hidden Mickeys. A pseudo-triangle looks like a hat on each Mickey head.

Hint 154: In the Library where you meet Belle, a book with Mickey-shaped bookmarks on its spine is at the right rear corner of the room. It's the fifth book from the right, above a blue and gold horizontal frieze midway up the wall.

Main Street, U.S.A.

- *Town Square Theater*

Hint 155: In the last room in the queue just before you enter Mickey's Dressing Room to *Meet Mickey*, there are mail slots for the theater cast. Mickey has his own personal mail slot.

Hint 156: A classic Mickey made of metal rings lies in an upper compartment of Mickey's open magic chest in the Greeting Room.

Hint 157: Inside Mickey's magic chest, on the right, there's a classic Mickey lock on a chain. (It's sometimes covered by a scarf.) Additional Mickey-shaped locks can often be spotted in various locations in the Greeting Room.

Hint 158: Oswald the Lucky Rabbit is drawn on a piece of paper at the upper part of a bulletin board at the back of the room. He's next to a drawing of Mickey Mouse.

Hint 159: Just before the exit door from the Greeting Room, three large Mickey Mouse playing cards are held upright by a long gold clip on the floor. In the middle of the clip, a classic Mickey wearing a triangular "hat" resembles a Sorcerer Mickey.

Hint 160: Classic Mickey locks hang from the side of several metal display tables in the gift shop, and more classic Mickey locks hang high on the front of the "Tank of Terror" display case.

Hint 161: A birdhouse from the now closed *Mickey's Toontown Fair* sits on a tall merchandise cabinet at the left side of the shop (as you enter from outside). The front door of the birdhouse is shaped like a classic Mickey.

Fantasyland

- *Fairytale Garden*

Hint 162: At the base of the first light pole on the right as you enter, a classic Mickey that looks like a piece of different-colored stucco is in the cement on the side next to the fence.

Chapter 2 : Magic Kingdom Scav. Hunt

Hint 163: A side profile of Pluto's head is on the wall, to the upper left of the stage. It's left of the brick circle and above the stairs.

Hint 164: A side view of Angus, Merida's horse, is outlined on the wall at the rear of *Fairytale Garden*. Angus is rearing up on his hind legs and is facing right.

- *Storybook Circus area*

Hint 165: Between the exit of the *Fantasyland Train Station* and *Dumbo the Flying Elephant* is a trail of large and small (mother and baby) elephant tracks. These prints in the pavement come together at times to form classic Mickeys.

Hint 166: On the "Giraffes" boxcar in *Casey Jr. Splash 'N' Soak Station,* a classic Mickey is hidden in the clouds behind a giraffe in a painting on the side of the boxcar that faces the restrooms. This cloud Hidden Mickey is behind the lower part of the neck of the tall giraffe, and it's tilted to the right.

Hint 167: Find the 'Elephants' train car in *Casey Jr. Splash 'N' Soak Station* for a Hidden Surprise. On the rear wall of this train car is the number '71,' representing 1971 - the year Magic Kingdom and Walt Disney World opened.

Hint 168: Under the entrance sign to *The Barnstormer,* two classic Mickeys are in the scrollwork below Goofy's picture. The images are at the top corners on each side of the faux ticket booth window.

Hint 169: On the huge billboard on the right side of *The Barnstormer* (the billboard the ride train hurtles through), a tiny gray classic Mickey hides in the middle of the propeller of the lower plane on the far right side of the billboard.

Hint 170: A poster of Daisy Duck ("Madame Daisy Fortuna") is outside to the left of the entrance to *Pete's Silly Sideshow*. A faint

75

classic Mickey is traced on the upper part of her light green blouse, just to the right of her right index finger.

Hint 171: Eight tiny Mickey balloons are scattered around the large "Storybook Circus" painting at the rear of a tent next to *Pete's Silly Sideshow*.

Hint 172: A classic Hidden Mickey is on a sleeping cheetah inside *Big Top Souvenirs*. The cheetah is on a wall painting behind a register counter and its leg hangs down from a tree branch. The reddish-brown Mickey spot is on the hanging left lower leg, just above the ankle area.

Hint 173: A classic Mickey is formed by a manhole cover (the "head") and two elephant tracks (the "ears") near the entrance to the Lightning Lane queue for *Dumbo the Flying Elephant*.

Hint 174: A classic three-circle Mickey metal design sits above the *Disney Vacation Club* sign.

Hint 175: Embedded in the cement walkway in front of the *Disney Vacation Club* kiosk and across from *Ariel's Grotto* is a classic Hidden Mickey formed of a survey marker and two adjacent pebbles. It's near a cart track indented in the cement.

- *Gaston's Tavern area*

Hint 176: A tiny classic Mickey made of dark impressions hides on the rock that forms the base of Gaston's Statue, which stands in front of *Gaston's Tavern*. The Hidden Mickey is near the waterline below the back of Gaston's left leg.

Hint 177: A Hidden Donald Duck is at the upper left corner of a portrait in the *Bonjour Village Gifts* shop. The portrait is centered on the wall at the rear of the store and hangs near the ceiling.

Chapter 2 : Magic Kingdom Scav. Hunt

Hint 178: A classic Hidden Mickey is formed by horseshoe prints in the sidewalk. Find it as you walk from *Gaston's Tavern* toward *Be Our Guest Restaurant*; it's near the end of the short rock wall on your right and close to a pole with lanterns. Two horseshoe prints form the "head" and two other prints form the "ears." (The image is sometimes covered by a trash can).

- *Near Enchanted Tales with Belle*

Hint 179: An image that resembles Oswald the Lucky Rabbit is formed by three embedded pebbles in the middle of a walkway. To find the image, stop across from the *Enchanted Tales with Belle* entrance (and waiting time) sign and look down in the middle of the main walkway to *Be Our Guest Restaurant*.

Liberty Square

- *Liberty Tree Tavern*

Hint 180: Look for a spice rack to the right of the fireplace on the rear wall of the waiting area. Three grapes in a small still-life painting on the spice rack form a classic Mickey.

Hint 181: Turn left from the waiting area and go up the stairs. Then turn right and enter a brown room with a fireplace on the inside. Go up to the fireplace (you'll have to climb a few more steps) and look for a classic Mickey in the clouds. You'll find it on the left side of the upper part of the painting that's hanging to the left of George Washington's portrait.

Frontierland

- *Frontier Trading Post store*

Hint 182: In the "How to Pin Trade" wall posters, a cowboy's lanyard has a black classic Mickey.

- Pecos Bill Tall Tale Inn and Cafe

Hint 183: Inside the cafe, find the plates sitting upright along a ledge near the ceiling behind the middle of the serving counter. On the third plate from the left, at the upper left and near the inside circle of the plate, three red spots behind the white bird form a classic Mickey.

Adventureland

- Tortuga Tavern

Hint 184: In a window display about pirates inside the *Tortuga Tavern* restaurant, three candles stuck in a bowl form a classic Hidden Mickey.

Main Street, U.S.A.

Hint 185: On the roof of *The Crystal Palace restaurant*, the circles in the middle row of the tower above the main entrance resemble Mickey ears.

Hint 186: A tiny classic Mickey is impressed in the cement outside the *Crystal Arts* store entrance. It's on a gray flagstone between the red cement and the bricks of the side street off *Main Street*. Find a long crack (between red cement sections) that's parallel to *Main Street* and starts in front of the entrance pillars at the store entrance. The gray flagstone is at the end of this crack, and the Hidden Mickey is at the lower right corner of the flagstone as you face the store.

Hint 187: Outside along *Main Street*, near the *Emporium* shop and next to the *Main Street Fashion and Apparel store*, a sign on a door has two classic Mickeys, at the top and bottom along the border.

Hint 188: The cupola above the *Emporium*, in the middle recessed area of the store, has stained-glass windows just below the highest eaves. The central flower circle in each window is joined with two frosted "ear" panels to form classic Mickeys.

Chapter 2 : Magic Kingdom Scav. Hunt

Hint 189: In the outside Aladdin display window of the *Emporium* store, you'll find a small classic Mickey window in the wall of a building. Look on the left side of the display for a window in a building in the second row.

Hint 190: The sign on the *Caffe Italiano cart*, which appears seasonally in front of *Tony's Town Square Restaurant*, includes a classic Mickey in its design.

Hints 191 and 192: When you enter the inside dining area of *Tony's Town Square Restaurant*, look left to the corner and find two classic Hidden Mickeys:
- spot the flowers on a high shelf. Three of the flowers, usually red roses, are arranged as a classic Mickey.
- locate the second tile from the corner on the floor along the far wall. There's a classic Mickey impression at the center right side of this black tile. If you view the Hidden Mickey from the seating area, it will appear upside-down.

Hint 193: A small classic Hidden Mickey is on the middle back of the overhanging entrance sign to *Tony's Town Square Restaurant*. Look up as you exit the restaurant.

Hint 194: A Hidden Surprise is traced in the walkway cement right in front of the outside seating area of *Tony's Town Square Restaurant*: paw prints of Lady and the Tramp are inside a heart pierced by Cupid's arrow.

Hint 195: Several classic Mickeys adorn the gear on the horse pulling the *Main Street Trolley*.

Hint 196: In *Town Square Plaza*, walk about seven or eight steps away from the island curb toward the train station. As you approach the station, a classic Mickey is formed by circles on the train station ceiling. You might call this a "positional" classic Mickey because you have to be in just the right position to see it.

Train Station Exit from Main Street

Hint 197: Classic Mickeys are repeated atop a tall gate, which is usually folded inside a recess beside the entrance and exit tunnel walkway under the *Main Street Train Station.*

Chapter 3

Epcot Scavenger Hunt

• • • • • •

Before You Start

* Many great Hidden Mickeys are in Standby queues, and you might miss them if you take the Lightning Lanes. So, for optimal Hidden Mickey hunting, (if you choose to spend the money), I recommend reserving Lightning Lane (by purchasing, on the My Disney Experience app, the current version of Disney Genie+ and/or Individual Lightning Lane) for the following attractions: **Soarin' Around the World, Living with the Land,** *and* **Spaceship Earth.** *In addition, consult your My Disney Experience app: if the Standby queue is not open for* **Guardians of the Galaxy: Cosmic Rewind,** *then join the Virtual Queue.*

* Be sure to keep track of your Lightning Lane windows and return to those attractions at the appropriate times. In the Scavenger Hunt below, if you come to your Lightning Lane attraction and it's not time for it yet, you can skip to the next stop in the Hunt and return to the Lightning Lane attraction during your time window. If you don't opt for the Lightning Lane options, try to line up for headliner attractions during Early Entry or right after park opening.

* Some of the Hidden Mickeys in this park are in restaurants and shops. Be considerate of fellow guests and Cast Members as you search. Tell them what you're looking for, so they can share in the fun. Avoid

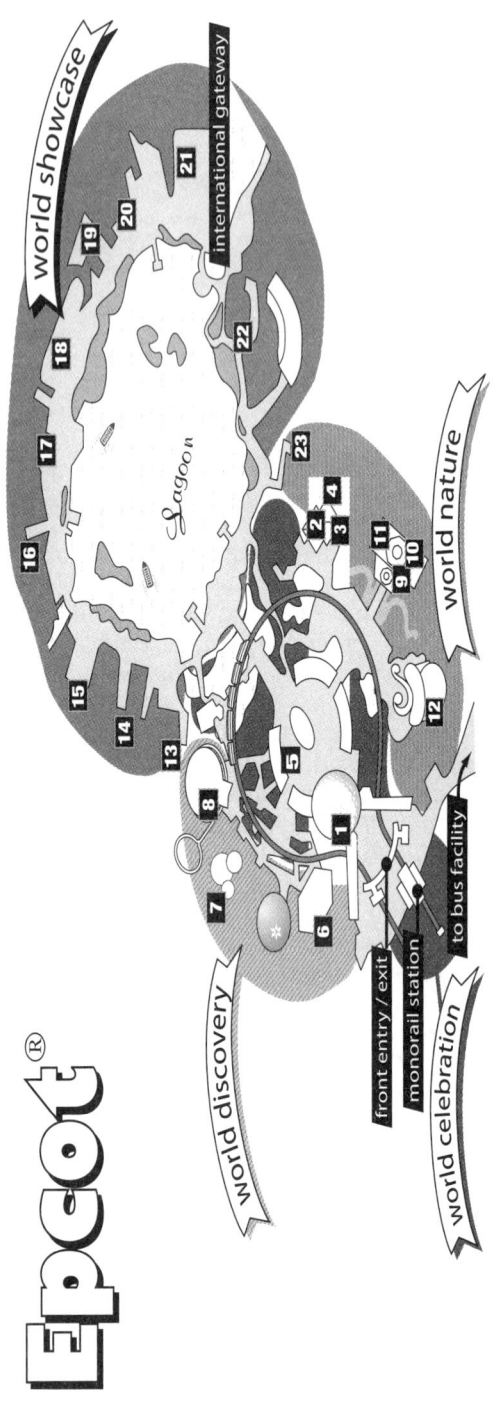

Chapter 3: Epcot Scavenger Hunt

World Celebration
1. Spaceship Earth® Pavilion
2. Disney & Pixar Short Film Festival
3. Journey Into Imagination with Figment
4. ImageWorks
5. Club Cool

World Discovery
6. Guardians of the Galaxy: Cosmic Rewind
7. Mission: SPACE® Pavilion
8. Test Track® Pavilion

World Nature
9. Living with the Land
10. Awesome Planet
11. Soarin'® Around the World
12. The Seas with Nemo & Friends® Pavilion
    Turtle Talk With Crush

World Showcase
13. Mexico: Gran Fiesta Tour Starring the Three Caballeros
14. Norway: Frozen Ever After
15. China: Reflections of China
16. Germany
17. Italy
18. The American Adventure: The American Adventure Show
19. Japan
20. Morocco
21. France: Impressions de France
    Remy's Ratatouille Adventure
22. United Kingdom
23. Canada Far and Wide in Circle-Vision 360

searching restaurants at busy mealtimes unless you are one of the diners.

* Each person has unique needs for sustenance. If I don't have specific suggestions for restaurants (related to Hidden Mickeys), then I leave it to you to decide when and where to break for snacks/meals.

*
    If the Standby queue is open, make a beeline for **Guardians of the Galaxy: Cosmic Rewind.** *(Or choose Virtual Queue.)*
Clue 1: <u>Along the entrance queue, search for a Hidden Mickey in a display behind glass.</u>
5 points

*
    Now it's time for **Remy's Ratatouille Adventure.** <u>(All new Hidden Mickeys!)</u>
Clue 2: Find four Hidden Remys as you stroll outside through Paris towards *Remy's Ratatouille Adventure.*
5 points for four Hidden Remys

Clue 3: Around the covered winding outside entrance queue for *Remy's Ratatouille Adventure*, study the pavement for Remy's footprints.
5 points

Clue 4: Spot classic Hidden Mickeys at the entrance to the building that houses *Remy's Ratatouille Adventure.*
3 points

Clue 5: Squint for Remy hidden on the wall of the inside queue.
3 points

Clue 6: Along the queue, walk slowly through the artist's studio to locate a tiny black classic Hidden Mickey on a painting.
5 points

Clue 7: At the end of the ride, right after you leave your "ratmobile," scan the wall alongside the ride vehicles for a small Hidden Mickey.
5 points

Chapter 3: Epcot Scavenger Hunt

✱
   Walk fast to ***Frozen Ever After.***
Clue 8: When you reach the inside Standby queue, look high for a Hidden Mickey.
4 points

✱
   Cross over to *The Land pavilion* now (or wait for your *Lightning Lane* time) and get in line for ***Soarin' Around the World***.

Clue 9: In the pre-show video, spot the Mickey ears.
2 points

Clue 10: In the pre-show video, stay alert for Hidden Character clothing logos.
4 points for spotting two

Clue 11: During the ride, search the hills to the left of the castle in Germany for a Hidden Mickey near a footbridge.
5 points

Clue 12: During the ride, focus on the sky for a floating Hidden Mickey.
4 points

Clue 13: Don't miss a classic Mickey on the Fiji island!
5 points

Clue 14: Look for some floating Mickeys below you near the end of the ride.
3 points

Clue 15: A huge classic Mickey in the sky greets you at the end of your *Soarin'* ride.
3 points

✱
   Walk to ***Test Track***.

Clue 16: In the Standby entrance queue, look for a classic Mickey traced on the wall.
5 points

Clue 17: Now spot a white classic Mickey on the wall.
4 points

Clue 18: Watch for an interactive touch screen on the right wall of the Standby entrance queue. Make your own classic Mickey on top of the car!
5 points

Clue 19: On the ride, look for a small, upright Hidden Mickey to your left during the "Drive Systems Analysis."
5 points

Clue 20: On the ride, watch for a road sign on your right to spot a Hidden Mickey.
5 points

Clue 21: Now, on your left, don't miss a Hidden Surprise quote from the movie "Cars."
5 points

Clue 22: Keep your eyes left for a small, purple Hidden Mickey on the wall.
5 points

*
Cross over to ***Mission: SPACE***.

Clue 23: <u>Along the entrance queue, scan the control room on your right for two full-body Hidden Mickeys.</u>
5 points for both

Clue 24: In the cockpit, before you're launched into space, smile at a Hidden Surprise reference to the Disney Imagineers.
4 points

Clue 25: Look for a Hidden Mickey on a video console in the exhibit area (at the exit).
2 points

Clue 26: Spot a Hidden Mickey on the ceiling of the gift shop at the attraction exit.
4 points

Clue 27: Search for Donald and Pluto on the ceiling.
4 points for spotting both

Chapter 3: Epcot Scavenger Hunt

Clue 28: Study the spaceship in a mural in the gift shop.
3 points

Clue 29: Now squint for a small black Hidden Mickey in the same mural.
3 points

Clue 30: While you're at it, examine the mural for an upside-down classic Mickey.
3 points

Clue 31: Now glance low for classic Mickeys near the floor.
2 points

Clue 32: Find two classic Mickeys and a side-profile Mickey on the wall of the gift shop.
2 points for spotting all three

Clue 33: Outside in the front plaza, search for a classic Mickey on the moon.
3 points

Clue 34: Look down for a classic Mickey in the blue tile area out front.
5 points

Clue 35: In a blue tile stripe out front, spot a white classic Mickey near a bluish and salmon-colored disk.
4 points

Clue 36: Find two more classic tile Mickeys near a drain cover.
4 points for spotting both

Cross over to *The Seas with Nemo & Friends* pavilion. Check out **Turtle Talk With Crush**. In the waiting area, search for two Hidden Mickeys.
Clue 37: Spot a tiny Mickey in the coral on the wall.
5 points

Clue 38: Admire a Hidden Mickey on a starfish.
4 points

Clue 39: During the show, study the undersea images on the show screen for a classic Mickey.
3 points

*
Head toward the *Mexico Pavilion* in World Showcase. Eat an early lunch to avoid the crowds. *The San Angel Inn Restaurante* in the Mexico pavilion is a good choice if you have 11:30 a.m. or so reservations. Ride *Gran Fiesta Tour Starring the Three Caballeros* before or after lunch.

If you eat in the *San Angel Inn*, look for classic Mickeys in the smoke rising from the volcano (see Clue 49).

* Ride **Gran Fiesta Tour Starring the Three Caballeros** in Mexico and keep your eyes peeled for Hidden Mickeys.

Clue 40: Squint for a classic Mickey in the water to the right of your boat.
5 points

Clue 41: At the beginning of the ride, take a close look at the smoke rising from the volcano.
4 points

Clue 42: In the first tunnel, search for Mickey on a necklace.
5 points

Clue 43: <u>Stay alert for three pots that make a classic Mickey.</u>
3 points

Clue 44: Find Mickey on a video screen on the wall.
5 points

Clue 45: Spot classic Mickeys in a small blue pond to the left of the boat.
4 points

Clue 46: Don't miss Mickey in a barge!
3 points

Chapter 3: Epcot Scavenger Hunt

Clue 47: Now, look for Mickey in a window.
5 points

Clue 48: In the final scene, turn on a light (your camera, phone, etc.) and highlight a Hidden Mickey under the platform to the left of your boat. (Psst! There are four of them. You might get lucky and see all four!)
5 points for one or more

After exiting the ride, walk to the outside of the *San Angel Inn Restaurante* (if you haven't already been there) and look for classic Mickeys that appear and disappear.

Clue 49: Observe the smoke rising from the volcano.
4 points

* Wander through **Norway**.

Clue 50: Check out *The Wandering Reindeer* gift shop for a Hidden Mickey inside.
3 points

* Stroll over to **China**.

Clue 51: Search for Hidden Mickeys on posts in the courtyard.
4 points

Now study the water in *China* for possible bonus points.
2 bonus points for one or more Hidden Mickeys

Cross over the bridge to the **Outpost**.

Clue 52: Check out the wooden poles.
3 points

Clue 53: Locate Mickey's name (twice) hidden high inside the *Village Traders Shop*.
5 points for both

Walt Disney World's Hidden Mickeys

* Walk left to **Germany**.

Clue 54: As you walk into the plaza, look for the classic Mickey on a suit of armor on the building to your right.
3 points

Clue 55: Spot Mickey behind a large bell.
3 points

Clue 56: Search for Mickey near a lion.
3 points

Clue 57: Just inside the *Karamell-Küche* shop, notice a Hidden Mickey design near a window.
3 points

Clue 58: Study the merchandise displays inside *Karamell-Küche* for a Hidden Mickey.
5 points

Check out the landscaping around the train attraction to earn yourself some possible bonus points. (Note: These Hidden Mickeys come and go.)

Try for more bonus points: someone recognizable might be sitting in a window seat of one of the passenger trains!
2 bonus points for each image you spot.

* Stop at **Italy** to inspect the shops, statues, and restaurants.

Clue 59: A classic Mickey is near the wine!
2 points

Clue 60: Look for Mickey behind a statue.
3 points

* Go to **The American Adventure** pavilion.

Clue 61: Search the walls inside for a classic Mickey in roses.
4 points

Chapter 3: Epcot Scavenger Hunt

Now inspect the rear wall of the rotunda, upstairs and down, for classic Hidden Mickeys:

Clue 62: Study a picture in the rotunda for Hidden Mickeys on two metal beams.
3 points for spotting both

Clue 63: Take a good look at the bronze eagle reliefs in the rotunda.
2 points for each floor; 4 points total

Clue 64: Enjoy the "American Indian Art" exhibit in the Gallery room for a Hidden Mickey.
4 points

Watch ***The American Adventure show***. (Tip: Try to sit on the right side of the theater for the best view of the Hidden Mickeys.)

Clue 65: At the beginning of the film, look at the rocks behind a kneeling female pilgrim.
4 points

Clue 66: Stay alert for a Mickey image on a stockade.
3 points

Clue 67: Study some fruit at the gas station.
3 points

Clue 68: At the end, watch the fireworks' explosions behind the *Statue of Liberty*.
4 points

Clue 69: At a time between stage performances, wander over to *America Gardens Theatre* and find a Hidden Mickey near the stage.
2 points

* Stroll over to ***Japan***.

Clue 70: Search for a classic Mickey in the koi fish pond.
2 points

Clue 71: Check out the grates at the bases of the trees in the courtyard.
2 points

Clue 72: Study the pond by *Katsura Grill*.
4 bonus points

Clue 73: Locate a classic Mickey in the *Kawaii exhibit* at the rear of the pavilion.
3 points

Clue 74: Now spot another Mickey Mouse image and two other Hidden Characters in the *Kawaii exhibit*.
4 points for all three

Clue 75: In the *Mitsukoshi store*, admire the oyster exhibit for a Hidden Mickey!
3 points

Clue 76: In the *Mitsukoshi store*, find three-circle Hidden Mickeys in glass walls.
3 points for one or more

Clue 77: Look around for Mickey in the bushes by the lagoon.
3 points

For more possible bonus points, scan the landscaping along the right side of the Japan Pavilion for a classic Hidden Mickey. (This image comes and goes).
5 bonus points

* Meander to **Morocco**.

Clue 78: Gaze at the front of the shop on the promenade for Hidden Mickeys.
2 points for one or more

Clue 79: Find a Mickey made of basket lids on the wall of a shop.
4 points

Clue 80: Study a mural at the rear of the pavilion for three Hidden Mickeys.
5 points for spotting all three

Chapter 3: Epcot Scavenger Hunt

* Go to **France**.

Clue 81: Examine the grates at the bases of the trees in the courtyard.
2 points

Clue 82: Find the classic Mickey bush on the right side of the ornamental garden.
3 points

Clue 83: Look high for classic Mickeys on the outside of a shop.
2 points

Clue 84: <u>Search for a classic Hidden Mickey on a wall inside a shop in the pavilion.</u>
3 points

Clue 85: In the movie *Impressions de France,* spot Mickey's head and ears in the background of the wedding scene.
4 points

* Enter the **United Kingdom**.

Clue 86: Check out a classic sports Mickey from the street.
2 points

* Now walk over to **Canada** to find more classic Mickeys.

Clue 87: Examine the totem pole on the left near the steps into the pavilion.
3 points

Clue 88: Study the front of the stone steps near the theater for a classic Mickey.
4 points

Clue 89: Step inside *Le Cellier Steakhouse* to find a Mickey made of wine.
3 points

*
   Go to the **Living with the Land** ride in *The Land pavilion* at your Lightning Lane time.

Clue 90: Take a good look at the bubbles in the mural at the rear of the entrance queue.
3 points

Clue 91: Don't miss a Hidden Surprise image on the far right wall that you pass by just before reaching the loading dock. Scan this wall for an outline of a Prince and Princess!
5 points

Clue 92: Examine the mural behind the loading area near the farmer's hat.
3 points

Clue 93: Now check the lower part of the mural behind the loading area. (You can spot this image from the boat).
3 points

Clue 94: Find a three-rock classic Hidden Mickey in a water garden.
5 points

Clue 95: Search for a garden hose classic Mickey.
4 points

Clue 96: Spot Mickey in a horizontal water tube. (Minnie may be in there, too!)
4 points for Mickey and 4 bonus points for Minnie

Clue 97: Don't miss a Mickey-shaped wire frame! You'll often see vines growing over it. (This frame is sometimes moved around to different areas).
2 points

Clue 98: Along the ride, stay alert for one or more plastic gourds shaped like Mickey. (These gourds sometimes appear in different areas along the boat ride).
3 bonus points

Clue 99: Look for plants arranged to form a Hidden Mickey.
4 points

Chapter 3: Epcot Scavenger Hunt

Clue 100: In the last room, scan inside a fish tank for a Hidden Mickey.
5 points

Clue 101: Toward the end of the ride, find the green Hidden Mickey in the round test tube holder in a lab room.
3 points

* Now relax and enjoy the ***Awesome Planet*** film.

Clue 102: <u>Pay attention during the last half of the film for a silver classic Hidden Mickey.</u>
3 points

* Go to the outside railing of ***The Garden Grill*** restaurant upstairs and take a good look at the back wall.

Clue 103: Find and then marvel at the green face of Mickey Mouse on the left side of the large mural of vegetation. He's in three-quarter profile on the right side of a single fern and he's well camouflaged by the fern's leaves. (He's easier to spot from inside the restaurant.)
5 points

Go to the *interior railing* to the left of the pavilion's main entrance.

Clue 104: Focus on the side of one of the globes hanging over the lobby to spot another Mickey.
3 points

Now walk *outside* under the overhang *and face the entrance doors.*

Clue 105: Study the mosaic mural on the wall to your right for a classic Mickey in jewels.
4 points

Clue 106: Search the same mosaic mural for a classic Mickey in grapes.
4 points

Walk down the sloping walkway (from the pavilion) until you come to *"The Land" sign* out front.

Clue 107: Search for a classic Mickey in the stones embedded in a support for "The Land" sign. (Tip: The support is covered with tiles and stone designs.)
4 points

* Head over to **The Seas with Nemo & Friends** pavilion.

Clue 108: Look up along the entrance queue for the ride for a Hidden Mickey.
3 bonus points (This image is not always present.)

Clue 109: On the ride, keep alert for a Mickey in the rock. Look below the fifth video screen to spot it.
5 points

Clue 110: Walk upstairs and search for one or more Hidden Mickeys on the aquarium floor.
5 points for one or more

Clue 111: Stroll to the upper level of the manatee viewing area and look for Hidden Mickeys on the wall. (These Hidden Mickeys come and go.)
3 bonus points

Clue 112: Cross to the upper display room above *Turtle Talk with Crush* to find two Hidden Mickeys on the wall in a lower panel.
5 points for both

Clue 113: Study an upper panel in this same display window for another Hidden Mickey.
5 points

Clue 114: Downstairs, find two Hidden Mickeys in bubbles on the wall near the manatees.
5 points for spotting both

Clue 115: <u>In the Ocean Life room, spot one of the creatures wearing a Mickey hat! (Note:</u>

Chapter 3: Epcot Scavenger Hunt

<u>the creatures don't always cooperate).</u>
5 points

Clue 116: In Bruce's room downstairs, look around for classic Mickeys in two different windows.
4 points for spotting both

Clue 117: Now search for Mickey near the exit gift shop.
3 points

✱
    Go to the Imagination! pavilion and ride ***Journey Into Imagination With Figment***.

Clue 118: Locate a small Buzz Lightyear figure along the entrance queue.
5 points

Clue 119: Near Buzz, find a tiny Tinker Bell and a figure wearing Mickey ears.
5 points for both

Clue 120: On the ride, find a Hidden Mickey on a greaseboard. (Note: It's not always there.)
5 bonus points

Clue 121: Squint for a black pair of Mickey ears in the Sight Room.
4 points

Clue 122: Look up at Figment's bathtub for a classic Mickey.
3 points

Clue 123: Now look up again in Figment's bathroom for another classic Mickey near the bathtub.
3 points

Clue 124: Find a classic Mickey on a cloud in the rainbow room.
3 points

Clue 125: Search for a Mickey in snow.
5 points

Clue 126: Look for a classic Mickey on the wall along the exit hallway.
3 points

When you reach **ImageWorks** ...

Clue 127: Locate a Hidden Mickey in big bubbles that rotate on a wall.
3 points

* Walk to **Club Cool**. Enjoy free exotic and refreshing soft drinks from other countries.

Clue 128: Search inside *Club Cool* for a few classic Mickeys on the wall.
3 points

* Head for **Spaceship Earth** at your Lightning Lane time.

Clue 129: During the ride, keep alert for classic Mickey light patterns on the floor to your right.
5 points

Clue 130: Now look quickly to your left for a Hidden Mickey in scrolls.
5 points

Clue 131: During the ride, notice the Hidden Mickey on the document in front of the sleeping monk.
4 points

Clue 132: In the Renaissance section, look quickly to your left to spot a classic Mickey formed by paint circles on a tabletop near a painter.
4 points

Clue 133: On your left, you'll soon approach another artist with a Hidden Mickey.
3 points

Clue 134: Scan left for a Hidden Surprise that references Walt Disney Imagineering.
3 points

Chapter 3: Epcot Scavenger Hunt

Clue 135: Watch for a chalkboard with the name of a famous Mickey Mouse cartoon.
4 points

Clue 136: Don't miss another Hidden Surprise behind a couch!
3 points

Clue 137: Stare at a cityscape on your left for a tiny classic Mickey.
5 points

Clue 138: On your journey back down from space, choose any options on your interactive screen that include the sea or underwater living and watch for bubbles.
4 points

Clue 139: After you exit the ride vehicle, look up for Mickey in the "Project Tomorrow" area.
3 points

Time now to tally your score.
Total Points for Epcot = _____

How'd you do?
Up to 202 points - Bronze
203 to 402 points - Silver
403 points and over - Gold
504 points - Perfect Score

If you earned bonus points in ***China***, ***Germany***, ***Japan***, ***Living with the Land***, ***The Seas with Nemo & Friends***, and/or ***Journey Into Imagination with Figment***, you may have done even better!

Chapter 3: Epcot Scavenger Hunt

- *Guardians of the Galaxy: Cosmic Rewind*

Hint 1: <u>A colorful display model of a city on planet Xandar is along the Virtual Entrance queue. Near the perimeter of the model, three small domes (blue "head" with one green and one blue "ear") sit in the grass in a park behind some tall buildings.</u>

- *Remy's Ratatouille Adventure* <u>(All new Hidden Mickeys!)</u>

Hint 2: Look for Hidden Remys everywhere:
* on the metal side supports of the benches
* along the top of the design swirls in the fence by the canal (you can see his ear, eye, and an outline of his head)
* in the middle of some manhole covers
* in the relief design of the large fountain (he appears to be running around just below the lip of the middle basin of the fountain).

Hint 3: Find Remy's footprints in the cement in a rear corner of the outside entrance queue for *Remy's Ratatouille Adventure*. They're near a blue door, and the footprints lead to a "Cast Members Only" door. You may have to step out of the main queue to wind over to the footprints.

Hint 4: At the entrance to the attraction building, swirls at the sides of the queue signs and clock above you form tilted classic Hidden Mickeys.

Hint 5: Small images of Remy are hidden in the red wallpaper along the inside queue.

Hint 6: Along the entrance queue, you'll enter an artist's studio filled with paintings. At the right side of the room, an abstract painting with dark blotches is propped on the lower shelf of a table - a tiny black classic Mickey is at the left side of the artist's signature at the bottom right of the painting.

Hint 7: At the end of the ride, as you step out of your "ratmobile" vehicle, study the wall to your left. A few feet to the lower right of the far left bottle-cap Exit sign, three tiny holes in the wall form a classic Hidden Mickey.

- *Frozen Ever After*

Hint 8: Along the inside entrance queue, three plates on the wall come together to form a classic Hidden Mickey. To find the image, after you walk into the room to the left (the "Ice Master & Deliverer of Arendelle" room) just inside the building, turn around back toward the entrance door and look above you. The three-plate Mickey is in the middle of a group of plates high up on the wall.

Chapter 3: Epcot Scavenger Hunt

The Land

-Soarin' Around the World

Hint 9: In the pre-show video, a man who is wearing Mickey Mouse ears is asked to take them off.

Hint 10: In the pre-show video, a boy sitting in his ride seat is wearing a red shirt with a Grumpy logo and shorts sporting Mickey Mouse.

Hint 11: Early in the ride, you'll see a castle in the hills to your right. Look left to a footbridge crossing a chasm between two hills. You can spot a small black classic Mickey marking, illuminated by sunlight, on the side of the hill to the right of the far end of the footbridge and at about the same level as the footbridge.

Hint 12: In the scene with hot air balloons floating above the desert, three colorful balloons in the distance merge together as a classic Hidden Mickey. The image is visible for only a few seconds.

Hint 13: Rocks on the Fiji Island beach form a classic Hidden Mickey, tilted slightly to the left. The image is best seen as it moves under you at the lower right of the screen.

Hint 14: As you approach Spaceship Earth near the end of the ride, some people walking below you are carrying Mickey balloons.

Hint 15: The last big image is a classic Mickey made of bursts of fireworks (Mickey's "ears") over *Spaceship Earth* (his "head").

- Test Track

Hint 16: On the wall, along the right side of the Standby entrance queue, is a photo collage of artists and designers. A classic Mickey is traced on a transparent drawing board, just above the right hand of a man wearing glasses and drawing with a Magic Marker.

Hint 17: In the middle of the photo collage of artists and designers, a tiny white classic Mickey lies above a white vertical dashed line. This Hidden Mickey is above the left forearm of a girl who is drawing on white paper.

Hint 18: A bit further along on the right wall of the Standby queue, look for an interactive screen with design criteria (efficiency, etc.) listed above a car. Touch the area along the top of the car and circles will appear. You can arrange these circles with your finger to form a classic Mickey.

Hint 19: On the ride, during the "Drive Systems Analysis," look for "Scan Complete" on the wall to the left of the vehicle. A small, upright classic Mickey is halfway down the screen under the "C" in "Complete."

Hint 20: On the ride, at the first part of the "Responsiveness Test," a sideways classic Mickey hides on the first triangular road sign on your right. Your car then rounds a bend, and you can spot this sign one more time!

Hint 21: A Hidden Surprise appears a few seconds later in the "Responsiveness Test" as a road sign whizzes by on your left - it says "Turn Right to Go Left," which is a quote from Doc Hudson in the movie "Cars."

Hint 22: Keep your eyes left just before you burst onto the outside track. A small, purple classic Mickey is on the wall, above eye level.

- *Mission: SPACE*

Hint 23: <u>Admire the details in a control room behind glass along the right side of the Standby entrance queue. Look for two Hidden Mickeys in the control room: a small Mickey sitting in a plane on top of the monitor workstation, usually on the middle section - and a full-body standing Mickey at the back of the room under the rear video screens and behind the last or left section of the workstation.</u>

Chapter 3: Epcot Scavenger Hunt

Hint 24: After you get seated in the cockpit, study the second blue control screen from the left for a Hidden Surprise - on the middle right side of the screen is the word "Imgneer." Sounds like "Imagineer," right?

Hint 25: In the *Expedition Mars* section of the exit exhibit area, you'll find small classic Mickeys in the design of the videogame joystick consoles at the upper left and upper right corners.

Hint 26: In the center of the gift shop near the exit doors, a large side profile of Mickey Mouse is painted on the ceiling in the middle square.

Hint 27: On either side of Mickey's side profile on the ceiling are reddish side profiles of Donald Duck and Pluto (or is it Goofy?).

Hint 28: On the right side of the mural behind the gift shop's cash register, the three round thrusters behind the blue X-2 spaceship form an upside-down classic Mickey.

Hint 29: Look for Minnie Mouse in the same mural. There's a small black classic Mickey in the red dirt under her left foot.

Hint 30: On the left side of the mural behind the gift shop's cash register, you'll find an upside-down classic Mickey on the lower part of the moon.

Hint 31: The bases of some of the merchandise stands near the gift shop exit contain "support arches" in the shape of Mickey.

Hint 32: You can spot Hidden Mickeys in the electrical tubing on the wall on both sides of the exit door from the gift shop. There's a classic Mickey on one side and both a classic Mickey and a side-profile Mickey on the other.

- In the entrance plaza

Hint 33: Spot three craters that approximate a classic Mickey at the upper left of the Luna 8 landing site on the back side of the moon.

Hint 34: In the middle of a blue tile area, very near and to the left of a gold strip (as you face the attraction), you'll find a tiny tile classic Mickey (black head and blue ears).

Hint 35: A small classic Mickey formed of white tiles is toward the bottom of a blue tile stripe. Look for a bluish and salmon-colored disc in the cement, near the lowest part of the stripe. Mickey is hiding about four feet from the disc as you go toward the Mars planet.

Hint 36: Two more tile or stone classic Mickeys (black head and white ears) lie next to a drain cover. Look for the cover in a circle of tiles to the left of the *Mission: SPACE* sign.

The Seas with Nemo & Friends

- Turtle Talk With Crush

Hint 37: In the waiting room, a tiny classic Mickey hides in the pink and brown coral in the first window painting to the right as you enter the room. At the lower part of the painting, the Mickey is left of the third tallest (leftmost) blue tube, about one quarter of the distance up the side of the tube. He's reclining to the right.

Hint 38: Also in the *Turtle Talk With Crush* waiting room, look at the upper left of the second window to the right (as you enter the room) to spot "Peach" the starfish. An upside-down classic Mickey lies above the left side of Peach's "eyebrow" (Peach's left, our right).

Hint 39: During the show, look closely at the middle left side of the rear screen, near the edge, to spot a classic Mickey made of coral circles on the rock. Mickey's ears are angled to the left.

Chapter 3: Epcot Scavenger Hunt

Mexico

- Gran Fiesta Tour Starring the Three Caballeros

Hint 40: During the boat ride, you'll pass a set of lily pads that forms a classic Hidden Mickey. It's to the right of your boat as you float through the small lagoon in front of the *San Angel Inn Restaurante*, before you pass in front of the volcano. These lily pads are in the shadows, but you can usually spot them from the boat.

Hint 41: While you're in the lagoon at the beginning of the boat ride, turn to your left and watch smoke rise from the volcano. Every half minute or so, holes in the smoke form classic Mickeys that quickly disappear.

Hint 42: Along the left wall inside the first tunnel, look at the fifth man from the far end. He is wearing green shorts and has a partially covered blue classic Mickey on the front of his necklace.

Hint 43: <u>Don't miss a classic Hidden Mickey made of pots. On the left side of your boat, three pots (two white ones for "ears" and a light brown pot for the "head") come together as a Hidden Mickey at the right front corner inside a boat full of pots.</u>

Hint 44: Watch for a video screen to the right of your boat that shows a broad expanse of water in the foreground and, in the background, a shoreline edged with modern buildings set against the backdrop of a mountain. Donald Duck is parasailing over the water, but you want to focus on the buildings on the shoreline. One building on the right side of the scene has a dark classic Mickey tree in front of it.

Hint 45: About halfway through the ride, in the small blue pond to the left of the boat, classic Mickeys appear in the bubbles after Donald is taken away. Look above and also to the lower left of the octopus.

Hint 46: Toward the end of the ride, as you enter the fireworks room, three drums form a classic Hidden Mickey at the lower right of the "Viva Donald" barge to the left of your boat.

Hint 47: Shortly after entering the fireworks room, a full body side-profile Hidden Mickey stands in a window one-third to one-half the way up the side of a tall building on the right side of your boat. Find this Mickey shadow to the left of a short, pink building and just past the third tall, black light pole.

Hint 48: These Hidden Mickeys can only be seen with a light from your camera, cell phone, etc. As your boat floats by the last scene of the ride with the map of Mexico on the wall, look down at tiles that line the base of the platform to your left. The tiles are just above the side of your boat. You can spot four Mickey stickers on the tiles! They're located about one-third of the distance along the row of tiles as you float along. The first one is a full-body Mickey on tile #17 (counting from the start). Several tiles further along, on tile #20, are Mickey's face and ears. Finally, two more full-body Mickey stickers are on tile # 24 (an upside-down Mickey) and # 25, which are halfway along the 50 tiles on the platform.

- *San Angel Inn Restaurante*

Hint 49: Smoke rising from the volcano by the river forms classic Mickeys that quickly disappear.

Norway

Hint 50: Inside *The Wandering Reindeer* gift shop, find a horizontal wooden slat on the wall close to the exit of *Meet Anna and Elsa at Royal Sommerhus*. Three small circles (one is a round, black head of a nail) at the left end of the slat form a classic Mickey, sideways to the left.

Chapter 3: Epcot Scavenger Hunt

China

Hint 51: Classic Mickey-shaped flowers are sculpted on the bases of several decorative light posts on the outside front of the pavilion.

Bonus Points Hint: In the ponds, the floating lily pads sometimes come together to form recognizable classic Mickeys.

Outpost (between China and Germany)

Hint 52: At the *Outpost*, three of the short wooden posts at the corner closest to the bridge form a classic Mickey when viewed from above.

Hint 53: At the *Outpost*, a piece of brown luggage is perched high on a rear wall in the left room inside the *Village Traders shop*. The luggage tag is signed "M. Mouse," and a red sticker on the bottom of the luggage says "Mickey Mouse" and "Disney Magic."

Germany

Hint 54: On the second floor of the building to your right, to the right of the glockenspiel clock, are three suits of armor. The one closest to the glockenspiel has a classic Mickey on its crown.

Hint 55: In the rear of the courtyard, a three-circle classic Mickey formation is in the ironwork support behind the bell on the front of the clock tower. It's a tilted Hidden Mickey formed by the circular metal support (not by holes in the metal).

Hint 56: At the left of the entrance to the *Biergarten Restaurant*, you can see a wrought-iron lion behind a lamp on the outside wall. The lion's front and rear paws are resting on an upside-down classic Mickey.

Hint 57: Inside the *Karamell-Küche* shop, check out the wood design border of a window along the wall that faces the World Showcase promenade. A circle and swirls in the wood form classic Hidden Mickeys in several corners of the window border design.

Hint 58: Inside the *Karamell-Küche shop*, a small orange classic Hidden Mickey is painted on the merchandise shelf siding. The image is about halfway up on a vine on the right shelf siding closest to the door to the main World Showcase promenade.

- Landscaping around the miniature train exhibit

Bonus Points Hint: Check the dirt, grass, decorations, and especially the bushes for Hidden Mickey images that come and go during the year. The landscapers often shape one or more of the tiny bushes into classic Mickeys.

Bonus Points Hint: Study the miniature passenger train(s) as it chugs by you. Tiny images of people sit by the windows of the train. You can often spot Daisy Duck in one of the windows, usually in one of the middle cars of the train. Be sure to change your vantage point around the exhibit to focus on both sides of the train(s). You may notice other tiny Disney Characters at times, even Mickey Mouse himself!

Italy

Hint 59: In the wine shop, *Enoteca Castello*, a classic Mickey appears in the woodwork along the relief design of the upper front counter.

Hint 60: Behind the statue on the right side of the walkway in front of the restaurants, a classic Mickey impression hides on the left side of the rock wall.

The American Adventure

Hint 61: A classic Mickey made of roses decorates a lady's hat in a painting on the first

Chapter 3: Epcot Scavenger Hunt

floor on the far left wall (as you enter). Look for the painting in which a man is speaking to a crowd in front of a hardware store. The lady with the rose-trimmed hat is at the lower middle of the painting and the Hidden Mickey is on the right side of her hat.

Hint 62: A painting on a first-floor wall at the right rear of the rotunda shows workers building a skyscraper. The tops of two vertical beams behind the workers sport classic Mickey holes.

Hint 63: On the rear walls, far left and far right, of the rotunda, first and second floors, large bronze eagle reliefs have classic Mickeys in the corners.

Hint 64: In the "American Indian Art" exhibit in the Gallery room, a classic Mickey copper bead or button is on the back of a white dress. Look for the "Ancient Resonance Dress."

- *The American Adventure show*

Hint 65: At the beginning of the film, an upside-down classic Mickey appears on the rock behind (and to your right of) a kneeling female pilgrim.

Hint 66: Early in the show, a classic Mickey lock hangs on the right side of a stockade in a scene of the American Revolution time period.

Hint 67: In the scene with the old gas station, a classic Mickey is formed by three apples in a crate at the lower right of the scene.

Hint 68: At the end of the show, fireworks light up the sky behind the *Statue of Liberty* Torch. At one point, one of the fireworks at the upper right explodes into a small (not perfect but close enough) classic Mickey, sideways to the left.

- *America Gardens Theatre*

Hint 69: Classic Hidden Mickeys are stuck on both sides of the stage apron / forestage, near the short brick wall that borders the front of the main stage.

Japan

Hint 70: In the koi fish pond across from the *Mitsukoshi store*, a drain cover in the water near the bamboo fence sports a classic Mickey.

Hint 71: Some of the trees in the courtyard are encircled by metal grates with classic Mickey designs.

Hint 72: Visit the pond next to *Katsura Grill* for a possible bonus Hidden Mickey. Cast Members sometimes arrange rocks in the pond to form a classic Mickey.

Hint 73: The rear exhibit area is showcasing "Kawaii - Japan's Cute Culture." In one of the displays, magnets on the upper left of a refrigerator door are arranged like a classic Mickey.

Hint 74: Also in the Kawaii exhibit, spot more Hidden Images - a Mickey Mouse container at the top rear of the refrigerator, and to the right of the fridge, a Hidden Donald Duck and a Hidden Duffy the bear.

Hint 75: In the middle of the *Mitsukoshi store*, look for Hidden Mickeys in the oyster-pearl display. Sometimes, you can find pearls arranged as a classic three-circle Mickey, and other times Cast Members arrange the oyster shells into a classic Mickey in the water. Once, I arrived right after store opening and watched the Cast Member form the familiar image with oyster shells.

Hint 76: Near the center of the *Mitsukoshi* store, circles in the glass walls at the entrance to the expensive jewelry section come together to make several decent classic

Chapter 3: Epcot Scavenger Hunt

Hidden Mickeys. Along the right side of the front glass wall on the left (as you enter the jewelry section), classic Mickeys are near the upper and lower corners.

Hint 77: Out on the promenade, next to the lagoon, three round bushes to the left of the *Torii Gate* form a classic Mickey.

(Bonus points) – Be sure to check the landscaping along the right side of Japan (the side closest to Morocco). Sometimes, you can spot a classic Hidden Mickey made of rocks sitting on the ground!

Morocco

Hint 78: Three brass plates are arranged to form a classic Mickey on a door at the entrance to the *Souk-alMagreb* "Gifts of Morocco" shop on the promenade. (Sometimes, the plates are on the nearby red door, and you might find more than one plate classic Mickey on the doors!)

Hint 79: Basket lids usually form a sideways classic Mickey on the wall inside the *Brass Bazaar shop* (located at the right side of the Morocco pavilion behind the *Tangierine Cafe*). As you face the rear of the pavilion from inside the shop, look above the right side of the archway.

Hint 80: Across from *Restaurant Marrakesh*, three small classic Mickeys hide on a mural on the rear wall of a small room. One is at the top of a tower on the right side of the mural's street. Another is on the left side of the street, next to a double archway. The third is a tiny black Mickey in an upper doorway on the left middle part of the mural.

France

Hint 81: A few of the trees in the pavilion courtyard and along the walkway to *Remy's Ratatouille Adventure* are encircled by metal grates with classic Mickey patterns.

Hint 82: In the patterned hedge (parterre) garden, a bush in the middle right area (on the side nearest the canal) is trimmed to the shape of a classic Mickey.

Hint 83: Classic Mickey images are high on the outside molding of *Les Vins de France* shop, near the entrance to *Impressions de France*.

Hint 84: <u>Inside the *L'Esprit de la Provence* shop, opposite the entrance door fom the outside walkway, three gold pots hanging on the wall come together as a classic Hidden Mickey.</u>

- *Impressions de France*

Hint 85: In the movie's outdoor wedding scene, you can see a Mickey head and ears in a second-floor window of the house in the background. It's in the center screen.

United Kingdom

Hint 86: Outside the *Sportsman's Shoppe*, a sign has a classic Mickey with a tennis racket head, a tennis ball nose, a soccer ball for one ear, and a rugby ball for the other ear.

Canada

Hint 87: Past the steps into the pavilion, the left totem pole has black classic Mickeys on both sides near the top by the raven's wings.

Hint 88: A classic Hidden Mickey is etched on the front facing of a stone step inside Canada, close to the theater. Start at the theater and walk up the steps. You will come to a landing with a light and a trail that branches off to the left. Continue walking up the steps. The Mickey image appears before you reach the next landing.

Hint 89: Behind the check-in desk at *Le Cellier Steakhouse*, three horizontal bottles at the center top of a wine display form a classic Mickey.

Chapter 3: Epcot Scavenger Hunt

The Land

- Living with the Land

Hint 90: In the middle section of the giant wall mural at the rear of the queue, bubbles align to form a classic Mickey, ears angled to the left.

Hint 91: A Hidden Surprise is on the first part of the far right wall of the entrance queue - the wall you pass by right before reaching the loading dock. It's a large, indistinct, bright white outline of a Prince and Princess holding each other. The image extends from the floor to near the ceiling, and the Prince faces left and bends slightly down over the Princess.

Hint 92: A classic Mickey is formed by shrubs (the "head" has white dots on it) to the right of the brim of the farmer's hat near the top of the loading dock mural.

Hint 93: In the lower right area of the mural behind the boat loading area, three circles form a small classic Mickey (a purple circle forms the head and blue circles form the ears). The head is tilted slightly to the right.

Hint 94: Small, round, light gray rocks on the right side of your boat come together as a classic Mickey. Find them on top of a rock wall in the middle of a water garden section—near the lily pads.

Hint 95: A garden hose is coiled into a classic Mickey to the right of the boat about halfway through the fish farming section. (Cast Members usually check on and arrange this Mickey image every morning.)

Hint 96: A classic Mickey made of wire mesh can be found in the aquaculture section. Cast Members generally place it in one of the horizontal display shrimp tubes that are part of the landscape on either side of your boat. (A wire mesh Hidden Minnie, with her hair bow, sometimes also appears in the aqua-tubes, not far from Mickey.)

Hint 97: Stay alert for a large, classic Mickey-shaped vine frame (sometimes covered with vines, sometimes not).

Hint 98: Along the ride, you can often spot hanging plastic gourds shaped like classic Mickeys. They're used to grow fruit or vegetables into Mickey shapes.

Hint 99: Plants of different colors are usually arranged in groups to form a classic Mickey in the greenhouses. Often the plants are lettuces.

Hint 100: In the last room of the ride, a fish tank—labeled "Integrated Aquaculture"—is on the left side of your boat. Vertical pipes are visible along the top section of the tank. Classic (three-circle) Hidden Mickey holes are in the pipe at the top middle of the tank. (Warning: sometimes this pipe is rotated so that the holes are harder to spot).

Hint 101: Near the end of the ride, a large circular test-tube holder on the right side of a "Biotechnology Lab" room has a green classic Mickey in the center. Mickey is formed by the test tubes' green stoppers.

- *Awesome Planet*

Hint 102: <u>Toward the end of the show, after the images of wind turbines, watch the center of the screen for an overhead video of the solar farm at Walt Disney World near Epcot. The silver solar panels are arranged as a huge classic Mickey.</u>

- *The Garden Grill*

Hint 103: On the left side of the large wall mural of vegetation inside the restaurant, a Mickey is hiding behind the most prominent fern that extends all the way to the top of the mural. Counting up horizontally from the bottom of the fern, his face is mostly behind the fifth through eighth leaves on the fern's right side. He's looking slightly downward and to the right in a three-quarter profile.

Chapter 3: Epcot Scavenger Hunt

Two black circles that form his eyes are visible above the sixth fern leaf on the right, more than halfway to the end of the leaf. Mickey's ears jut above the seventh leaf, and his mouth and nose are below the sixth leaf. His face and ears are green, and his mouth is slightly open. This Hidden Mickey is a real classic!

-Around The Land's main entrance

Hint 104: From the upper-level railing, just to the left as you walk in the main entrance, a classic Mickey is on the Earth above the lobby. It's in water swirls, to the left of the tip of South America, and it's sideways to the right.

Hint 105: A classic Mickey hides in the mosaic mural on the pavilion's right outside wall (as you enter). Find the word "LAND" on the mural and look slightly above and to the right about six feet or so to a reddish plateau. Just above the left side of the flat upper part of the plateau are three round stones - a green "head" and two reddish "ears."

Hint 106: In the same mosaic mural, look for a cluster of grapes to the upper left of the word "LAND." A classic Mickey, tilted down to the right, is formed by three grapes.

Hint 107: The Land sign outside the pavilion's entrance rests on two large stone- and tile-covered supports. On the end of the right-hand support, embedded stones decorate the upper portion of the green-tiled area. A small classic Mickey, formed of three stones and sideways to the left, lies near the center of the stone decoration.

- The Seas with Nemo & Friends

Hint 108: As you reach the wooden rails of the walkway along the inside entrance queue for the ride, a classic Mickey made of blue moving water circles lies above you on the right side. (Note: This image isn't always present.)

Hint 109: On the ride, a classic Mickey impression in rock lies below the fifth video screen from the start. It's slightly above and between two pink clusters of standing corals, to the right of center in the rock ledge.

Hint 110: Spot one or more classic Mickeys formed of rocks at the bottom of the aquarium. They're best seen from the upstairs viewing corridor and circular viewing area. At one time, one of the images had starfish-shaped rocks for its "ears."
Note: These rock Mickeys may change locations on the aquarium floor, and some may disappear at times. You may need to look through several windows in the observation area to find them.

Hint 111: You can often see classic Mickeys on the chalkboard at the upper level of the Manatee viewing area. The board lists the names and other information about the manatees in the pool. Hidden Mickeys on this chalkboard come and go.

Hint 112: Search the room upstairs directly above *Turtle Talk with Crush*. In the far left display window (as you enter the room), look for two classic Hidden Mickeys in bubbles in the lower row of panels. You'll find them in the upper right corner of the second panel from the right side of the large window.

Hint 113: In this same display window, look high in the upper left panel under the words "Finding Solutions" for another bubble classic Hidden Mickey.

Hint 114: In the manatee viewing room, lower level, bubbles in wall displays form two classic Mickeys. One is on the left wall (as you exit), in the left middle square containing the words "Manatee Zone ... Slow Speed." Another is on the right wall (as you exit) in the lower left square with the polar bear.

Chapter 3: Epcot Scavenger Hunt

Hint 115: <u>In the Ocean Life room, a few Mickey hats lie on the floor of the small seahorse aquarium, where you may be lucky enough to spot one of the sea urchins wearing a Mickey hat! Because it makes them feel protected or hidden from predators, sea urchins often wear (hide under) items - like Mickey hats! - on their "heads."</u>

Hint 116: As you enter Bruce's room on the lower level, check out the second windows on both the right (labeled "Did You Know?") and left (labeled "Bruce's Scrapbook"). In both windows, an oyster contains three pearls arranged as a classic Mickey.

Hint 117: Bubbles come together to form several classic Mickeys on the garbage cans you see in the pavilion.

- *Journey Into Imagination With Figment*

Hint 118: On the right side along the entrance queue, a small Buzz Lightyear is hiding in a display across from Professor Phillip Brainard's office door. Recently, he's been lying down and is harder to spot.

Hint 119: Directly above Buzz Lightyear, on the upper shelf, a tiny black silhouette of Tinker Bell can be spotted inside a pyramidal container. Look through a hole in the front of the container; Tinker Bell stands on the right side, and a figure wearing Mickey ears is two people to the left of Tinker Bell.

Hint 120: As you enter the *Sight Room*, a tiny classic Mickey is hidden at the lower right of a greaseboard on a wall to your right. The greaseboard is below the words "Focus Group." (Note: This Hidden Mickey may change colors or locations on the board or even disappear at times.)

Hint 121: In the center of the *Sight Room*, headphones on the left of two tables have Mickey ears on an earpiece!

Hint 122: Three bubbles make a classic Mickey near Figment's hand on the edge of his bathtub.

Hint 123: In *Figment's Upside-Down House*, his toilet forms a classic Mickey with two red circles on the floor.

Hint 124: When you feel a blast of air and the walls open, you'll see a rainbow and balloons. Look down and to the right to see classic Mickey circles appear on a cloud at the bottom right of the stage.

Hint 125: In this same scene at the end of the ride, find the letters that spell "Action" that stand in the middle of the scene. Snow covers the top of the letter "A," and a tiny classic Mickey sits in the snow at the bottom left of the snow cap. The Hidden Mickey image tilts to the left.

Hint 126: On the left wall of the exit hallway, a sideways classic Mickey is behind and between the "I" and "M" of the *ImageWorks* sign.

- *ImageWorks*

Hint 127: Inside *ImageWorks,* a group of big circles (bubbles?) rotates in place on a wall. At times, three circles come together at the lower right to form a classic Hidden Mickey.

- *Club Cool*

Hint 128: Study the collections of small bubbles in the design on the red right wall just inside *Club Cool*. In several areas, the bubbles come together as classic Mickeys.

- *Spaceship Earth*

Hint 129: After the fall of Rome, you see three scholars seated around a table on the floor. They are illuminated by lights that form patterns on the floor. The outer circles of light patterns form classic Mickeys.

Chapter 3: Epcot Scavenger Hunt

Hint 130: Across from the seated scholars, on a wall to your left, are shelves with cubbyholes full of scrolls and books. In one of the last cubbyholes you pass before you leave the scene, the round ends of three stacked scrolls lying horizontally form a classic Mickey. It's on the second shelf up from the bottom, in the right lower corner of the second cubbyhole from the right wall.

Hint 131: During the ride, in a scene to the left, monks are writing at desks. In front of the sleeping monk is a document with a small ink blot at the upper right corner. The blot is shaped similar to a classic Mickey and becomes visible as your vehicle passes by.

Hint 132: Just after the Gutenberg printing press scene, in the first part of the Renaissance section, look for the first painter to the left of your ride vehicle. Three white paint circles form a classic Mickey on the top left of the table near the painter. You have to look fast for this one.

Hint 133: Now, on your left, you'll pass by an artist painting fruit. On his canvas, an orange for the "head" with two smaller fruits (one light brown and one yellow) for "ears" come together as a classic Hidden Mickey, tilted right.

Hint 134: On your left, check out a Hidden Surprise. A radio announcer is speaking into a microphone, which is labeled with "WDI" - a reference to Walt Disney Imagineering.

Hint 135: On the right side, as you're passing the section showing black and white movies, a chalkboard marquee on the ground lists upcoming features. One is "The Band Concert," a famous Mickey Mouse cartoon.

Hint 136: On your left, a "Mouse Trap" game - a Hidden Surprise - is set up on the floor behind the couch in the room with the family watching TV.

Hint 137: Just past the scene with the family watching TV, a cityscape in the dark appears on the left of your vehicle. At the middle bottom of the row of buildings, three tiny lights close to the lakeshore come together as a classic Hidden Mickey.

Hint 138: On the journey back down from space, you can play an interactive game about choosing your future. On the touch-screen in front of you, choose any options that include the sea or underwater living. Watch for bubbles that float up the screen and try to spot several groups of bubbles that form sideways classic Mickeys.

Hint 139: At the exit of *Spaceship Earth*, several classic Mickeys float along on overhead blue screens in the *Project Tomorrow* interactive area.

Chapter 4

Disney's Hollywood Studios Scavenger Hunt

• • • • • •

Before You Start

* Many great Hidden Mickeys are in Standby queues, and you might miss them if you take the Lightning Lanes. So, for optimal Hidden Mickey hunting, (if you choose to spend the money), I recommend reserving Lightning Lane (by purchasing, on the My Disney Experience app, the current version of Disney Genie+ and/or Individual Lightning Lane) for the following attractions: **Voyage of The Little Mermaid**, **Disney Junior Play & Dance!**, and **Fantasmic!**

* Be sure to keep track of your Lightning Lane windows and return to those attractions at the appropriate times. In the Scavenger Hunt below, if you come to your Lightning Lane attraction and it's not time for it yet, you can skip to the next stop in the Hunt and return to the Lightning Lane attraction during your time window. If you don't opt for the Lightning Lane options, try to line up for headliner attractions during Early Entry or right after park opening.

* Line up for shows 20-30 minutes ahead of start time.

* Many of the Hidden Mickeys in this park are in restaurants and shops. Be considerate of fellow guests and Cast Members as

Walt Disney World's Hidden Mickeys

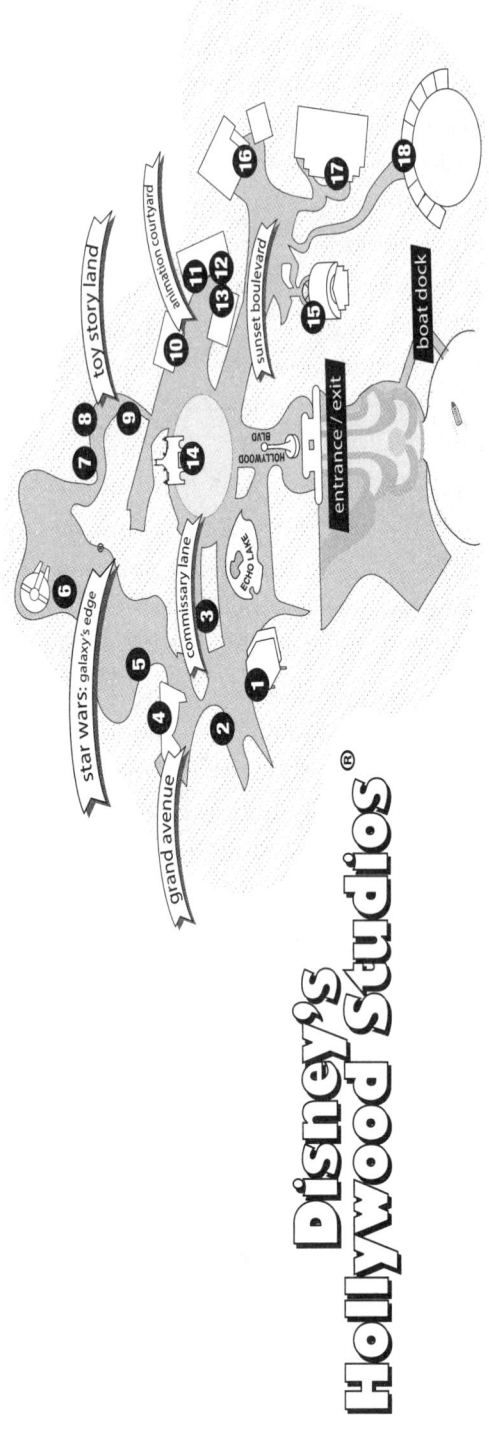

Chapter 4: DHS Scavenger Hunt

Disney's Hollywood Studios®

1. Indiana Jones™ Epic Stunt Spectacular!
2. Star Tours® – The Adventures Continue
3. Mickey and Minnie at Red Carpet Dreams
4. Muppet*Vision 3D
5. Star Wars: Rise of the Resistance
6. Millennium Falcon: Smugglers Run
7. Alien Swirling Saucers
8. Slinky Dog Dash
9. Toy Story Mania!®
10. Walt Disney Presents
11. Voyage of The Little Mermaid
12. Star Wars Launch Bay
13. Disney Junior Play & Dance!
14. Mickey & Minnie's Runaway Railway
15. Beauty and the Beast - Live on Stage
16. Rock 'n' Roller Coaster® Starring Aerosmith
17. The Twilight Zone Tower of Terror™
18. Fantasmic!

125

Walt Disney World's Hidden Mickeys

you search. Tell them what you are looking for, so they can share in the fun. Avoid searching restaurants at busy mealtimes unless you are one of the diners.

* Each person has unique needs for sustenance. If I don't have specific suggestions for restaurants (related to Hidden Mickeys), then I leave it to you to decide when and where to break for snacks/meals.

*
  Hurry to ***Mickey & Minnie's Runaway Railway.*** (All new Hidden Mickeys!)

Clue 1: Be alert for Hidden Mickeys above you along part of the outside entrance queue.
3 points

Clue 2: Enjoy Hidden Mickeys in a corner of the cartoon panels on the walls of the inside queue.
2 points

Clue 3: Search for one of these cartoon panels with a pink paint classic Mickey.
4 points

Clue 4: Along the inside queue, scan overhead light fixtures for side-profile Hidden Mickeys.
5 points

Clue 5: In the pre-show video room, find a tiny classic Hidden Mickey near a bird on the wall.
5 points

Clue 6: Scan the pre-show room for a classic Hidden Mickey on a steeple.
3 points

Clue 7: Note classic Hidden Mickeys near the ceiling.
2 points

Clue 8: Enjoy at least three white classic Hidden Mickeys on the large painting on the screen at the front of the room.
5 points for three

Chapter 4: DHS Scavenger Hunt

Clue 9: When the pre-show cartoon video begins, don't miss the Hidden Mickey on Mickey's car.
3 points

Clue 10: On the ride, in the Carnival Room, check out the classic Hidden Mickey in the 'Frontier Toss' game.
4 points

Clue 11: As you're floating fast toward the waterfall, scan left for a classic Hidden Mickey in a tree.
4 points

Clue 12: At the bottom of the waterfall, focus on the third large clam from the right for a (split-second) classic Hidden Mickey.
5 points

Clue 13: As you enter the room with the city scene, look up for a classic Hidden Mickey on a billboard.
5 points

Clue 14: Spot an ice cream Hidden Mickey to your right.
3 points

Clue 15: Squint for Mickey Mouse on a clothesline above Donald Duck's delivery truck.
5 points

Clue 16: As you leave the city scene, look up for a tiny classic Hidden Mickey near an antenna.
5 points

Clue 17: In Daisy Duck's dance class room, check out classic Hidden Mickeys on the wall.
3 points

Clue 18: While leaving the dance class room, enjoy moving light Hidden Mickeys.
3 points

Clue 19: After the dance class room, spot a classic Hidden Mickey behind a trash can.
4 points

Clue 20: In the Factory Room, notice a small red-and-yellow classic Mickey to your right.
3 points

Clue 21: Watch a classic Mickey with moving ears on your right near the ceiling.
4 points

Clue 22: To your right, study dots that move up and down and form intermittent classic Hidden Mickeys.
5 points

Clue 23: On the left side of the room, spot a blue classic Mickey made of gears.
3 points

Clue 24: Look below this gear Hidden Mickey for a small blue Hidden Mickey.
3 points

Clue 25: Now glance to the right of the small blue Hidden Mickey for a sideways classic Hidden Mickey.
3 points

Clue 26: As you exit the Factory Room, note the small rotating classic Hidden Mickey on your left.
3 points

Clue 27: In the last room, marvel at fireworks Hidden Mickeys.
2 points

Clue 28: As you're leaving the last room, be alert for a classic Hidden Mickey on a directional sign.
5 points

Clue 29: After you leave your ride vehicle, stay alert for the Hidden Mickeys on the walls and ceiling that you spotted before in the pre-show video room!
2 points

Chapter 4: DHS Scavenger Hunt

★ Hike across the park to ***Millennium Falcon: Smugglers Run***.

Clue 30: Along the inside Standby entrance queue, study a large engine for a small, silver Hidden Mickey.
4 points

Clue 31: Look around the briefing room (just before you enter the cockpit) for a classic Hidden Mickey.
3 points

Clue 32: In the cockpit, scan the ceiling for a classic Hidden Mickey.
4 points

Clue 33: Outside in Star Wars: Galaxy's Edge, admire the Millennium Falcon's exterior for—not a Hidden Mickey—but a Hidden Millennium Falcon!
5 points

Clue 34: Continue squinting at the exterior (both sides) of the Millennium Falcon for another Hidden Surprise: three tiny TIE Fighters!
5 points for all three

Clue 35: Walk up the stairs to the left (as you face the entrance to the attraction) of the Millennium Falcon and gaze high to your right for one more Hidden Surprise: numbers that relate to Star Wars movies.
5 points

Clue 36: In "The Market Merchants" shopping area, search for a three-gear Hidden Mickey.
3 points

Clue 37: Notice small classic Mickeys in metal window (or vault) coverings near the three-gear Mickey.
3 points

*
Walk to Toy Story Land and queue up for ***Slinky Dog Dash***.

Clue 38: In the queue, check out the top of a box for a Hidden Mickey.
5 points

Clue 39: At the loading dock, don't miss a Hidden Mickey in the sky.
4 points

Clue 40: At the loading dock, study Andy's drawings on the wall for an upside-down Hidden Mickey.
3 points

Clue 41: Glance to the side of the loading dock area for a Hidden Surprise: numbers that relate to a 'Toy Story' movie.
5 points

* It's time to play on ***Toy Story Mania!***
Clue 42: At the beginning of the Standby entrance queue, find a dinosaur with a Hidden Mickey.
3 points

Clue 43: Further along the queue, search high for a cloud Hidden Mickey.
2 points

Clue 44: Along the entrance queue, look low for a classic Mickey behind a beaver.
4 points

Clue 45: Study the wall posters along the inside queue for a Hidden Mickey. Look familiar?
3 points

Clue 46: Near the loading dock, in Andy's Bedroom, squint high for a tiny Hidden Mickey.
5 points

Clue 47: As you get close to loading, spot a classic Mickey on the wall.
2 points

Chapter 4: DHS Scavenger Hunt

Clue 48: On the ride's interactive screens, look behind the target balloons in front of the volcano to spot a classic Mickey.
5 points

Clue 49: Trixie and her Hidden Mickey may be nearby!
2 points

Clue 50: On another screen, watch the white plates for a classic Mickey image.
3 points

Clue 51: Stay alert for a classic Mickey below an exclamation point on the wall.
5 points

Clue 52: Study a book along the exit for a tiny classic Mickey.
5 points

Clue 53: Along the exit hallway, check out the coloring book posters on the walls for a Hidden Mickey. (You may be able to access this exit hallway from outside the attraction).
5 points

* Get in the queue for **Alien Swirling Saucers**. (You can exit before the ride if you wish).

Clue 54: Stay alert for a Hidden Mickey in the queue.
2 points

Check your Times Guide or *My Disney Experience* app for convenient show times for *Beauty and the Beast- Live on Stage*.

*
   Now go to **Rock 'n' Roller Coaster Starring Aerosmith.** (You can find the Hidden Mickeys here without riding the coaster; just exit before the ride.)

Clue 55: Study the tile floor along the entrance queue for two classic Mickeys.
5 points for both

Clue 56: Don't miss the tiny Mickey on a wall poster just before the pre-show room.
4 points

Clue 57: Search around the pre-show room for a classic Mickey.
4 points

Clue 58: In the limo countdown-to-takeoff area, stare across the track for a Hidden Surprise (a Castle).
4 points

Clue 59: Now locate five Hidden Characters on a big poster.
5 points for spotting all five

Clue 60: Pay attention to the instructional video overhead for 2 Mickeys and a Donald.
4 points for all three

Clue 61: Stare across the track for Mickey on the wall.
5 points

Clue 62: At the loading gate, look at the rear license plates of the limo ride vehicles. (Then exit if you wish.)
4 points

Clue 63: As you step out of your ride vehicle at the end, glance to your far left to spot Mickey on a wall. (If you haven't taken the ride, walk in through the gift shop to find this and the following images.)
3 points

Clue 64: <u>Admire moving lights near the coaster track for Hidden Mickeys!</u>
3 points

Clue 65: Search for a box with a classic Mickey in a word.
5 points

Clue 66: In the gift shop, spot a Hidden Mickey on a guitar.
4 points

Chapter 4: DHS Scavenger Hunt

Clue 67: In the gift shop, look around for a Hidden Oswald the Lucky Rabbit (with long ears).
3 points

Clue 68: Also in the shop, find Mickey and Minnie made of guitar picks!
4 points for both

Clue 69: Outside in the courtyard, locate a Hidden Mickey on a food kiosk sign.
3 points

Clue 70: Also in the courtyard, search for three Hidden Mickeys on the wall of the attraction.
5 points for spotting all three

* Walk to ***The Twilight Zone Tower of Terror***.

Clue 71: Look around along the Standby entrance queue for coins that make Mickey.
4 points

Clue 72: During the pre-show film in the library, find the plush Mickey Mouse doll held by a little girl.
3 points

Clue 73: Linger in the left library to spot the words "Mickey Mouse" on sheet music on a desktop.
4 points

Clue 74: Notice a classic Mickey stain on the wall in the boiler room.
4 points

(Tip: For the best vantage point for the falling elevator Hidden Mickeys that follow, take the right queue when the line for the ride splits. Then tell the Cast Member you're hunting for Hidden Mickeys and ask to be seated in the rightmost ride vehicle.)

Clue 75: At the first stop on the ride, search for a Hidden Mickey above you.
4 points

Clue 76: Also look for a Mickey Mouse doll here.
4 points

Clue 77: Stare at the star field (the doors to the elevator shaft just before they open!) to spot a classic Hidden Mickey in the stars.
5 points

*
Your next stop is ***Star Tours—The Adventures Continue***.

Clue 78: Don't miss a classic Mickey on a tree along the outside queue.
5 points

Clue 79: Along the inside entrance queue, look for a Hidden Mickey near C-3PO.
3 points

Clue 80: Now wait for a shadow Hidden Mickey in a video on a wall display along the entrance queue. (Note: You may have to cool your heels awhile to spot this one!)
4 points

Clue 81: Next, study the entrance queue luggage scanner for Mickey and other Disney characters and images.
5 points total for finding Mickey and two or more other Disney images

Clue 82: Just after you're seated for the ride, watch C-3PO to your right for a tiny Hidden Mickey.
5 points

Clue 83: At the end of the ride, if you land on the *Coruscant* planet (as opposed to other random end destinations for the ride), look for classic Mickeys on a rear wall.
5 bonus points

*
Go to ***Muppet*Vision 3D***.
Clue 84: Along the entrance queue, as you enter the building, stop for a Hidden Surprise: a sign will lead you to a key!
4 points

Chapter 4: DHS Scavenger Hunt

Clue 85: As you enter the pre-show waiting room, don't miss a net with a Hidden Surprise.
4 points

Clue 86: In the waiting room for the pre-show, find bicycles that form a Hidden Mickey.
2 points

Clue 87: During the first part of the pre-show on the video monitors, observe the test pattern.
4 points

Clue 88: In the first part of the movie, keep your eyes open for shelves on a wall with trophies. Look for Mickey there!
5 points

Clue 89: During the finale of the movie, listen for a Hidden Surprise: a snippet from a well-known Disney song.
5 points

Clue 90: After the cannon shoots holes in the theater, watch for a plush Mickey.
3 points

Clue 91: Try to spot the Mickey balloons while Kermit rides in on a fire truck.
3 points

Clue 92: Study the license plate on the fire truck for a Hidden Surprise.
4 points

Clue 93: Don't miss Pluto's appearance!
2 points

*
Walk to ***Voyage of The Little Mermaid*** at your Lightning Lane time.

Clue 94: Look for a classic Mickey in the inside waiting room.
3 points
(You can stay for the show in the theater or exit out the doors you just entered to continue your Hidden Mickey search.)

★
  Catch a performance of ***Beauty and the Beast—Live on Stage***.

Clue 95: Watch for Mickey on the back of one of the characters.
3 points

★
  Enjoy ***Walt Disney Presents***.

Clue 96: During your walk through the attraction, locate a Hidden Mickey in a painting that Walt is holding.
3 points

Clue 97: Search for a tiny classic Mickey on a small gazebo in an exhibit.
5 points

★ Check out the show ***Disney Junior Play & Dance!*** in Animation Courtyard at your Lightning Lane time.

Clue 98: Watch for Mickey in the lighting and stage effects.
3 points for two or more

★
  On Commissary Lane, get in line for ***Meet Disney Stars at Red Carpet Dreams***.

Clue 99: Don't miss a Hidden Mickey while you're smiling at Minnie!
2 points

Clue 100: In the hallway of the Meet and Greet area, pay attention to the posters on the wall.
2 points

★
  Get ready to meet *BB-8* at ***Star Wars Launch Bay***.

Clue 101: While you're waiting, scan the walls for a Hidden Mickey.
4 points

Chapter 4: DHS Scavenger Hunt

Clue 102: Admire the display of spaceships inside *Star Wars Launch Bay* and squint for a Hidden Mickey.
5 points

* Walk to the **entrance arch to Animation Courtyard**.

Clue 103: Search this area for Hidden Characters.
4 points for finding two characters

Clue 104: Find a Hidden Mickey outside above the entrance to *Voyage of The Little Mermaid*.
3 points

*
   Stroll over to **The Chinese Theater** behind Center Stage. Find two classic Mickeys among the celebrity impressions in the cement in front of the Theater.

Clue 105: Check Harry Anderson's square.
3 points

Clue 106: Now see if you can spot a Mickey in Carol Burnett's square.
3 points

*
   Cross the park to **Woody's Lunch Box**.

Clue 107: Look around inside the food order window for Hidden Mickeys.
3 points for one or more

Clue 108: In front of *Woody's Lunch Box*, locate a Hidden Surprise: a reference to Disney animators!
5 points

*
   Go to **The Hollywood Brown Derby** restaurant.
Enjoy the pictures in the waiting area inside the restaurant.

Clue 109: Spot the man with Mickey Mouse ears.
3 points

Walt Disney World's Hidden Mickeys

*
  Turn left as you leave and *head down Sunset Boulevard*.

Clue 110: Find a coin Hidden Mickey near a store entrance.
4 points

Clue 111: Search for a classic Mickey in scrollwork on a blue building.
4 points

* Walk to **Rosie's All-American Cafe**.

Clue 112: Look around the food order area for Mickey.
4 points

*
  Turn left onto Hollywood Boulevard, then right to **Hollywood & Vine restaurant**.

Clue 113: Seek a Hidden Character above the restaurant's entrance.
3 points

Enter the restaurant and examine the left wall.

Clue 114: Find a stick-figure Mickey.
2 points

Clue 115: Search the wall for some classic Mickeys.
3 points

* Step inside the waiting area for the **50's Prime Time Cafe** and look closely at the tables.

Clue 116: Check out what's holding them together.
1 point

* Admire the area outside of **Indiana Jones™ Epic Stunt Spectacular!**

Clue 117: Interact with a Hidden Surprise in a well!
3 points

Chapter 4: DHS Scavenger Hunt

* Go to the **Backlot Express restaurant**.

Clue 118: Locate two Hidden Mickeys on the drink station near the exit door that faces *Star Tours*.
4 points for both

Clue 119: Look for standing Mickeys.
4 points for finding four or more

*
  Ask a restaurant Cast Member to let you check out the **Sci-Fi Dine-In Theater Restaurant** inside.

Clue 120: Look for a classic Mickey in the waiting area.
3 points

Clue 121: Find a full-body Mickey in the waiting area.
3 points

Clue 122: Study the right rear mural in the dining area. Look for two Hidden Mickeys along the treetops.
5 points for both

Clue 123: Stare at a small mosaic mural at the rear of the restaurant for a side profile of Mickey Mouse.
5 points

Clue 124: Watch the movie reel for three full-body Hidden Characters.
8 points for spotting all three

Clue 125: Stay alert during the movie for a classic Hidden Mickey on a spacesuit.
4 points

Clue 126: When popcorn appears on the movie screen, search for a Hidden Mickey.
5 points

Clue 127: Find a Hidden Mickey on a dining car.
3 points

* Walk to the **BaseLine Tap House.**

Clue 128: Locate a classic Hidden Mickey on a wall inside **BaseLine Tap House**.
3 points

* Wander into the **Stage 1 Company Store**.

Clue 129: Take a good look at the old bureau that's loaded with hats and paint cans.
3 points

Clue 130: Spot a classic Mickey on the wall.
3 points

Clue 131: Search for some famous shorts.
3 points

Clue 132: Now find several Hidden Mickeys outside the store.
5 points for four or more

* In the waiting area for **Mama Melrose's Ristorante Italiano**:

Clue 133: Check out the Dalmatian.
3 points

Clue 134: Examine the plaster on the right wall.
3 points

Clue 135: Find a classic Mickey leaf near the check-in podium. (Note: This Hidden Mickey moves around or disappears at times!)
4 bonus points

Clue 136: Locate a small Hidden Mickey marking on the wall behind the check-in podium.
5 points

Clue 137: Now look at the plaster on the wall to the left of the check-in podium.
3 points

Chapter 4: DHS Scavenger Hunt

* Stroll *toward* **Hollywood Boulevard**.

Clue 138: While in the central plaza, stare toward the **Dockside Diner** for a Hidden Mickey.
3 points

Clue 139: At the intersection of *Hollywood and Sunset Boulevards*, discover Mickey Mouse's previous moniker. (Psst! Read the impressions in the sidewalks, near the curb.)
5 points

* Enter **The Trolley Car Cafe.**

Clue 140: Scan the walls inside for a Hidden Surprise: a reference to Disney animators!
5 points

* Walk behind **Keystone Clothiers**

Clue 141: Search for a classic Mickey at a drink stand.
2 points

Clue 142: Study three door signs in this area for Hidden Surprises. One door has three "homophone" names (the names sound like funny phrases when pronounced) related to entertainment.
5 points

Clue 143: Another door has homophone names related to dentistry.
4 points

Clue 144: A third door has a historical reference to Walt and Roy Disney's first office (in 1923) for the Walt Disney Company!
5 points

Clue 145: Check this general area for another Hidden Surprise: famous names stamped on wood.
5 points

* Walk to **Mickey's of Hollywood**.

Clue 146: The tiniest Hidden Mickey in the park is on the store's outside black wall column that's closest to the park entrance.
5 points

* Go to the **Cover Story** store and take a good look at the outside.

Clue 147: See any classic Mickeys in the design?
2 points

* Stroll to the area just inside the **park entrance**.

Clue 148: Locate a Hidden Mickey on an animal.
4 points

*
In the evening, arrive 30 to 40 minutes before show time (even if you have a Lightning Lane entry pass). Enjoy the Hidden Images in the **Fantasmic!** show.

Clue 149: Look for large bubbles floating up the water screen that form one or more classic Mickeys.
5 points

Clue 150: Stay alert for a classic Mickey in the water during the scene with the whale and Mickey.
5 points

Clue 151: Wave at Tinker Bell on the water screen.
3 points

* *Scan your Studios Guidemap* for Hidden Mickeys.

Clue 152: Turn the Disney's Hollywood Studios map upside down and search for Mickey.
4 points

Chapter 4: DHS Scavenger Hunt

Clue 153: Now study the map for a group of tiny classic Hidden Mickeys.
3 points

It's time to tally your score.

**Total Points for
Disney's Hollywood Studios =**

_____

How'd you do?

Up to 228 points - Bronze
229 to 455 points - Silver
456 points and over - Gold
570 points - Perfect Score

You may have done even better if you earned bonus points in ***Star Tours—The Adventures Continue***, and/or the check-in podium of ***Mama Melrose's Ristorante Italiano***.

Chapter 4: DHS Scavenger Hunt

-Mickey & Minnie's Runaway Railway (All new Hidden Mickeys!)

Hint 1: Along the outside queue, some of the light fixture covers have a gold design with a repeating pattern of side-profile Hidden Mickeys.

Hint 2: Along the walls of the inside queue, changing panels with titles of Disney cartoons show a small classic Mickey logo in each panel at the lower left corner.

Hint 3: In these changing panels, a pink paint classic Mickey is at the lower right side of the panel with the advertisement for the cartoon "Potatoland."

Hint 4: Further along the inside queue, covers of overhead light fixtures include subtle repeating side-profile Hidden Mickeys.

Hint 5: More than six Hidden Mickeys are in the room with the pre-show cartoon video: first, on the left-side wall, a tiny classic Mickey sits high in the branches of a tree to the right of a bird sitting on a branch.

Hint 6: #2 - on the right-side wall, a small classic Mickey sits near the top of a steeple on a temple.

Hint 7: #3 - small classic Mickeys encircle the outer ring of a large chandelier on the ceiling.

Hint 8: #4, 5, and 6 - At the front of the room, on the stationary screen with an Oriental white painting on a red background, three of the trees or bushes have circular leaves or flowers. At times, these white circles come together as classic Hidden Mickeys.

Hint 9: In the pre-show cartoon video, the front of Mickey's car has a silver classic Mickey ornament.

Hint 10: Along the ride, in the Carnival Room, a classic Mickey (a bullseye 'head' and two blue 'ears') sits in the upper middle of the background of the 'Frontier Toss' game, which is on the left side of the room.

Hint 11: Along the ride, just before the waterfall, look quickly to your left to spot a tree bending over the left side of the river. Three coconuts on the tree make a decent classic Mickey.

Hint 12: At the bottom of the waterfall, the third large clam from the right opens and shows three pearls in a classic Mickey formation, tilted to the right. The image appears for only a split second.

Hint 13: In the room with the city scene, look for four Hidden Mickeys: high on a rooftop straight in front of you, a white classic Mickey is on a bottle on a billboard advertising 'Delux-O-Detergent.'

Chapter 4: DHS Scavenger Hunt

Hint 14: #2 - a large classic Mickey is formed by ice cream scoops, tilted left, in a cone at the right side of the room.

Hint 15: #3 - in a recess in shadows at the left side of the city scene, a T-shirt with a full-body Mickey Mouse hangs high on the left side of a clothesline, to the left of a window in a building and just above Donald Duck's purple delivery truck.

Hint 16: #4 - high on a rooftop, a tiny classic Mickey is on a horizontal electrical cord on the right side of an arrow-shaped antenna. You can spot this Hidden Mickey for just a second or two before your car leaves the scene.

Hint 17: In Daisy Duck's dance class room, sideways classic Hidden Mickeys are repeated in the design along the lower walls.

Hint 18: While leaving Daisy Duck's dance room (and en route to the 'Factory Room'), watch the walls in and after the dance room for moving white light classic Mickeys.

Hint 19: Just after Daisy Duck's dance room, a classic Mickey sits low on a wall to the left, behind a trash can.

Hint 20: Many Hidden Mickeys adorn the 'Factory Room': a red-and-yellow classic Mickey on a green background is midway up on the mid-right side of the room.

Hint 21: A blue classic Mickey with moving ears appearing and disappearing is high near the ceiling just past the middle of the right side of the room and to the upper left of the red-and-yellow classic Mickey.

Hint 22: Below the blue moving classic Mickey mentioned above, colored dots move up and down between two larger yellow dots. At times, the moving dots come together with the upper and lower yellow dots to make classic Mickeys.

Hint 23: A teal blue three-gear classic Mickey sits on a rectangular piece of metal midway up at the mid-left side of the room.

Hint 24: A small blue classic Mickey hides straight down below the teal blue gear Mickey.

Hint 25: A classic Mickey, sideways to the left, can be seen to the right of the small blue classic Mickey mentioned above.

Hint 26: A blue classic Mickey rotates on the upper left side of the exit door from the Factory Room.

Hint 27: In the last room, fireworks on the far wall come together at times to form classic Mickeys.

Hint 28: As you move along the last stretch before the unloading dock, a directional sign stands on your left. Part of the sign pointing left says "Fishing Hole." The "o" in "Hole" makes a classic Mickey.

Hint 29: As you exit, you walk back through the room that had the pre-show video, so you can spot the chandelier Hidden Mickeys and the two wall Hidden Mickeys one more time!

- *Millennium Falcon: Smugglers Run*

Hint 30: The inside Standby entrance queue loops around a large silver engine. Two small metallic slag smudges are stuck on the middle of the far side of the engine. Depressions in the upper smudge make a classic Mickey tilted to the left.

Hint 31: Two sideways classic Mickeys made of round silver metal wheels or rings sit on one side of the wall video monitor along the entrance queue in the room before the cockpit and on the side of the wall video monitor along the exit.

Chapter 4: DHS Scavenger Hunt

Hint 32: On the middle front of the cockpit ceiling, a small metal classic Mickey is visible at times between two small flexible pipes at the point where the pipes separate and angle away from each other.

Hint 33: Outside in Star Wars: Galaxy's Edge, walk up to the side of the Millennium Falcon and find a Hidden Surprise beneath the end of the black band that's curving around the side of the cockpit. A tiny Hidden Millennium Falcon is stuck on the real starship! Spot the nose of the Falcon poking out above a silver pipe and the body of the ship behind the pipe.

Hint 34: Another Hidden Surprise awaits you on the Millennium Falcon. Three tiny TIE (Twin Ion Engines) Fighters of the Galactic Empire hide on the Millennium Falcon. A TIE Fighter sits among two rows of irregular-shaped bolts in each of three small rectangular boxes, two on the right (near) side and one on the left side of the starship.

Hint 35: One more Hidden Surprise is not far away from the Millennium Falcon. Face the entrance to *Millennium Falcon: Smugglers Run* and look up to your left to spot a spaceship sitting on a roof. Now, walk up the stairs to your left and stare high to your right as you walk away from the Millennium Falcon. Large numbers: "77," "80," and "83" on side doors of the spaceship become visible. These numbers are shortened for the years of the first released Star Wars movie trilogy. (The middle door with "80" is sometimes retracted and not visible).

Hint 36: While walking past shops and food stalls in "The Market Merchants," search high along the walls for round silver gears that connect to pipes jutting out from the wall. Three gears at the top come together as a classic Hidden Mickey, tilted to the left.

Hint 37: Long, rectangular metal window or vault coverings sit to the left of the silver gears. One of the panels in each window covering has holes of different sizes that make repeating classic Hidden Mickeys.

- *Slinky Dog Dash*

Hint 38: About halfway through the Standby queue, look for a Squeaky Penguin Bath Toy box on the right side of the queue. In the left lower corner of the lid on top of the box, three bubbles form an upside-down classic Hidden Mickey.

Hint 39: In the queue at the loading dock, on a mural of Andy's drawings (blueprints) for the ride, you can see a cloud that is shaped like a classic Mickey. It's above the parachutes in the upper right corner of the wall mural of drawings.

Hint 40: At the loading dock, at the left side of Andy's drawings on the wall, holes at the left of the upper border of the paper form an upside-down classic Hidden Mickey. Look near the blue pin and above the "y" in "Slinky."

Hint 41: From the right side of the loading dock or looking left from the coaster as it takes off, you can spot a Tyrannosaurus Rex painted on a large toy box. "11, 22, and $19.95" are stamped on a price label at the top left of the front of the box. These numbers are a Hidden Surprise: they represent the release date, 11/22/1995 - for the first 'Toy Story' movie.

- *Toy Story Mania!*

Hint 42: At the beginning of the Standby entrance queue, Trixie – a gray triceratops from the "Toy Story" movies – shows up on the back wall of the "Midway Games Play Set," in front of which you can meet Woody and Jessie. Three spots near her left upper horn come together as a classic Mickey, tilted to the right.

Hint 43: In the first part of the inside queue, look up to your left. A classic, three-circle

Chapter 4: DHS Scavenger Hunt

Hidden Mickey cloud sits high on the wall in the corner.

Hint 44: A series of animal cutouts ("Pop-Outs") are in a standing board on the right side of the queue. Behind the beaver cutout, a dark red sideways classic Mickey sits on a "fire ball" on the board behind the beaver.

Hint 45: Further along the inside queue, Trixie the dinosaur, with her Hidden Mickey spots, appears again on a "Dino Darts" poster on the wall.

Hint 46: Near the loading dock, the entrance queue sometimes winds through Andy's Bedroom. In the first window above you to the right, a tiny, black classic Hidden Mickey sits just above the left side of the window ledge and to the immediate right of a vertical tree branch.

Hint 47: On the wall next to the ride vehicles, a classic Mickey is formed by three ovals that outline Mr. Potato Head, Slinky Dog, and Bullseye the horse.

Hint 48: Watch for the screen with target balloons in front of the volcano spewing lava. If you pop the middle 100-point balloon on the second tier, a faint classic Mickey appears on the rear surface in the lava behind the balloons.

Hint 49: Before you leave the volcano, glance to the right and say hello to Trixie again with her Hidden Mickey spots! She's on a sign for "Dino Darts."

Hint 50: Be alert for the screen with moving white plates. At one point, a large plate aligns with smaller plates behind it to form a classic Mickey.

Hint 51: Look for the words "Circus Fun!" on the wall to your right as you rotate into position for the last screen stop. The dot below the exclamation point is a classic Mickey.

Hint 52: On the upper spine of the large "Tin Toy" book along the exit, a tiny white classic Mickey is in a chicken's eye. It's the fourth image from the top of the spine.

Hint 53: As you exit, a faint, yellow full-body Mickey Mouse is at the lower right of the last coloring book poster along the right wall of the exit hallway. At the top of the poster are the words "It's Fun to Take a Spin with Your Friends." (If you don't ride on the third track, you may be able to access this part of the exit hallway from outside the attraction).

- *Alien Swirling Saucers*

Hint 54: In a "Docking Control" mural along the left side of the entrance queue, three buttons (red, green, and blue) on the right side of a console are arranged as a classic Mickey.

- *Rock 'n' Roller Coaster Starring Aerosmith*

Hint 55: Look down for a tiled floor just as you step inside the building along the Standby entrance queue. In the middle of the walkway at the end of this tiled-floor section, before you enter the carpeted room, two classic Mickeys are each formed by three tiny round tiles. The circles are all the same size, but these images are purposeful and they're sentimental favorites.

Hint 56: On the last wall before you enter the lower level of the pre-show video room, a poster labeled "Cosmic Car Show" has a tiny classic Mickey on the bottom right under the front tire of the car. The Mickey image is at the end of the signature of "J. Mouse."

Hint 57: Cables coiled into a classic Mickey lie on the rear right side of the floor in the pre-show room with *Aerosmith's* musical instruments. This image is moved around in the room at times.

Hint 58: Along the entrance queue, soon after you enter the limo countdown-to-take-

Chapter 4: DHS Scavenger Hunt

off area, look across the track and check out the red "Rock Rack" magazine stand next to a bench. An image of Cinderella Castle is on the cover of the (Free!) magazine displayed in the stand.

Hint 59: You'll find five Hidden Characters (three images of Mickey Mouse and one each of Minnie and Goofy) along the right side of a framed collage. First, look for two stickers of Mickey's face, one at the upper right and a smaller one at the middle right (to the left of a red square). Just below the middle right Mickey face is a small drawing of Goofy, Minnie, and Mickey walking to the right. This large poster is on the wall to your left along the inside queue and near the boarding area.

Hint 60: Near the loading dock, an instructional safety video about the roller coaster plays continuously overhead on several screens. At one point, you'll see a girl remove her Donald Duck hat. After an animated car speeds away, a tiny, black classic Mickey floats behind other black smoke exhaust circles. An illustration of a child wearing Mickey ears appears several times.

Hint 61: On a wall across from the front of the loading dock area, various items are hanging from a row of hooks to the left of a wall cabinet and to the right of a garage door. One of the hanging items is a pink hat with the word "Mickey" across the front. (Note: These items and/or their arrangement change from time to time.)

Hint 62: On the rear license plate of each limo ride vehicle, the year sticker at the upper right is a classic Mickey.

Hint 63: Look to your far left as you exit the ride vehicle. A black classic Mickey is on the wall where the side of a gate connects to the wall.

Hint 64: <u>Now glance to your right, before reaching the exit gate, to spot round colored lights merging as classic Mickeys that move over the walls of the coaster track.</u>

Hint 65: After exiting the ride vehicle, you'll walk past black boxes on the right side of the room with the guest photo screens. On one box, "Sash Cord" is written at the left side of a piece of tape. The "o" in "Cord" is a black classic Mickey. This Hidden Mickey is fading over time.

Hint 66: A blue guitar is stuck horizontally on the ceiling above you in the middle of the gift shop. Three tiny classic Mickeys are on a silver plate at the base of the guitar. They're formed of holes for the "ears" and screws for the "heads."

Hint 67: An image of Oswald the Lucky Rabbit's head and ears is made of wires. Find him behind the glass door of a cabinet on the right wall of the room that's at the left side of the gift shop (as you exit the ride).

Hint 68: On cashier's counters at the right rear of the gift shop, just before you reach the exit walkway, spot a Hidden Mickey and a Hidden Minnie made of guitar picks under laminated surfaces. Look for Mickey on the left countertop and Minnie (with her red bow) on the right.

Hint 69: Walk outside into the courtyard of *Rock 'n' Roller Coaster* and glance above the order windows of "The Rock Station" snack kiosk. Holes in the "R" form a distorted image that resembles a classic Hidden Mickey.

Hint 70: In the front courtyard, check the outside wall mural to your left for:
  - a boy wearing Mickey ears.
  - black classic Mickeys on a singer's light blue shirt.
  - a gold "bling" Mickey on the necklace of the man in the black suit.

Chapter 4: DHS Scavenger Hunt

- The Twilight Zone Tower of Terror

Hint 71: Along the entrance queue in the hotel lobby, just before you're directed to the pre-show rooms, glance to your left at coins in a wooden inbox container sitting on a counter. Usually, three coins in the container - often at the lower left - form a classic, sometimes upside-down, Hidden Mickey.

Hint 72: During the pre-show film in the library, the little girl on the elevator holds a plush Mickey Mouse doll.

Hint 73: Look for sheet music on a desktop and under a trumpet to the right of the television in the left library. The words "Mickey Mouse" are part of a song title: "What! No Mickey Mouse?"

Hint 74: A black, slightly distorted classic Mickey stains the wall of the boiler room at the spot where the queue branches. He's about eight feet up from the walkway, between an "Exit" sign and a red electrical box.

Hint 75: At the first stop on the ride, a small, dark classic Mickey can be seen above the ghostly images in the lower center of the ornate design on the closest archway.

Hint 76: Also at this first stop, the little girl in the ghostly images is still holding her Mickey doll.

Hint 77: On the ride itself, you'll see a bright star field just before the doors open into the elevator shaft. Look closely as the stars you're watching converge in the middle into a small bright classic-Mickey shape for a split second. (Tip: You see it best from the rightmost ride vehicle.)

- Star Tours—The Adventures Continue

Hint 78: About halfway along the outside winding queue, a white classic Mickey is high on a tree trunk, just below the walkway platform for the Ewok village above. It's on the huge central tree, directly across from the Imperial Walker.

Hint 79: Along the right of the inside entrance queue, blue circles make a Mickey hat with ears on the upper part of the control panel behind C-3PO's head. It's at the lower center of the upper screen.

Hint 80: In a wall display along the entrance queue, the silhouette of R2-D2 appears several times in a continuous video loop of moving shadow figures. At one point, R2-D2 sprouts satellite ears that rotate into round "Mickey ears" for a few seconds.

Hint 81: Along the entrance queue, a robot watches a continuous scan of luggage. You can spot images of a plush Mickey Mouse and a plush Goofy, along with images of Buzz Lightyear, Aladdin's lamp, a Sorcerer Mickey hat, a Mr. Incredible shirt, Madame Leota's crystal ball, and some other Disney images.

Hint 82: Just after you're seated, C-3PO appears on a screen at the front right of the room. A small bright classic Mickey is on his right forearm near his wrist.

Hint 83: At the end of the Star Tours ride, there are four classic Hidden Mickeys in the Coruscant landing sequence, which is one of three different and random end destinations for the ride. After the Star Tours vehicle crash lands on the platform and is lowered below into the hanger, look for four recessed panels in the top half of the back wall of the hanger. A classic Mickey is in the center of each panel. To see them, focus on the background wall instead of the droid in the foreground that's flying around with the two light batons.

- Muppet*Vision 3D

Hint 84: As you walk into the inside entrance, stop at the window on your right. A sign in the window says "Back in 5 mintues -

Chapter 4: DHS Scavenger Hunt

key is under mat." Go ahead, lift up the front edge of the floor mat to find the key!

Hint 85: As you enter the pre-show waiting room, glance up to your left. Hanging from the ceiling is a net full of orange and green jello. Sounds like 'Annette Funicello,' right? She was one of the original Mouseketeers on the Mickey Mouse Club show and later became a successful singer and actress.

Hint 86: Near the middle of the left wall of the waiting room for the pre-show, bicycles sit on luggage, which is, in turn, on top of a wooden chest. A round black hotbox at the side of the luggage forms a classic Hidden Mickey with two bicycle wheels above it.

Hint 87: During the first part of the preshow on the video monitors, a test pattern appears after you see the words "Video Display Test." The black lines on a white background form a classic Hidden Mickey.

Hint 88: During the first part of the movie, as Kermit walks past the long hall and toward the lab, look for shelves with trophies on the wall before he reaches the lab entrance doors. It appears that a full-body Mickey Mouse trophy is at the middle of the top right shelf.

Hint 89: During the finale, listen for the refrain "It's a small world after all" from the familiar song after you see trombone and trumpet players and when you see one player with a tuba stuck on his head.

Hint 90: After the cannon shoots holes in the theater, a person holding a plush Mickey Mouse walks left to right in front of the crowd outside.

Hint 91: After the cannon shoots holes in the theater and Kermit rides in on a fire truck, you can see that some of the observers outside are holding Mickey Mouse balloons.

Hint 92: An image of Cinderella Castle (a Hidden Surprise) is on a license plate at the right lower corner of the fire truck Kermit is riding.

Hint 93: As the fire truck backs out, Pluto shows up at the right side of the screen.

- *Voyage of The Little Mermaid*

Hint 94: Opposite the entrance doors to the inside waiting room, an ornate map of the Earth's hemispheres hangs on the left side of the wall. The brass frames encircling the hemispheres form the "head" of a sideways classic Mickey, while the decorative circular elements between them form a set of "ears." (Note: There's just one set of "ears" but two possible "heads.")

- *Beauty and the Beast—Live on Stage*

Hint 95: A classic Mickey is on a wind-up device on Cogsworth's back. The device has two holes for the "ears" and a larger circle for the "head." Sometimes this image is upside down.

- *Walt Disney Presents*

Hint 96: On the left side of the display aisle, in the 1940 Fantasia exhibit, a young Walt Disney holds a painting. Three large round bushes in the painting form an upright classic Mickey.

Hint 97: About halfway down the hallway of exhibits is a 1954 model of Disneyland's *Adventureland*. At the left side of the exhibit, study the fence around a small gazebo perched on a roof at the Jungle Cruise loading dock. A classic Mickey-shaped hole is at the right side of the front of the fence.

- *Disney Junior Play & Dance!*
Hint 98: Classic Mickeys appear at times in the lighting and stage effects as well as on various costumes and stage props during the live show.

Chapter 4: DHS Scavenger Hunt

- *Meet Disney Stars at Red Carpet Dreams*

Hint 99: A gold classic Mickey is on the middle of the back of the chair next to Minnie.

Hint 100: In the hallway of the Meet and Greet area, you'll pass "The Sweethearts of Swing" poster on the wall to your left. In the poster, Goofy holds a classic Hidden Mickey.

- *Star Wars Launch Bay*

Hint 101: In the second room of the queue to meet *BB-8*, a dark classic Mickey is on the rear wall near the ceiling, above an exit sign and behind a light fixture.

Hint 102: Model spaceships are displayed in a large room to the left of the Meet and Greet areas. Find the Tantive IV ship and stare into the front window. A tiny Star Wars poster with Mickey and Minnie is on the left side of the wall that you can see through the window. You may have to shine a light or take a flash photo through the window to spot this great image.

- *Animation Courtyard*

Hint 103: Donald Duck and Goofy are etched on the ornamental arches that are adjacent to Animation Courtyard's main entrance arch.

Hint 104: On the large sign over the entrance for the *Voyage of The Little Mermaid,* a classic Mickey made of bubbles floats high above Ursula's left hand.

- *The Chinese Theater*

Hint 105: Harry Anderson's celebrity impression is at the front left of the Chinese Theater (as you face the front facade). Look for a classic Mickey on Harry's tie.

Hint 106: Four squares to the right of Harry Anderson's impression, Carol Burnett's square has classic Mickey ears in the upper right side.

- *Woody's Lunch Box*

Hint 107: Stand at the order counter at Woody's Lunch Box and study the rear and side walls inside. Various berries painted on the walls come together at times as classic Hidden Mickeys.

Hint 108: In a small, fenced-off area at the front left of "Woody's Lunch Box," find an 'A113' - a reference to the classroom in the California Institute of the Arts where many Disney animators have studied. 'A' is on a block, the '1' and '1' are on the bottom of dominoes standing in the grass, and the '3' is on another block near the front fence.

- *The Hollywood Brown Derby*

Hint 109: On a wall to the left in the waiting area, in the second row of pictures, you'll find a caricature of Jimmy Dodd (with his Mouse ears), who was the MC or "Leader of the Club" for the 1950s "Mickey Mouse Club" TV show.

- *Sunset Boulevard*

Hint 110: Just past "The Trolley Car Cafe," a faux ticket booth sits at a store entrance. Coins are scattered over the front counter inside the booth, and three coins at the upper left come together as a classic Hidden Mickey.

Hint 111: Midway down Sunset Boulevard toward the *Tower of Terror,* the outside scrollwork about halfway to the top of a blue building on the right side of the street has a tilted upside-down classic Mickey in its design. Look inside the circular swirls.

Chapter 4: DHS Scavenger Hunt

- *Rosie's All-American Cafe*

Hint 112: Mickey's smiling face is at the right lower corner of a photo collage at the right side of Rosie's leftmost food order window.

- *Hollywood & Vine*

Hint 113: Outside the restaurant, a silhouette of Roger Rabbit is in a window above and to the left of the entrance.

Hint 114: On the left wall inside, the "San Fernando Valley" mural has a stick-figure Mickey on the far right, behind a pole.

Hint 115: Bushes form several classic Mickeys to the immediate left of the stick-figure Mickey and also above him.

- *50 's Prime Time Cafe*

Hint 116: In the waiting area, washers shaped like classic Mickeys secure the white tabletops.

- *Indiana Jones™ Epic Stunt Spectacular!*

Hint 117: Hidden Surprise - Outside and to the left of the entrance to the show, a sign by an excavation well says "Do Pull Rope." When you pull the rope, you'll often hear a surprised response from the explorer down in the well.

- *Backlot Express*

Hint 118: Stacks of paint cans are on top of the drink station near the exit door facing *Star Tours*. A yellow paint-splotch classic Mickey is on the second can up in a stack of cans next to a pillar, and a smaller blue paint-splotch classic Mickey is on the fourth can up. The Hidden Mickeys are on the side of the cans facing the exit door.

Hint 119: Several full-body two-dimensional Mickeys are on the bulletin boards inside the *Backlot Express* restaurant. One bulletin board is near the exit door facing *Star Tours*. A second is close by at the side of the seating area across from the mural of the city park.

- *Sci-Fi Dine-In Theater Restaurant*

Hint 120: In the waiting area on the left wall (as you enter) is a poster for the movie *Attack of the 50 Ft. Woman*. A yellow classic Mickey is behind her right knee, just off the highway.

Hint 121: Mickey Mouse in a graduation outfit is on an "Educational Reimbursement Program" notice on the lower middle of a bulletin board on a wall in the waiting area.

Hint 122: Face the kitchen, then look to the right of it at the tall fence. You'll find two Hidden Mickeys in the mural above the right side of the tall fence. Look at the treetops. A classic Mickey, tilted slightly to the right, is above the right corner of the tall fence. Another classic Hidden Mickey is just to the left of the first one; this second one appears to be waving with his left hand.

Hint 123: In the multicolored tiles above the kitchen door entrance (on the right as you face the kitchen) is a side profile of Mickey. He's outlined in yellow tiles and appears to be looking to his left (our right). Look first for his jaw, a curving line of yellow tiles at the lower middle of the mosaic square.

Hint 124: Watch the movie reel for Donald Duck, Mickey Mouse, and Tinker Bell. Donald is in a cartoon segment about a secretary who is kidnapped to another planet; Donald is one of the characters who chases her. The segment follows a clip of Walt Disney. Mickey appears in person later in the reel, in a "News of the Future" segment; he wears a spacesuit and waves to the crowd. Tinker Bell flies around above the word "Tomorrowland."

Chapter 4: DHS Scavenger Hunt

Hint 125: Stay alert for a youngster in a spacesuit during the movie reel, when the words "Calling All Boys! All Girls!" appear on the screen. A classic Mickey formed by a circle and two knobs is on the upper chest of the spacesuit, just below the helmet.

Hint 126: Watch for popcorn popping all over the movie screen. Two morsels of popcorn, in the lower middle between the popcorn popper and the box of popcorn, form upside-down classic Hidden Mickeys (actually more of a Mickey hat and ears).

Hint 127: Faint silver classic Mickeys are at the sides of the dining-car seats, on the running boards.

- *BaseLine Tap House*

Hint 128: Inside the BaseLine Tap House, a 'Drill Hole Point Size Chart' is at the bottom of a framed group of 'Notices' on the rear wall to the right of the bar. Three circles, a black 'head' and two brown 'ears,' on the chart make a classic Hidden Mickey.

- *Stage 1 Company Store*

Hint 129: Look for an old bureau that's loaded with hats for sale and has paint cans at the very top. You'll find a green, painted classic Mickey near the center of the desktop.

Hint 130: In the middle of the store, across from the green-paint Hidden Mickey on the bureau, circles in the middle of a cloud at the upper left of a mural with a rainbow approximate a classic Mickey tilted slightly to the left.

Hint 131: Mickey Mouse's shorts (red with white buttons) are hanging on a line near one of the exit doors.

Hint 132: Walk around the outside of the *Stage 1 Company Store* and admire five or more Mickey images formed by paint that's spilled on the ground. One yellow classic

Mickey is between a Cast Member door and a big bull's-eye on the walkway between the *Muppet*Vision 3D* building and the Stage 1 Company Store.

- *Mama Melrose's Ristorante Italiano*

Hint 133: Just inside the entrance, to your right, the Dalmatian has a black classic Mickey spot on its right shoulder (your left).

Hint 134: A slightly distorted classic Mickey hides in the plaster of the right wall between the waiting room and the dining area. Look in the upper right corner, near the entrance door.

Hint 135: To the right of the check-in podium (as you face it), a green classic Mickey leaf is about two feet above the bottom of the window trellis, along the left edge. (Note: This Hidden Mickey moves around or disappears at times!)

Hint 136: Look for a red classic Mickey marking on the exposed brick wall behind the check-in podium and to the left of the hanging grapes and grape leaves. It's about six feet up from the floor and near the edge of the wall next to the window trellis with the hanging grapes.

Hint 137: The left wall between the waiting room and the dining area has a smaller classic Mickey plastered on the brick. You'll find it in the middle of the left wall, just above the counter.

- *Toward Hollywood Boulevard*

Hint 138: Maneuver around the plaza in front of Center Stage and stare toward the *Dockside Diner*. Above the food order windows, the diner's oval sign lines up with the portholes ("ears") to produce a classic Hidden Mickey.

Chapter 4: DHS Scavenger Hunt

- Intersection of Hollywood & Sunset Blvds.

Hint 139: On both sides of Sunset Boulevard near its intersection with Hollywood Boulevard, you'll find small impressions in the cement sidewalks, near the curb. They read, "Mortimer & Co, 1928, Contractors." "Mortimer Mouse" was Mickey Mouse's first (and soon discarded) name; 1928 was the year he was "born." (Two more of these stamps are at the other end of Sunset Boulevard. One is near the curb just before the walkway to *Rock 'n' Roller Coaster*. The other is across the street close to the entrance walkway to the *Fantasmic!* show.)

- The Trolley Car Cafe

Hint 140: On the right-side wall is a switchboard with a tiny 'A113' on the upper right side. This is a reference to the classroom in the California Institute of the Arts where many Disney animators have studied.

- Keystone Clothiers

Hint 141: At *Peevy's Polar Pipeline* drink service, behind *Keystone Clothiers*, gauges or regulators form a classic Mickey, especially when viewed from behind.

Hint 142: To the far left of *Peevy's Polar Pipeline*, look for a door labeled with "Sights and Sounds." Notice the three names on the door: Ewell M. Pressem, Singer B. Flatt, and Bill Moore. If you say each name aloud, it sounds like a funny phrase which relates to the job title!

Hint 143: To the left and closer to *Peevy's Polar Pipeline* is a doorway with a sign listing some offices. If you say each name on the sign aloud, it suggests something related to dentistry.

Hint 144: To the right of *Peevy's Polar Pipeline* is a door sign with a historical reference: 'Holly Vermont Realty.' In 1923, Walt and

Walt Disney World's Hidden Mickeys

Roy Disney set up their first office for the Walt Disney Company in a small room at the back of the Holly Vermont Realty office. They produced the Alice Comedies in that room.

Hint 145: A stack of shipping crates sits near the *Dockside Diner*. A few interesting names are stamped on different areas of the crates, including Rick Blaine from the 'Casablanca' movie and George Bailey from 'It's a Wonderful Life.'

- *Mickey's of Hollywood*

Hint 146: The tiniest classic Hidden Mickey in Disney's Hollywood Studios is on an outside wall of the store along Hollywood Boulevard. Go to the inside of the black wall column that's closest to the park entrance. You'll be standing by a store window. The Mickey is made of tiny paint spots—a white one for the "head" and light brown spots for the "ears." The surface of the black wall column has ridges. Starting from the edge of the column closest to the street, count seven ridges back to the first flat ridge. On the fourth horizontal section up from the base of the wall, the Mickey image is on the left side of this flat section, about an inch up from the bottom of the horizontal section.

- *Cover Story*

Hint 147: You'll find a design containing classic Mickeys on the outside of the store, next to *The Darkroom*. Look on the horizontal frieze below the second-floor windows.

- *Sid Cahuenga's One-of-a-Kind*

Hint 148: Just inside the park entrance, a statue of a Dalmatian stands on the porch to the left of the shop's entrance doors. A black classic Mickey spot hides on the dog's left rear thigh.

Chapter 4: DHS Scavenger Hunt

- *Fantasmic!*

Hint 149: At one point in the show, animated characters float up in large bubbles on the water screen. The bubbles are different sizes and form classic Mickeys at times. For example, the second dancing Genie's bubble is the "head" of a decent classic Mickey.

Hint 150: Watch for the scene with the whale coming after Mickey. Just after Mickey yells for help, an outline of a classic Mickey forms for a few seconds in the foam on the wall of water gushing towards you.

Hint 151: Near the end of the show, after Mickey vanquishes the villains, Tinker Bell flies across the water screen.

- *Disney's Hollywood Studios Guidemap*

Hint 152: The face of Mickey Mouse on the park map has been distorted over time, but you can still spot it. The ear on the right is formed by *Echo Lake*, while the buildings on the left (for *The Hollywood Brown Derby* and *Disney Junior Play & Dance!*) form the distorted ear on the left. His round head is the central plaza, and his forehead "widow's peak" shows up at the end of Hollywood Boulevard. Two faint gray patches in the center of the plaza form his eyes, and his nose is an oval patch where *Center Stage* is located.

Hint 153: On the park map, tiny pink classic Hidden Mickeys adorn the right side of the entrance plaza.

Chapter 5

Disney's Animal Kingdom Scavenger Hunt

• • • • • •

Before You Start

* Many great Hidden Mickeys are in Standby queues, and you might miss them if you take the Lightning Lanes. So, for optimal Hidden Mickey hunting, (if you choose to spend the money), I recommend reserving Lightning Lane (by purchasing, on the My Disney Experience app, the current version of Disney Genie+ and/or Individual Lightning Lane) for the following attractions: **Kilimanjaro Safaris**, **DINOSAUR**, *and* **Festival of the Lion King.**

* Be sure to keep track of your Lightning Lane windows and return to those attractions at the appropriate times. In the Scavenger Hunt below, if you come to your Lightning Lane attraction and it's not time for it yet, you can skip to the next stop in the Hunt and return to the Lightning Lane attraction during your time window. If you don't opt for the Lightning Lane options, try to line up for headliner attractions during Early Entry or right after park opening.

* Some of the Hidden Mickeys in this park are in restaurants and shops. Be considerate of fellow guests and Cast Members as you search. Tell them what you're looking for, so they can share in the fun. Avoid

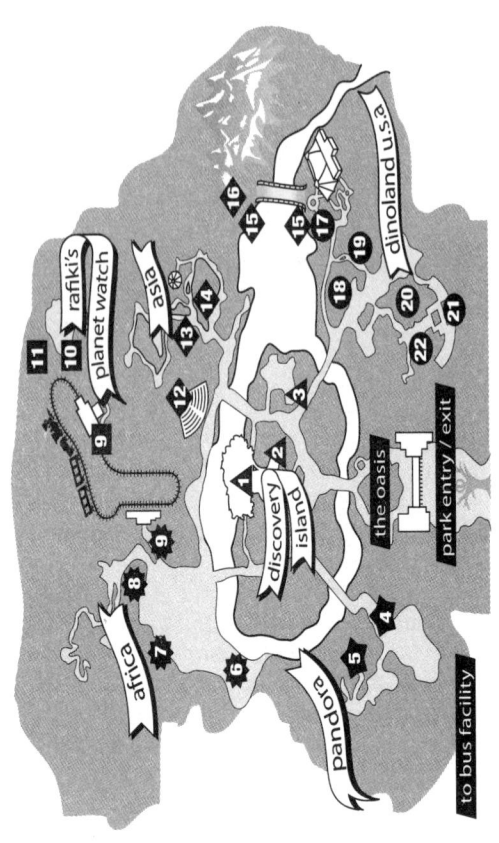

Chapter 5: DAK Scavenger Hunt

▲ Discovery Island
1. The Tree of Life
2. It's Tough to be a Bug!®
3. Flame Tree Barbecue

Pandora – The World of Avatar
4. Na'vi River Journey™
5. Avatar Flight of Passage™

Africa
6. A Celebration of Festival of the Lion King
7. Kilimanjaro Safaris®
8. Gorilla Falls Exploration Trail
9. Wildlife Express Train

■ Rafiki's Planet Watch
10. Conservation Station®
11. Affection Section

◆ Asia
12. Feathered Friends in Flight!
13. Maharajah Jungle Trek®
14. Kali River Rapids®
15. Disney KiteTails
16. Expedition Everest – Legend of the Forbidden Mountain®

● DinoLand U.S.A.
15. Disney KiteTails (main seating)
17. Finding Nemo – The Musical
18. The Boneyard®
19. TriceraTop Spin
20. Cretaceous Trail
21. DINOSAUR
22. Dino-Sue T Rex

Disney's Animal Kingdom®

searching restaurants at busy mealtimes unless you are one of the diners.

* Each person has unique needs for sustenance. If I don't have specific suggestions for restaurants (related to Hidden Mickeys), then I leave it to you to decide when and where to break for snacks/meals.

*
Your first stop is ***Avatar Flight of Passage.***

Clue 1: Stay alert along the Standby entrance queue (and on the ride) for bioluminescent Hidden Mickeys. Look for the first one on the right side of the initial inside portion of the queue.
5 points

Clue 2: As you continue along the queue, look high for another bioluminescent Hidden Mickey.
4 points

Clue 3: Search for small bottles that make one or more Hidden Mickeys.
2 points

Clue 4: Pore over a researcher's note paper for a Hidden Mickey.
5 points

Clue 5: On the ride, when you stop in a cave, glance around for a classic Mickey.
4 points

Clue 6: Along the Exit 2 lower level exit corridor, don't miss a Hidden Surprise: special handprints!
5 points

* Get in line for ***Na'vi River Journey***.

Clue 7: Look up in the covered portion of the Standby queue to find one or more classic Mickeys in lights.
3 points

Chapter 5: DAK Scavenger Hunt

Clue 8: Scan the ceiling of the covered portion of the Standby queue for holes that make a classic Mickey.
5 points

Clue 9: On the boat ride, analyze the chanting Shaman for a Hidden Mickey.
5 points

Clue 10: Outside in front of *Na'vi River Journey*, admire a large abstract figure and zoom in on a classic Hidden Mickey made of colored beads.
3 points

Clue 11: Outside in Pandora, study the cement walkways for a classic Mickey. (Tip: it's by a seating area.)
3 points

*

Cross the park to **Expedition Everest** in Asia. One of the queue Hidden Mickeys (Clue 31) is only visible from the Single Rider or Lightning Lane queues. Join the Standby queue to search for the Mickeys in Clues 12 through 24. After you exit the ride, you can look for Hidden Mickeys in and just outside the gift shop and then step into the Single Rider queue to look for Clue 31.

Clue 12: In the Standby queue, search for a classic Mickey in the first sunken courtyard.
3 points

Clue 13: Locate Mickey depressions on a red wall.
4 points

Clue 14: Look around for cloud Hidden Mickeys in a mural.
4 points for spotting two

Clue 15: Keep alert for pipes on a shelf that form a classic Mickey.
3 points

Clue 16: Find small Mickey ears in this room.
5 points

Clue 17: Look for a Hidden Mickey made of light-switch devices in a display.
3 points

Clue 18: Stay alert for Mickey on a book.
4 points

Clue 19: Search for Mickey on a handrail.
5 points

Clue 20: Spot a Hidden Mickey on a kettle.
4 points

Clue 21: Squint for a Hidden Mickey in an animal track.
5 points

Clue 22: Search for an animal with Mickey's ears!
3 points

Clue 23: In the last room before boarding for both the Standby and Lightning Lane lines, glance around for Sorcerer Mickey near something blue.
5 points

Clue 24: In the loading area outside the Standby and Lightning Lane lines, look for a classic Mickey.
3 points

Clue 25: After the ride starts, stay alert for a classic-Mickey melted spot in the snow on the mountain.
5 points

Clue 26: Don't miss a small, white snow Hidden Mickey before and after your coaster comes to a stop.
5 points

Clue 27: Find a small classic Mickey made of gold balls in the gift shop at the ride exit.
3 points

Clue 28: Look around the gift shop for classic Mickey circles on a brown chest.
3 points for one or more

Chapter 5: DAK Scavenger Hunt

Clue 29: Admire a Hidden Mickey on a yellow flower near the ceiling.
4 points

Clue 30: Search outside, near the Serka Zong Bazaar shop, for a classic Mickey.
3 points

Clue 31: In either the Single Rider or the Lightning Lane queue, find a Hidden Mickey on a lantern.
4 points

Clue 32: Locate a cloud Hidden Mickey outside on a truck.
4 points

Clue 33: Now walk around to spot a classic Mickey in camp supplies near a post.
3 points

*
 Stroll to Africa at your Lightning Lane time to enjoy riding **Kilimanjaro Safaris**.

Clue 34: Along the queue, watch a video monitor for spots on a leopard.
5 points

Clue 35: Observe the island in the flamingo pond.
4 points

Clue 36: Near the lions, watch for Donald in the rocks.
4 points

Clue 37: Locate Hidden Mickey(s) on a drink cart as you exit from *Kilimanjaro Safaris*.
4 points

★
 Go to **Kali River Rapids** in Asia and find three classic Mickeys on your way to the ride. (You can exit when you get to the loading dock if you don't want to get on the raft. Ask a Cast Member to point the way out.)

Clue 38: You're getting close to the first Hidden Mickey when you see stone statues in the grass.
2 points

Clue 39: Gaze high for a classic Hidden Mickey inside the next room. (The room may be roped off. If so, ask a Cast Member if you can explore the room).
4 points

Clue 40: Scan the banks at the loading dock for a Hidden Mickey.
4 points

★
 Visit **DINOSAUR** at your Lightning Lane time.

Clue 41: Study along the inside entrance queue for a classic Hidden Mickey on a tree.
4 points

Clue 42: After the ride begins, be alert for a Hidden Mickey on a whiteboard. (Note: This Mickey image changes locations and even disappears at times.)
4 bonus points

Clue 43: Find a classic Mickey on the red dinosaur in the mural behind the counter in the ride's photo-purchase area.
4 points

★
 Walk into the queue for **It's Tough to be a Bug!** on Discovery Island.

Clue 44: When you get inside *The Tree of Life,* look for Mickey above the handicapped entrance doors.
4 points

Chapter 5: DAK Scavenger Hunt

✱
Stroll over to the ***Maharajah Jungle Trek***.

Clue 45: At the tiger exhibit area, check the water in the painting to the right of the first arch.
2 points

Clue 46: Look for the earring Mickey on the left mural inside the first arch.
2 points

Clue 47: Find a bush Mickey on the left mural inside the first arch.
2 points

Clue 48: Search the right mural inside the first arch for a Hidden Mickey on a man.
2 points

Clue 49: Inside the building with arches, on the right wall, check the flowers on two square panels to find classic Mickeys.
2 points for one or more

Clue 50: Look for a classic Mickey in the mountains inside the second arch.
2 points

Clue 51: Now find a classic Mickey in the cloud formation inside the same arch.
2 points

Clue 52: As soon as you exit the temple ruins, search for two Hidden Mickeys in the leaves to your left.
8 points for spotting both

Clue 53: Walk left to the Elds Deer Exhibit for a Hidden Mickey in the wall mural.
4 points

Clue 54: Further along the trail, before you get to the aviary entrance, try to spot a classic Mickey in a man's necklace in a carving on the wall.
2 points

Clue 55: On another carving, locate a Hidden Mickey on an ear.
2 points

*
  Before or after lunch, wander over to the ***Gorilla Falls Exploration Trail*** in Africa.

Clue 56: <u>In the bird aviary, spot a classic Hidden Mickey in the water.</u>
4 points

Clue 57: Past the gorilla viewing area, search for a Hidden Jafar.
5 points

Clue 58: In the last part of the trail, you walk under a Hidden Surprise!
3 points

*
  See ***Finding Nemo: The Big Blue... and Beyond!*** at Theater in the Wild in DinoLand. Arrive 30 minutes before showtime.

Clue 59: Look around for a Hidden Mickey near the stage.
3 points

Clue 60: Find two Hidden Mickeys in the show-time signs outside.
4 points for spotting both

*
  Go to Africa and see ***Festival of the Lion King*** at your Lightning Lane time.

Clue 61: Along the Lightning Lane queue, watch for some poles near the ceiling that make a classic Hidden Mickey.
3 points

Clue 62: Be alert for an upright classic Mickey on Timon the meerkat's float.
4 points

Clue 63: Now search for an upside-down classic Mickey on Timon's float.
4 points

Chapter 5: DAK Scavenger Hunt

Clue 64: Check out a classic Mickey image on Pumbaa the warthog's float.
3 points

Clue 65: Study the center stage for a classic Mickey.
4 points

Tip: If the floats and props are still there after the show has ended, you can look for the Hidden Mickeys in the Clues above as you exit. If you need help, ask a Cast Member. However, don't dillydally, as the Cast Members need to empty the theater for the next show.

*
Take the *Wildlife Express Train* to Rafiki's Planet Watch to search **Conservation Station** for a Hidden Mickey bonanza. (Note: Some of the Hidden Mickeys here may be covered up or inaccessible depending on the current shows and entertainment activities inside the building).

Clue 66: Look at the mosaic in the pavement outside the main entrance to *Conservation Station* for a small classic Mickey.
4 points

Clue 67: On the wall mural just to the right, spot a Mickey Mouse profile on an opossum.
4 points

Clue 68: Look for a butterfly wearing classic Mickeys.
3 points

Clue 69: Gaze closely at a spider nearby with a classic Mickey marking.
3 points

Clue 70: Spot a classic Mickey on an ostrich.
3 points

Clue 71: Look for a classic Mickey on a green snake.
3 points

Clue 72: Search for another classic Mickey on a lizard's ear.
4 points

Clue 73: Locate a side-profile Mickey on a hippo.
4 points

Clue 74: Glance at a llama for a classic Mickey.
3 points

Clue 75: A squirrel nearby sports a classic Mickey.
3 points

Clue 76: Look for a classic Mickey on an alligator.
3 points

Clue 77: Find a frog bearing a tiny image of Mickey's face.
5 points

Clue 78: Scan a walrus for a Hidden Mickey.
4 points

Clue 79: Find the Hidden Mickey on an owl.
3 points

Clue 80: Search for the amazing Mickey image on a second butterfly!
5 points

Clue 81: Look up for a classic Mickey on a frog behind a monkey.
5 points

Clue 82: Scan the mural for a fish with a partially hidden classic Mickey.
5 points

Clue 83: Locate a butterfly with two Hidden Mickeys.
4 points for both

Clue 84: Look around carefully for a frog with a side-profile Mickey.
5 points

Chapter 5: DAK Scavenger Hunt

Clue 85: Find a yellow butterfly with a classic Mickey.
3 points

Clue 86: Look lower for a chameleon with Mickey spots.
3 points

Clue 87: Admire this chameleon a bit longer so you don't overlook another Hidden Mickey!
4 points

Clue 88: Scan overhead for a Mickey in tree leaves.
3 points

Clue 89: Next to the "Song of the Rainforest" area, spot a fly with a tiny classic Mickey on its back.
5 points

Clue 90: Search for a tiny flower Hidden Mickey at the first entrance to the "Song of the Rainforest" area.
4 points

Clue 91: Look for a classic Mickey indentation on a tree toward the front of the *Rainforest* area.
3 points

Clue 92: Don't stray far for a Mickey hole in a leaf.
4 points

Clue 93: Check the trees inside the *Rainforest* area for a side-profile Mickey shadow.
4 points

Clue 94: Look for the classic Mickey shadow on the ceiling near door number eight in the "Song of the Rainforest" area.
4 points

Clue 95: Now find a Hidden Mickey on a tree near door number six.
3 points

Clue 96: Search for a green moss sideprofile Mickey in the *Rainforest* area.
4 points

Clue 97: Walk out to the front of the *Rainforest* area and search for a sideprofile Mickey.
4 points

Clue 98: Spot a classic Mickey made of short plant stalks on the Grandmother Willow tree.
3 points

Clue 99: Also in the *Rainforest* area, spot a classic Mickey on a cockroach.
4 points

Clue 100: Now find a classic Mickey on a lizard on the same tree.
3 points

Clue 101: Stay with this tree and admire a berry Hidden Mickey.
4 points

Clue 102: Look for a butterfly wearing a tiny Hidden Mickey on this tree.
5 points

Clue 103: Examine the grates around the bottoms of the trees in the main lobby.
2 points

Clue 104: Locate a Hidden Mickey on a plate in a window display at the rear of the lobby.
3 points

Clue 105: Search for a Hidden Mickey on the wall of one of the rooms at the rear of the lobby.
3 points

Clue 106: Spot a reptile classic Mickey on a ledge in the rear area displays and laboratories.
3 points

Chapter 5: DAK Scavenger Hunt

* Walk outside to **Affection Section** to spot another classic Hidden Mickey.
Clue 107: Study the animals in the petting zoo. (Note: These Hidden Mickeys come and go.)
4 bonus points

* Wander on over to the **Wildlife Express Train station** and look for classic Mickeys.
Clue 108: Examine the rafters inside the station.
2 points

* Ride the train to Africa, then check out **Harambe Fruit Market** for a cool Hidden Mickey.

Clue 109: This full-body Mickey is somewhere inside the *Fruit Market*.
4 points

Clue 110: Check the beginning of the cement and flagstone path at the side of the *Fruit Market*.
4 points

Clue 111: Turn left at the opposite end of the path and follow the cement walkway a few feet to find a large, faint classic Mickey in the cement.
5 points

* Stroll inside **Tusker House Restaurant**.

Clue 112: Locate a classic Mickey on an Assignment Board on a wall.
4 points

* Go to the far side of **Tamu Tamu Refreshments**.

Clue 113: Find another classic Mickey formed by a small utility cover and adjacent pebbles.
5 points

Clue 114: Marvel at a Hidden Baloo the bear inside the small seating area behind *Tamu Tamu Refreshments*.
5 points

Clue 115: Search for another Hidden Character here.
4 points

* Walk a short way down the *path to Asia*.

Clue 116: Look over to **The Tree of Life** and spot the Hidden Mickey on it. (Psst! It's near the hippo.)
4 points

*
Cross the bridge from Africa to Discovery Island and amble on into **Pizzafari restaurant**.

Clue 117: Spot Mickey in the room across from the food order counters.
3 points

Clue 118: In the first dining room to the left as you walk down the hall, search for a tiny orange classic Mickey.
5 points

Clue 119: In the Nocturnal Room (the dining room directly to the left of the food counters as you face the counters), study the firefly wings.
3 points

Clue 120: In the Nocturnal Room, look around for a classic Mickey in the trees.
4 points

*
Stroll a short distance into **Pandora – The World of Avatar**.

Clue 121: While on the bridge from *Discovery Island* to *Pandora*, admire a Hidden Surprise: a dragon near the water!
3 points

Clue 122: Check out the main entrance path for a Hidden Mickey on a rock seat.
4 points

Chapter 5: DAK Scavenger Hunt

*

Return to DinoLand U.S.A. Enter **The Boneyard**.

Clue 123: Look around the children's dig area for Hidden Mickey hard hats.
2 points

* Enter **Restaurantosaurus** through a rear door (from near the restrooms).

Clue 124: Locate a Hidden Mickey near the ceiling of the large dining room closest to *DINOSAUR*.
4 points

* Walk to the **Cretaceous Trail** in the middle of DinoLand and go dino hunting.

Clue 125: Find a dark Mickey on a dinosaur's back.
3 points

* Go to **TriceraTop Spin**.

Clue 126: Search in front of the attraction for a classic Mickey on a dinosaur with a ball.
3 points

Clue 127: Spot a classic Mickey in one of the parking spaces near the attraction.
3 points

Clue 128: Study the nearby horned dinosaur studded with gems and find a Mickey pin.
4 points

* Check inside **Chester & Hester's Dinosaur Treasures** shop.

Clue 129: Find a marionette Mickey in the shop.
2 points

Clue 130: Scan inside the store near the rear entrance for a black classic Mickey.
5 points

Clue 131: Study the pavement outside the store entrance that faces *TriceraTop Spin* for a classic Mickey.
5 points

* Walk along the outer walkway *behind the* **Fossil Fun Games** area.

Clue 132: Check out the fence signs for a classic Hidden Mickey.
3 points

*
   On *Discovery Island,* enter the **Island Mercantile** shop.

Clue 133: Look for three classic Mickeys made of spots.
5 points for all three

* Back outside the shop, find a classic Mickey made of green moss.
Clue 134: Study the front of **The Tree of Life**.
5 points

* Step inside the **Riverside Depot** shop.

Clue 135: Scan the walls for a Hidden Mickey.
3 points

* Wind your way over to the **Discovery Trading Company** next door.

Clue 136: Locate a Hidden Mickey in a constellation high on a wall.
5 points

Clue 137: Search outside the exit door closest to *Flame Tree Barbecue* for a tiny classic Mickey in the pavement.
4 points

* Stroll to the **Flame Tree Barbecue Restaurant**.

Clue 138: Study the ground in the food order area for a rock classic Mickey.
4 points

Chapter 5: DAK Scavenger Hunt

Clue 139: Now find a classic Mickey in the seating area outside.
2 points

* Go to the **Rainforest Cafe** *entrance sign* inside the park.

Clue 140: Look for a Hidden Mickey on the sign.
3 points

* Keep your eyes open *as you leave the park.*

Clue 141: Search the outside walls of the ticket booths for Hidden Mickeys.
4 points for two

Clue 142: Outside the entrance turnstiles, check the metal grates around some of the trees near the tram loading area.
2 points

**Total Points for
Disney's Animal Kingdom =**

　　　　———————

How'd you do?

Up to 206 points - Bronze
207 to 412 points - Silver
413 points and over - Gold
516 points - Perfect Score

You may have done even better if you earned bonus points in **DINOSAUR**, and/or ***Affection Section***.

Chapter 5: DAK Scavenger Hunt

Pandora - The World of Avatar

-Avatar Flight of Passage

Hint 1: A bioluminescent classic Mickey is on the right wall of the cave soon after you enter the inside queue. The image is at the upper part of a cluster of flower-like growths about halfway up the wall.

Hint 2: After you pass by the "Attention" message painted on the right wall, begin scanning near the ceiling for a bioluminescent classic Hidden Mickey sideways to the left. You can spot the image up high as you make a U-turn in the queue along the upsloping walkway.

Hint 3: When you reach the lab along the Standby entrance queue, look on a countertop for a collection of small, different-sized bottles with black caps. Several sets of three bottle caps come together as classic Hidden Mickeys. These images may change from time to time.

Hint 4: Further along in the lab, you'll come across drawings (or prints or doodles) on a researcher's note paper. Three of the small black circles—along the upper left border of the drawings—form a classic Mickey, sideways to the right. The "ear" circles are lighter than the "head" circle.

Hint 5: On the ride, when your banshee stops in a cave, look down over the left side to find another bioluminescent Hidden Mickey, similar to the ones along the entrance queue.

Hint 6: In the exit corridor - Exit 2 - on the lowest level, search the wall on your right for a Hidden Surprise: three handprints in red paint with initials below the prints. These are the handprints and initials of James Cameron, the director of the Avatar movie, Jon Landau, a producer of Avatar, and Joe Rohde, lead Imagineer and creator of Pandora and all of Disney's Animal Kingdom.

- Na'vi River Journey

Hint 7: Along the Standby entrance queue, glance up at one or more light fixtures. From certain vantage points, a center large bulb lines up with smaller bulbs to make a classic Mickey.

Hint 8: Leaves with holes blanket the ceiling of the covered portion of the Standby entrance queue, so this classic Mickey made of holes is difficult to locate! It's about halfway along the inside queue, above a large lantern and next to a small rope tie, not far from the outer perimeter of the queue.

Hint 9: Toward the end of the boat ride, study the cloak on the chanting Audio-animatronic 'Shaman of Song' on your right. A classic Mickey-shaped hole is in the lower part of the cloak hanging from the Shaman's

Chapter 5: DAK Scavenger Hunt

left arm (to your right of the Shaman's chest, between the hand and chest). Look for black holes in the reddish fabric that form a classic Hidden Mickey tilted to the left. The image appears a couple of times as the Shaman lifts and moves the left arm.

Hint 10: Outside in front of *Na'vi River Journey*, walk to the front of an abstract figure made of branches and woven plant material and festooned with colorful beads. At the lower left of the figure, a group of beads contains a three-bead Hidden Mickey tilted right. It has a purple "head," a green right "ear," and an orange left "ear." Other groups of beads in this display also come close as classic, three-circle Hidden Mickeys.

Hint 11: Outside, walk away from *Pongu Pongu* refreshment stand and locate a small seating area by a lightpost. On the cement walkway by the lightpost are rust circles left by barrels that have been moved. Three of these circles come together as a classic Mickey. First, spot the smaller "ears" and then the larger "head" under them. One side of the "head" has a ragged appearance.

Asia

- *Expedition Everest*

Note: Hints 12 through 24 apply to Hidden Mickeys you'll find in the Standby queue. The Hidden Mickey in Hint 31 can only be spotted from the Single Rider or Lightning Lane queues.

Hint 12: A classic Mickey made of a central circle with swirls for ears hides in the base of a Yeti statue. You'll find it in a sunken outdoor courtyard past the first room (an office).

Hint 13: Just past the first room, a classic Mickey is formed by shallow depressions in the left wall of a small red building. The upright image is at the far left lower corner of the wall, below and to the left of a small curved drainpipe.

Hint 14: On the rear wall of the same red building just past the first room, classic Mickeys lie in the clouds on the left and right sides of a Yeti mural.

Hint 15: As you enter the second building (*Tashi's Trek and Tongba Shop*), an upside-down classic Mickey is formed by the highest pipes on the top shelf in the right corner.

Hint 16: Along the far wall of *Tashi's Trek and Tongba Shop*, a small white Yeti doll on a far right upper shelf inside a cupboard wears black Mickey ears.

Hint 17: In *Tashi's Trek and Tongba Shop*, light-switch devices in a glass case on the left side of the queue form a classic Mickey.

Hint 18: Inside the *Yeti Museum*, on the right side of the queue after the first left turn, look for a Yeti book at the far left of the book display. A partial image of Mickey's head and ears is imprinted in the snow on the book's front cover.

Hint 19: Just past the snow Mickey of Hint 18, a classic Mickey is etched into the top end of a wooden handrail.

Hint 20: Dents in a kettle in the *Yeti Museum's* second display form a classic Mickey.

Hint 21: Also in the *museum*, a classic Mickey is hiding in an "animal track." It's at the lower left of a tall glass cabinet in a display labeled "Documenting Biodiversity." Look near the top of the third paper from the left, above the label "Small Mammal Tracks."

Hint 22: The next-to-last display cabinet in the *museum* has a photo of a bear with ears that look like Mickey's ears. The bear is on the right side of the cabinet, under the words "The Yeti, Interpreting the Findings."

Hint 23: In the last room before boarding, look for a photo of a woman in blue listening

Chapter 5: DAK Scavenger Hunt

to a hand-held radio. Mickey in his Sorcerer's Hat is etched on a wall to the left of the woman's head.

Hint 24: Outside in the loading area, look for a classic Mickey in the blue scrollwork above the first window. (You can see this Hidden Mickey from both the Lightning Lane and Standby queues.)

Hint 25: In the first part of the ride, as your train is climbing the mountain, a dark, melted classic Mickey-shaped spot appears in the snow to your left. The "ear" farthest away from the train is contiguous with a larger dark spot above it.

Hint 26: As your coaster approaches the torn track rails, a small white upright classic Hidden Mickey is in the snow on your left. You can spot it before your coaster comes to a stop and as you're going backward. When your coaster is stopped, the Hidden Mickey is to the left of the rear of the train. It's on the brown rock wall, a few feet up from the ground.

Hint 27: Small gold balls form classic Mickeys at the bottom of both sides of a merchandise display in the middle of the gift shop at the ride exit. The display is across from the photo pickup area.

Hint 28: Brown chests sit on an upper shelf of a merchandise cabinet at the right side of the gift shop's right exit door (as you exit the ride). Circles along the front and sides of the lower chest form several classic Mickeys. One is at the right lower corner of the front of the chest. It's tilted to the left.

Hint 29: Find a yellow flower at the top center of this same merchandise cabinet (at the right side of the right exit door). A petal at the seven o'clock position on the flower forms a classic Mickey.

Hint 30: Outside and across from the *Serka Zong Bazaar* gift shop, a large upside-down classic Mickey is etched near the top of the second stone tablet from the edge closest to the shop.

Hint 31: In the *Yeti Museum* as seen from both the Lightning Lane and Single Rider queues, a sideways classic Mickey is formed by three dents in a lantern in the second glassed-in display. (Note: You cannot spot this lantern image from the Standby queue.)

Hint 32: At the front of the left side of the *Anandapur Ice Cream Bus*, look for a painting with two towers. A classic Hidden Mickey, tilted to the left, hides in the clouds at the upper right of the painting. (Note: the images on this truck change from time to time.)

Hint 33: Outside the attraction, base camp supplies hang in the *Gupta's Gear* area. A three-circle Mickey image hangs among these supplies, near the second post from the end nearest the restrooms.

Africa

- *Kilimanjaro Safaris*

Hint 34: Near the end of the entrance queue, just before you reach the final loading dock, a monitor above you shows a continuous video loop. Look for the resting orange-and-white leopard with black spots. Three spots on white fur form a classic Mickey on the left side (your right) of the leopard's neck.

Hint 35: In elephant country, and about halfway through the ride, the island in the flamingo pond is shaped like a classic Hidden Mickey. It's to the left of your ride vehicle. The "head" and "ears" are often darker than the outer sand of the island.

Hint 36: The rocks in the lion area are arranged to resemble Donald Duck. Spot his cap first, then his face, eyes, and beak. (Note: These rocks have shifted positions slightly over time.)

Chapter 5: DAK Scavenger Hunt

Hint 37: Walk to a cashier's cart at the end of the exit path from *Kilimanjaro Safaris* and not far from the entrance to the *Gorilla Falls Exploration Trail*. Look for tiny tile Hidden Mickeys on the top (not the side or front) of the counter of the drink and merchandise cart.

Asia

- Kali River Rapids

Hint 38: Along the entrance queue, keep your eyes peeled for stone statues in the grass. As you approach the next room to your right, look at the lower left corner of the outer wall. Three of the plates on the wall form a classic Mickey, tilted down to the right. (Note: These images change from time to time.)

Hint 39: Inside the next room to your right—a museum—a dark classic Mickey is on the back of a light brown boot, which is high on a shelf near the ceiling in the middle of a collection of boots. To find it, walk through the first door to the museum and look up behind you to the shelf. Continue to look around - you may discover more boots with Hidden Mickeys! (If the room is roped off, ask any Cast Member nearby if you can just look around in the museum for a few minutes).

Hint 40: At the loading dock, study the right side of the shore and rock wall across the waterway for a classic Mickey made of wheels with spokes - one large wheel topped by two smaller ones.

DinoLand U.S.A.

-DINOSAUR

Hint 41: Just inside the building entrance, on the right side of the queue, look at the tree at the far left of the mural. A classic Mickey made of round, light brown spots is on the tree trunk, next to the lower right branch.

Hint 42: Just as the ride starts and before you travel back in time, a classic Mickey at the lower left corner of a white greaseboard appears to the left of your vehicle. (This Mickey image changes locations and may even disappear at times.)

Hint 43: On the mural behind the counter in the ride's photo-purchase area, a large red dinosaur has a small classic Mickey on its lower neck.

Discovery Island

- It's Tough to be a Bug!

Hint 44: Inside *The Tree of Life*, look for the handicapped entrance doors to *It's Tough to be a Bug!* (You reach them before you get to the main entrance doors to the theater.) Look at the upper left area near the doors—and just to the right of the "Cast Members Only" door—to find a small dark classic Mickey.

Asia

- Maharajah Jungle Trek

Hint 45: To the right of the first arch, swirls in the water under a tiger form a classic Mickey.

Hint 46: Inside the first arch, on the left mural, the king's gold earring forms a solid upside-down classic Mickey.

Hint 47: Inside the first arch, on the left mural, a dark green bush under the wrist of the king's extended arm forms a small upright classic Mickey.

Hint 48: Inside the first arch, on the right mural, a man is wearing an upside-down classic Mickey gold earring.

Hint 49: On the right wall inside the building with arches, two square panels are decorated

Chapter 5: DAK Scavenger Hunt

with flowers. Some of the outer flowers have circles at the bases of their petals that form classic Mickeys.

Hint 50: Inside the second arch, on the left mural, there's a small classic Mickey in a brown rock formation on the left side of the mountains.

Hint 51: Inside the second arch, on the right mural, a classic Mickey appears in the upper part of the left cloud formation.

Hint 52: As you exit the temple ruins, turn to your immediate left to a large wall mural. Among the leaves is a dark green classic Mickey. It's about nine feet above the ground and one foot from the bricks at the left side of the mural. Another even darker green classic Mickey is further to the right on this mural. It's above the tiger running toward the left, and between two large, light green fan-shaped leaves.

Hint 53: Just past the temple ruins where the tigers are, turn left to the Elds Deer Exhibit. Study the huge outdoor painted mural on the wall to your left. Mickey is hiding in the right center of the mural—below the third (from the left) of four vertical brick cracks—in some orange flowers and green leaves. Look for a classic Hidden Mickey with an orange and white head and green ears.

Hint 54: On a wall to the right, just before you reach the aviary entrance, you can spot an upside-down classic Mickey in the necklace of a man in the middle carving.

Hint 55: On the wall carving to the left of the above Hidden Mickey, an earring on a crouching man (his right ear—on the left as you face the man) forms a classic Hidden Mickey.

Africa

- Gorilla Falls Exploration Trail

Hint 56: While you're observing and listening to the colorful birds in the aviary, search the duck pond on your left for a classic Hidden Mickey formed of dark rocks. You'll find it along the shoreline of the pond, usually under water.

Hint 57: A three-dimensional head of Jafar is carved out of a 25- to 30-foot rock. You'll find it past the gorilla viewing area, to the right of the first section of the first suspension bridge.

Hint 58: At the last part of the trail, look up to see a Hidden Surprise as you walk under the head and body of a huge turtle sculpted in the rocks.

DinoLand U.S.A.

- Finding Nemo: The Big Blue... and Beyond!

Hint 59: Three bubbles touch to form a classic Mickey at the lower left of the stage.

Hint 60: Two sideways classic Mickeys formed by bubbles hide in each of the two outdoor signs announcing the show times for the day. One is in the bottom right corner of the signs, and the other is under the word "The" and near the bottom of the signs. These signs are posted on both the walkway from Asia and the walkway from the rest of DinoLand U.S.A.

Africa

- Festival of the Lion King

Hint 61: Near the end of the Lightning Lane queue, round poles are stacked two deep in a crate on a plank near the ceiling and next to the outside main walkway. Three poles to the right of the middle of the stack form a classic Hidden Mickey tilted down to the right.

Chapter 5: DAK Scavenger Hunt

Hint 62: A white classic Mickey is painted on the lower middle front of Timon's (and the giraffe's) float. You can see it as the float enters the arena.

Hint 63: An upside-down white classic Mickey is on the lower right side of Timon's float, under the giraffe's front leg.

Hint 64: Three circles form a classic Mickey at the front left (Pumbaa's left) side, and near the top of the side, of Pumbaa's float.

Hint 65: A classic Mickey in relief is on the lower side of the movable center stage, to the right of some steps. It is usually facing the *Elephant section* of the audience.

Rafiki's Planet Watch

- Conservation Station

(Note: Some of the Hidden Mickeys here may be covered up or inaccessible depending on current shows and entertainment activities inside the building).

Hint 66: A classic Mickey made of circles (two dark and one light) hides in the circular mosaic in the pavement right outside the main entrance to *Conservation Station*. Mickey is above the second "T" in "Station" and below the elephant's trunk.

Hint 67: Find an opossum on the right side of the mural just inside the entrance. There is a side profile of Mickey Mouse in its left eye.

Hint 68: Above the opossum, at the upper right, a butterfly has classic Mickeys on its wings.

Hint 69: About six feet up from the floor, not far from the opossum, a spider has a light pink classic Mickey marking on its thorax.

Hint 70: On the wall to the left of the restrooms, near the entrance, the pupil of an ostrich's eye is a classic Mickey.

Hint 71: Toward the middle of the mural at the front, near the entrance, a green snake sports a black classic Mickey on its upper back.

Hint 72: Near the upper right border of the screen (on the wall facing you as you enter the building), a dark classic Mickey marking is at the top of a green lizard's ear, above a deer.

Hint 73: A hippopotamus is the fifth animal from the left at the bottom of the entrance mural on the left wall. A side-profile Mickey is on its lower jaw, under the middle tooth.

Hint 74: To the immediate left of the hippopotamus, a llama sports a dark brown classic Mickey on its neck.

Hint 75: Under the hippopotamus, a squirrel's eye has a black classic Mickey pupil.

Hint 76: On the hippo's right side, an alligator has a small dark classic Mickey to the left of its green eye.

Hint 77: To the right of the alligator, Mickey Mouse's smiling face is under a frog's right eye.

Hint 78: Directly above the frog with the smiling Mickey is a walrus with a dark classic Mickey on the left side (your right) of his neck.

Hint 79: A bit farther along on this left wall mural, the pupils of an owl's eyes are classic Mickeys.

Hint 80: The entrance murals curve toward the inside of the building. On the right curving mural, look closely for the butterfly with an image of Mickey's face on its body (not on its wings!).

Chapter 5: DAK Scavenger Hunt

Hint 81: Midway along the right curving mural, high up near the ceiling, a classic Mickey-shaped marking is on the white skin of the chin under the middle of a frog's face. The frog is behind a red-faced monkey.

Hint 82: Toward the top and near the end of the left side of the entrance mural, a dark classic Mickey, partially hidden by an octopus nearby, is on the side of a fish, to the left of the fish's fin.

Hint 83: Along the bottom of the right mural as you approach the inside show area, two black classic Mickeys are near the bottom of the wings of an orange butterfly under a monkey.

Hint 84: Near the bottom of the same mural, a side-profile Mickey is in a silver frog's left pupil.

Hint 85: Before the first entrance to the "Song of the Rainforest" area, about halfway up the wall and above a bat, a yellow butterfly has a black classic Mickey on its left wing.

Hint 86: In the same area, a tan and green chameleon has a group of spots directly behind the eye that form an upside-down classic Mickey.

Hint 87: This same chameleon sports a small dark classic Mickey behind the neck and just above the front leg. It's at about the same level as the upside-down Hidden Mickey described above.

Hint 88: A hole in the tree leaves overhead resembles a classic Mickey. It's directly above the first entrance.

Hint 89: The fly with a tiny classic Mickey on its back is on the left panel of the first entrance to the "Song of the Rainforest" area.

Hint 90: On the same panel, a tiny yellow-flower classic Mickey blooms on a green plant near the floor.

Hint 91: Turn to the right panel mural at the same entrance to the *Rainforest* area to see a classic Mickey indentation on a tree. It's about four feet up from the floor.

Hint 92: Look for a classic Mickey hole in a green leaf near the Mickey indentation in Hint 86.

Hint 93: Now go inside to see a side-profile Mickey shadow about seven feet up from the floor on the front of a tree inside the *Rainforest* area.

Hint 94: Above and in front of door number eight in the *Rainforest* area, you can spot a dark classic Mickey shadow on the ceiling to the right.

Hint 95: A white classic Mickey is outlined on a tree by door number six, to the left of the words "The Accidental Florist."

Hint 96: Turn around and walk out toward the lobby to look at the right side of the tree with "The Song of the Rainforest" sign (the Grandmother Willow tree). A rear horizontal panel has a green moss sideprofile Mickey about six feet up from the floor.

Hint 97: A side-profile Mickey indentation appears on the same tree under the sign and to the lower right (as you face her) of Grandmother Willow's face. (Tip: You have to walk farther into the lobby to spot it.)

Hint 98: Three plant stalks form a classic Mickey in the mural near the floor on the bottom left of the Grandmother Willow tree (as you face it from the lobby).

Hint 99: To the right of the Grandmother Willow tree, there is a cockroach display inside a tree in front of the "Song of the Rainforest" area. A cockroach inside and toward the back of the tree bears a dark, upside-down classic Mickey on its back.

Chapter 5: DAK Scavenger Hunt

Hint 100: A lizard above the "Giant Cockroach" sign on the same tree has a classic Mickey above its front leg.

Hint 101: On the right front side of this tree, locate a long strand of red berries. The three berries at the very bottom of the strand form a classic Mickey.

Hint 102: On the left front of the tree with the cockroach display, a light brown butterfly about six and a half to seven feet up from the floor has a tiny black classic Mickey on its back between the wings.

Hint 103: The grates around the bottoms of the trees in the lobby have classic Mickey patterns, as do those outside by *Affection Section*.

Hint 104: A classic Mickey on a "Microtiter Plate" is usually in the first display room to the right in the rear of the lobby. Look into the second window of the "Wildlife Tracking Center." The colors in the plate change from time to time.

Hint 105: A Hidden Mickey made of black insect nets hangs on a rear wall of the Veterinary Treatment room, which is one of the middle rooms at the back of Conservation Station. The nets are next to the doors to the Treatment/Prep Room.

Hint 106: A classic Mickey made of three containers with reptile skins is on a ledge in the far left window of a room with reptiles.

- *Affection Section*

Hint 107: One of the animals usually has a classic Mickey shaved into its coat.

Wildlife Express Train station

Hint 108: High up in the rafters inside the train station, look for classic Mickeys where the beams intersect.

Africa

- In and around Harambe

Hint 109: At the *Harambe Fruit Market* in Harambe village, a tiny Mickey Mouse doll is hiding on support poles halfway to the top of the ceiling. (He is moved around at times inside the hut).

Hint 110: At one side of the *Harambe Fruit Market*, a short cement and flagstone path with benches leads through some trees. A large Mickey Mouse head in the cement marks the beginning of the path. It's several feet in diameter.

Hint 111: At the opposite end of this short path, turn left onto the cement walkway and walk a few feet. Nearby you'll find a faint depression in the cement that forms a very large classic Mickey (six feet or more in diameter). This Hidden Mickey is best seen after a rain when the pavement is wet. It's often partially covered with parked strollers.

Hint 112: In *Tusker House Restaurant*, walk to a small dining room on the left side of the hallway to the restrooms. A classic Mickey is formed by one of the magnets on a display Assignment Board on a wall inside the room.

Hint 113: Near *Tamu Tamu Refreshments*, on the walkway that connects Africa and Asia, a small utility cover and the pebbles adjacent to it form a classic Mickey. Here, the utility cover has the letter "S" in the middle.

Hint 114: Inside the small seating area behind *Tamu Tamu Refreshments*, a white Hidden Baloo (the bear) is on the wall nearest the path to Asia. He's often covered by a curtain.

Hint 115: Also inside the small seating area behind *Tamu Tamu Refreshments*, a Hidden Scar (the lion) is formed by the exposed brown brick on a corner wall and under a vase in a recessed opening.

Chapter 5: DAK Scavenger Hunt

Hint 116: On the back of *The Tree of Life,* and visible from the path between Africa and Asia, is an upside-down classic Mickey. Look above the eye of the hippopotamus to spot him.

Discovery Island

- Pizzafari restaurant

Hint 117: A yellow classic Mickey image is under a bat, which is on a wall in the seating area across from the food order counters. As you enter the room, turn left to face the rear wall and look for the bat on the right.

Hint 118: On the rear wall of the first dining room to the left (as you walk down the hall away from the food order area), a tiny orange classic Mickey is at the lower left of a turtle shell.

Hint 119: On the left rear wall of the Nocturnal Room (the dining room directly to the left of the food order counters as you face the counters), the wings of the lower left firefly resemble Mickey Mouse ears.

Hint 120: In the same room, a classic Mickey made of tree leaves lies above the head of a reddish raccoon. It's tilted with the "ears" to the left as you face the wall.

Pandora – The World of Avatar

Hint 121: A Hidden Surprise - as you're walking alongside the right wall of the bridge from Discovery Island to Pandora, check out the Hidden Dragon peeking out from the trees on the left shore of Discovery River. This dragon was part of the proposed but never-completed mythical land: Beastly Kingdom.

Hint 122: Along the main entrance to *Pandora*, check out an image on one of the rock seating areas. Find a rock seat on the right side of the walkway (as you enter), just past a split in the walkway and not far past the interactive tree that stands near the bridge at the main entrance. Three small holes in the top of the short rock seat come together as a classic Mickey.

DinoLand U.S.A.

- *The Boneyard*

Hint 123: On the right side of the children's dig area, in a small display, a fan and two hard hats form a classic Mickey.

- *Restaurantosaurus*

Hint 124: A black smudge classic Mickey is on the bottom of a boot wedged high in the rafters over the large dining room closest to *DINOSAUR*.

- *Cretaceous Trail*

Hint 125: At one end of this short trail in the middle of DinoLand, you'll find a large dinosaur. Three dark spots on its middle back make a classic Mickey.

- *TriceraTop Spin*

Hint 126: In front of *TriceraTop Spin,* a green dinosaur balances a red and yellow-striped ball on its horns. A classic Mickey, tilted to the right, appears in the scales on the dino's right side, under the front horn.

Hint 127: Across from *TriceraTop Spin,* a classic Mickey is formed by cracks in the cement at the front middle of the cement area near the horned dinosaur.

Hint 128: On the right side of the horned dinosaur (as you face it), a gold "Steamboat Willie" Cast Member pin is located on a spine on the dinosaur's upper back, near a large silver medallion.

Chapter 5: DAK Scavenger Hunt

- Chester & Hester's Dinosaur Treasures shop

Hint 129: Inside, near the middle of the shop, look up to see a Mickey Mouse marionette.

Hint 130: Near the rear entrance, a classic Hidden Mickey is made of dark spots at the lower left of the left side of a "Cold Drinks" dispenser. It's just above the lower red horizontal band.

Hint 131: In front of the store, near the restrooms, a tiny orange image is embedded in the cement a few feet to the right of the leftmost post (as you face the store with your back to *TriceraTop Spin*).

- Behind Fossil Fun Games

Hint 132: Along the outer walkway behind the *Fossil Fun Games* area, look for a sign on the fence that says "Games of Chance." An upside-down classic Mickey made of gold spots lies on the upper left thigh of the blue dinosaur, on the right side of the sign.

Discovery Island

- Island Mercantile shop

Hint 133: Three classic Mickeys made of spots hide on two orange and blue bumblebee honeycombs on posts inside the shop. These posts are along a rear wall opposite the entrance doors closest to the walkway to the Oasis. Two classic Mickeys are on the honeycomb on the right as you face the rear wall. Find the bee inside a hexagon at the upper center of the honeycomb. One Hidden Mickey is in the hexagon adjacent to the bee at the upper right, and a second Hidden Mickey is one hexagon away to the lower left of the bee. A third classic Mickey hides on the left honeycomb, three hexagons away from the central bee, counting down and to the right. Collections of spots in other hexagons on the honeycombs may also resemble the classic Mickey shape, but these three images are the best proportioned.

- *The Tree of Life*

Hint 134: On the front of *The Tree of Life*, facing the Oasis and about one-third the distance up the tree trunk from the bottom, is a classic Mickey made of dark green moss. You'll find it to the left of the buffalo. (This Hidden Mickey is becoming more distorted over time.)

- *Riverside Depot*

Hint 135: Along a rear wall opposite the entrance door from the walkway between the Oasis and Discovery Island, three round, shallow baskets come together as a classic Mickey, tilted to the left. Find the baskets on top of a tall merchandise cabinet. (Note: the location and form of this Hidden Mickey is changed at times).

- *Discovery Trading Company*

Hint 136: At the far left room of the shop, look for the group of constellations above an inside doorway. One of the constellations (on the right side of the group and near the dolphin) has three stars with round gems in their centers that form a Hidden Mickey. It's near the upper tip of the constellation, and the dolphin's tail points to it.

Hint 137: Walk out the exit of the shop nearest *Flame Tree Barbecue*. In the pavement is a classic Hidden Mickey made of small stones. It's about 15 to 20 feet from the exit door and about one foot or so from the right-angle intersection of two crack lines.

- *Flame Tree Barbecue Restaurant*

Hint 138: In the food order area, rocks embedded in the ground form a classic Mickey at the front edge of the rock border and just to the right of the second inside post from the right wall.

Chapter 5: DAK Scavenger Hunt

Hint 139: At the outside seating area behind the food order counters, some of the grates on the ground around tree trunks have classic Mickey circles.

Oasis

- Rainforest Cafe

Hint 140: A green lizard at the *Rainforest Cafe* entrance sign that is inside the park has an upside-down classic Mickey in the middle of the circles on its neck.

-Outside the entrance turnstiles to the park

Hint 141: When you head out of the park, turn back as you pass the ticket booths. You'll find two rock classic Mickeys, one on the right-hand lower corner near the bottom of the wall of the rightmost ticket booth and the other in the wall of the leftmost ticket booth near the ground and toward the front of the booth's left side wall.

Hint 142: Outside the entrance turnstiles, near the tram loading area, the metal grates at the bases of some of the trees incorporate classic Mickeys in their design.

Notes

Chapter 6
Resort Hotel Scavenger Hunt

• • • • • •

Walt Disney World's resort hotels are filled with Mickeys, hidden and otherwise. The majority are what I like to call décor Mickeys, imaginative decorations that vary among the hotels and change periodically over time. Hidden and decor Mickeys can be found along hotel hallways in the carpet, wallpaper, and lampshades. They appear in the guestrooms on covers for drinking glasses, bedspreads, pillows, day beds, furniture, lamps, lampshades, room curtains, shower curtains, wall pictures, wallpaper, carpets, soap, the outer wrapping of toilet paper rolls, and other items. The housekeeping staff sometimes create Mickey images out of towels on the bed or elsewhere in your room for you to enjoy upon your return! Guest laundry rooms sometimes have Hidden Mickeys on the soap vending machines and in the bubbles on wall paintings, and resort laundry bins and carts show off classic and side-profile Mickeys.

In the restaurants, pancakes, waffles, butter pats, pasta, pizza, pepperoni on the pizza, and the arrangement of dishes and condiments, among other items, are sometimes Mickey-shaped. Sample menu displays in food order areas often have food items arranged to form classic Mickeys. Mugs, paper plates, and other items in the gift shops can sport Mickeys. Even the utilities embrace Mickey. Manhole covers and survey markers throughout Walt Disney World often have classic Mickey designs in the center.

Walt Disney World's Hidden Mickeys

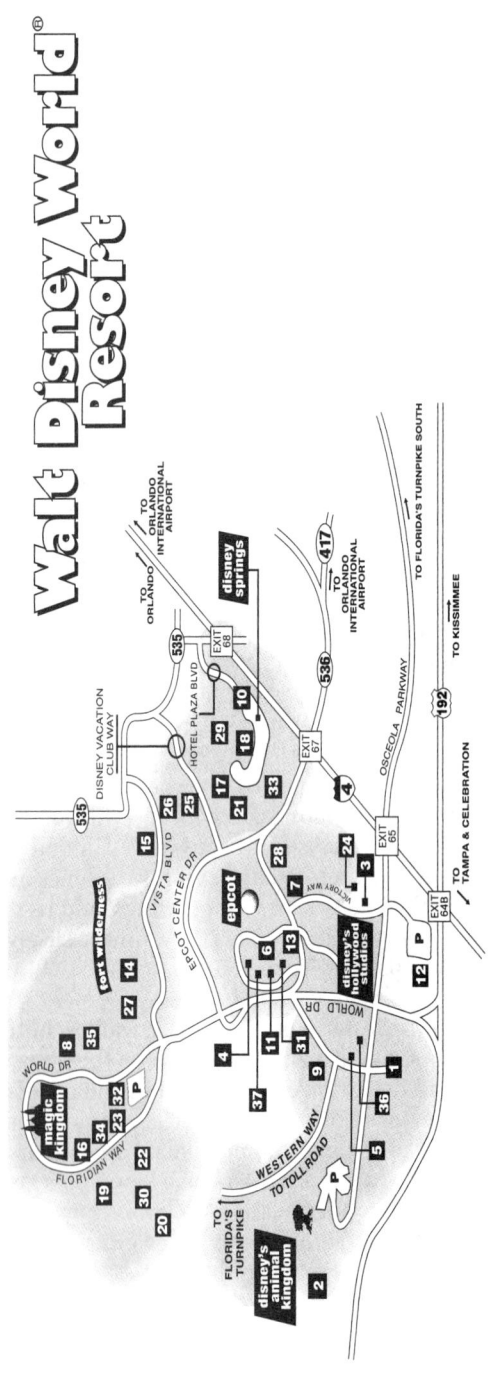

Chapter 6: Resort Hotel Scavenger Hunt

Walt Disney World Resort®

1. All-Star Resorts
2. Animal Kingdom Lodge
3. Art of Animation
4. Beach Club
5. Blizzard Beach
6. BoardWalk
7. Caribbean Beach
8. Contemporary
9. Coronado Springs
10. Disney Springs
11. Dolphin
12. ESPN Wide World of Sports Complex
13. Fantasia Gardens Mini Golf
14. Fort Wilderness
15. Golden Oak
16. Grand Floridian
17. Lake Buena Vista Golf Course
18. The Landing, in Disney Springs
19. Magnolia Golf Course
20. Oak Trail Golf Course
21. Old Key West
22. Palm Golf Course
23. Polynesian Village
24. Pop Century
25. Port Orleans – French Quarter
26. Port Orleans – Riverside
27. Reflections – A Disney Lakeside Lodge
28. Riviera
29. Saratoga Springs
30. Shades of Green
31. Swan
32. Transportation and Ticket Center
33. Typhoon Lagoon
34. Wedding Pavilion, Disney's Fairytale
35. Wilderness Lodge
36. Winter Summerland Mini Golf
37. Yacht Club
P Parking

213

Generally, I do not include decor Mickeys in the scavenger hunts unless they are truly unique (as many of the carpet Mickeys are) and are easily accessible to Hidden Mickey hunters at the hotels and in other WDW areas. So, don't be surprised to discover dozens of Mickeys at the hotels you visit that aren't included in this scavenger hunt. They're fun to spot but you don't get points for finding them.

The most efficient way to access the Disney Resorts is by car. However, you won't be allowed to park at most of the Resorts (the Swan and Dolphin hotels are exceptions) unless (1) you have reservations to stay at the Resort or (2) you made a meal reservation at the Resort (you can park within 30-60 minutes of your meal reservation time). Guests without hotel reservations can park at the Swan or Dolphin hotels for about $33.00 a day. (Disney may modify the above Resort parking rules at any time).

Buses to all the WDW hotels are available from Disney Springs. If you choose to bus around, be prepared for leisurely hunting. You won't be able to visit as many hotels in a given time frame as you would with a car.

Other transportation options (boat, monorail, or Disney Skyliner) may exist for the Resorts you want to explore. If you're really lucky, you may have a spouse, friend, or family member who is willing to drop you off and pick you up. I mention the transportation options, other than by car, for accessing the Disney Resorts.

Again, be considerate of other guests and Cast Members. Ask permission to look around restaurants and avoid searching for Hidden Mickeys at mealtimes unless you are one of the diners. Even then, be careful to stay out of the way-especially of waiters with full trays. Let others share in the fun by telling them what you are up to if they notice you looking around.

Chapter 6: Resort Hotel Scavenger Hunt

Two important notes:

I've arranged this hunt in a logical, efficient progression. However, you may want to hunt just one hotel or group of sister hotels at a time. That's why I list the perfect score for each resort hotel in parentheses after the hotel name in the Clues section.

This scavenger hunt includes only those WDW resorts in which I found Hidden Mickeys. If I found no convincing (to me) Hidden Mickeys in a hotel, I didn't include it in the hunt. Keep your eyes open; you may spot one that I haven't found (yet).

* **Bonus Points Opportunity.** During your Hidden Mickey hunt around WDW property, pay attention to the ***Disney buses***. You may get lucky! The ***Disney Cruise Line bus*** has a Hidden Pluto on each side of the gold scrollwork on the front of the bus between the headlights. Look for a green classic Mickey on the back of some buses that are diesel. General ***Disney transport buses*** sometimes sport a classic Mickey on the rear of the vehicle, usually related to rear upper or lower lights. Even more subtle are faint classic Mickey images in the windows of some buses, only visible if the lighting is just right! If you spot one or more of these images, give yourself 5 bonus points for each one.

Animal Kingdom Area Resorts

I'll start this scavenger hunt with the seven Animal Kingdom Area resorts (*Animal Kingdom Lodge*, the three *All-Star Resorts*, *Coronado Springs*, *Art of Animation*, and *Pop Century*). You can start (and stop) wherever you want. Have fun!

Disney's Animal Kingdom Lodge (104 points) * includes *Kidani Village* points [bus]

Clue 1: Look up for a classic Mickey outside near the hotel's main entrance.
2 points

Clue 2: Find a classic Mickey on a mural between the outer and inner entrance doors to the main lobby.
2 points

Clue 3: Inside the main lobby, spot a classic Mickey on a chandelier.
3 points

Clue 4: Check the logs banded to wood supports around the main lobby. Find any classic Mickeys?
2 points

Clue 5: Look for a classic Mickey on the rock formation next to the short bridge on the right side of the main lobby (as you face the lobby on entering).
4 points

Clue 6: Search the *Kudu Trail* at the rear of the lobby for a classic Mickey on a post.
4 points

Clue 7: Try to spot a green Hidden Mickey in side profile outside the rear doors of the main lobby. He's on the vine-covered column, on your right as you exit, and he's looking into the lobby.
5 points

Chapter 6: Resort Hotel Scavenger Hunt

Clue 8: On the trail to *Arusha Rock Overlook*, outside the rear exit from the main lobby, explore the decorative reliefs on the rock wall for a giraffe sporting a classic Mickey.
3 points

Clue 9: Spot another classic Mickey along the walkway in *Arusha Rock Overlook*.
4 points

Clue 10: Search for a classic Mickey on the rock wall as you descend the stairs from the right side of the main lobby to *Boma restaurant*.
4 points

Clue 11: Inside *Jiko restaurant*, check out the ceiling above the large oven exhausts.
2 points

Clue 12: From inside *Jiko*, spot a classic Mickey out the window.
5 points

Clue 13: From the path alongside the walkway to the pool's water slide, find a classic Mickey impression low on a rock.
4 points

Clue 14: Farther along this walkway, around the back of the swimming pool, look for a classic Mickey cut into the rock wall.
4 points

Clue 15: From a fence at the flamingo overlook, study the rock wall for a classic Mickey.
4 points

* Go to to *The Mara* and then turn and walk toward the pool.
Clue 16: Search the wall outside in the back of *The Mara* eatery seating area for a classic Mickey.
4 points

Now look around inside *The Mara* food area.
Clue 17: One Hidden Mickey is on the left upper wall.
3 points

Clue 18: Another is on the right upper wall.
3 points

- Back inside the Lodge

Clue 19: Spot a classic Mickey in the elevator to the Fitness Center.
2 points

Clue 20: Walk around to spot some classic Mickeys in the carpet below the fifth floor as well as either on or above the fifth floor.
4 points for two or more different classic Mickeys

Clue 21: Go to the second floor of the Zebra Trail for a Hidden Mickey near the elevators to *Simba's Cubhouse*.
4 points

- Walk to **Kidani Village**. (32 points)

Clue 22: Look for Mickey on a clock.
4 points

Clue 23: Search high for Mickey in the lobby.
5 points

Clue 24: Spot him as you approach *Sanaa restaurant*.
4 points

Clue 25: Locate Mickey on a wall inside *Sanaa*.
3 points

Clue 26: Study *Sanaa's* dining tables.
3 points

Clue 27: Now leave the restaurant and find Mickey on a rock near the exit door to the outside walkway.
4 points

Clue 28: Stroll the hallways for carpet Mickeys.
4 points for two or more

Chapter 6: Resort Hotel Scavenger Hunt

Clue 29: Check out the cement walkway from the main lobby to the *Samawati Springs Pool* for a classic Mickey traced in the cement.
5 points

Disney's All-Star Resorts (19 points)
[bus]

* *All-Star Sports Resort*

Clue 30: Search for small Hidden Mickeys near the entrance of the gift shop.
3 points

Clue 31: Look for classic Mickeys on a wall in the food court.
2 points

Clue 32: If you know what I (the author of this book) look like, I'm a spectator at a hockey game in the food court!
5 bonus points

Clue 33: Find the classic Mickey in the cement outdoors behind and to the right of the registration building. (Psst! It's near the Mickey Mouse statue.)
2 points

* *All-Star Music Resort*

Clue 34: Scan the *Intermission Food Court* order area for a Hidden Mickey.
3 points

Clue 35: Search in the *Intermission Food Court* seating area for a Hidden Mickey in a painting.
3 points

Clue 36: Examine the *Jazz Inn* courtyard to spot classic Mickey ears.
3 points

Clue 37: Take a look at the boots in the *Country Fair* area.
2 points

* All-Star Movies Resort

Clue 38: Check out *Andy's Room* in the resort's "Toy Story" section for Hidden Mickeys.
1 point

Disney's Coronado Springs Resort (52 points) *includes *Dig Site* points [bus]

Clue 39: Take a good look at the large wooden doors at the front entrance to the main lobby.
3 points

Clue 40: Search in the registration area for a spotlight Mickey.
4 points

Clue 41: Look around for a statue of a bird with a Hidden Mickey.
3 points

Clue 42: Now study the wooden doors at the exit labeled El Centro.
3 points

Clue 43: Admire the walls of *Rix Lounge* for a Mickey image.
2 points

Clue 44: Walk to the hallway outside the *Veracruz Exhibit Hall* in the Convention Center and look around for two classic Mickeys.
4 points for spotting both

Clue 45: Near the merchandise gazebo outside, examine the cement near a lamppost.
4 points

- Around the *Dig Site*

Clue 46: Spot a classic Mickey at the *Dig Site* swimming pool on a wall facing the lake.
3 points

Clue 47: Now find a classic Mickey on a wall facing the *Dig Site* pool.
3 points

Chapter 6: Resort Hotel Scavenger Hunt

Clue 48: Look for a whitish classic Mickey on a stone block on the Mayan pyramid at the *Dig Site*.
4 points

Clue 49: Spot Mickey near the *Dig Site* restrooms.
3 points

Clue 50: Locate one or more classic Mickeys made of rocks in the sidewalk near *Ranchos Building* 6A.
4 points

Clue 51: Enjoy Hidden Mickeys in the main lobby of the *Gran Destino Tower*.
5 points for 4 or more

Clue 52: Go down one floor and admire a large Hidden Mickey in the Barcelona Lounge.
5 points

Clue 53: Check the bus stop signs around the periphery of the resort.
2 points for one or more

Disney's Art of Animation Resort (45 points) [bus or Disney Skyliner]

Clue 54: In the *Landscape of Flavors* food court seating area, find a classic Mickey floating with jellyfish.
4 points

Clue 55: In the same food court seating area, study the light covers for Lightning McQueen.
4 points

Clue 56: Search for Mickey on the bottom of another light cover in the food court seating area.
5 points

Clue 57: Walk behind *The Big Blue Pool* and find Mickey inside the blue coral reef kids' play area.
5 points

Clue 58: Behind the blue coral reef kids' play area, look among the colorful standing corals for a Hidden Mickey.
3 points

Clue 59: Now face *Animation Hall* and head to the sidewalk to your right that borders the fence around *The Big Blue Pool*. Spot a Hidden Mickey on a fish.
5 points

Clue 60: In the resort's *Lion King* section, smile at Rafiki's Hidden Mickey.
3 points

Clue 61: Explore the *Boneyard* outdoors in the resort's *Lion King* section for a Hidden Mickey.
5 points

Clue 62: In *The Little Mermaid* section, locate a Hidden Mickey near a clam.
4 points

Clue 63: Check the hallway carpets of the various sections.
5 points for three or more

Clue 64: Step inside a guest building elevator for Hidden Mickeys.
2 points

Disney's Pop Century Resort (48 points)
[bus or Disney Skyliner]

Clue 65: Search for a fishbowl with a Hidden Mickey near the check-in area.
3 points

Clue 66: Find two classic Mickeys behind the registration counter.
5 points for both

Clue 67: Look low for three Hidden Mickeys at the *Everything Pop Food Court*.
6 points for all three

Chapter 6: Resort Hotel Scavenger Hunt

Clue 68: Now raise your eyes up for a Mickey in the lights. (Note: It's not always there!)
5 bonus points

Clue 69: Locate Hidden Mickeys on walls in the food court.
4 points for four or more

Clue 70: In the gift shop adjoining the *Everything Pop Food Court*, find Hidden Mickeys on the merchandise stands.
2 points

Clue 71: Also in the gift shop, search for two classic Mickeys on the wall.
4 points for both

Clue 72: Scan a large map/directory outside for a Hidden Mickey.
3 points

Clue 73: Step into a guest elevator for a Hidden Mickey.
3 points

Clue 74: Spot a classic Mickey on a wall near the *Computer Pool*.
4 points

Clue 75: Now look near the *Computer Pool* for two Hidden Mickeys that could help you type.
2 points for both

Clue 76: Marvel at a Hidden Mickey on a wall behind Mowgli on the *'60s building*.
5 points

Clue 77: Search for Mickey's name near the *Bowling Pool* (and, just for fun, a nearby reference to "Disneyland").
4 points

Clue 78: Look around for a Hidden Mickey near the bus stop out front of the Pop Century lobby.
3 points

223

Disney Springs Area Resorts

The Disney Springs area resorts with Hidden Mickeys are the *Caribbean Beach, Riviera, Old Key West*, the *Port Orleans Resorts*, and *Saratoga Springs Resort & Spa*.

Disney's Caribbean Beach Resort
(15 points) [bus or Disney Skyliner]

Clue 79: Examine a group of logs in the ground between *Martinique* Buildings 24 and 25 for a classic Hidden Mickey.
4 points

Clue 80: Spot a classic Mickey on the lighthouse behind *Old Port Royale*.
2 points

Clue 81: Search for a classic Mickey in the children's water play area near the main *(Old Port Royale)* pool.
4 points

Clue 82: Walk around just outside the main pool to marvel at this Mickey image.
5 points

Disney's Riviera Resort (40 points)
(All new Hidden Mickeys!)
[bus or Disney Skyliner]

Clue 83: Outside, in a colorful mural that arches over you, search for a classic Hidden Mickey above a castle.
4 points

Clue 84: In the same mural, locate a classic Hidden Mickey near a red cloud.
4 points

Clue 85: Look for Minnie Mouse (next to Mickey) outside a guest room window.
5 points

Clue 86: Glance around for classic Mickeys in the top part of the design of various outside structures of the Resort.
2 points

Chapter 6: Resort Hotel Scavenger Hunt

Clue 87: Don't miss Mickey on some outside posts!
3 points

Clue 88: Have a sip at *Bar Riva* and spot Mickey.
2 points

Clue 89: Search for a classic Mickey on a wall in the main lobby.
3 points

Clue 90: Admire the Fab Five inside the Resort, near an elevator.
4 points

Clue 91: Check guest hallways for Mickey.
2 points

Clue 92: Mickey greets you at the door of *Topolino's Terrace Restaurant*.
1 point

Clue 93: A large Hidden Mickey is just outside the Resort's main entrance doors.
3 points

Clue 94: While outside, smile at Mickey in the ornate design work of the Resort.
3 points

Clue 95: Squint for several classic Mickeys in a map outside.
4 points

Disney's Old Key West Resort (14 points) [bus or boat]

Clue 96: Find Hidden Mickeys in the interior design and with the merchandise in the *Conch Flats General Store*.
3 points for both

Clue 97: Take a close look at the fence railings in the registration area.
2 points

Clue 98: At the pool, spot a Mickey with a big mouth.
3 points

Clue 99: Find a Hidden Mickey near the steps to the water slide.
4 points

Clue 100: Notice the design of certain railings on the guest buildings outside.
2 points

Disney's Port Orleans Resort - French Quarter
(5 points) [bus or boat]

Clue 101: Find a classic Mickey in the registration area.
3 points

Clue 102: Look up for a classic Mickey in the food court area.
2 points

Disney's Port Orleans Resort - Riverside
(13 points) [bus or boat]

Clue 103: Look for classic Mickeys in the latticework of the registration area.
2 points

Clue 104: Also in the registration area, find more classic Mickeys near the giant fans.
2 points

Clue 105: Now spot Hidden Mickeys on the fans themselves.
3 points

Clue 106: Study a surrey bike (available for rent) for a Hidden Mickey.
3 points

* Cross the river and visit *Parterre Place*.

Clue 107: Find some Mickeys outside the *Parterre Place* building.
3 points

Chapter 6: Resort Hotel Scavenger Hunt

Disney's Saratoga Springs Resort & Spa
(78 points) [bus or boat]

Clue 108: Don't miss some Hidden Mickeys just outside the entrance to the registration lobby.
3 points

Clue 109: Locate Mickey in the registration lobby.
2 points

Clue 110: Behind *The Artist's Palette shop*, look around for Mickey on a door handle.
5 points

Clue 111: Glance around for a golf course Mickey behind *The Artist's Palette shop*.
3 points

Clue 112: Notice classic Mickeys on a jacket near *The Turf Club Bar and Grill*.
2 points

Clue 113: Find more Mickey images inside on a wall.
2 points for one or more

Clue 114: Look around inside *The Turf Club* for a classic Mickey on a wall.
3 points

Clue 115: Check out a statue outside the main lobby for three pairs of Hidden Mickeys. (Note: This statue also sports a decor Mickey.)
10 points for finding all six

Clue 116: Search for two Hidden Mickeys near stairs outside *The Artist's Palette*.
5 points for spotting both

Clue 117: In the children's play area of the pool, find a large classic Hidden Mickey.
5 points

Clue 118: Locate three Hidden Mickeys near the zero-grade pool entrance.
5 points for all three

Clue 119: Admire the guest buildings for small Mickeys.
2 points for one or more

Clue 120: Search for a Hidden Mickey on an outdoor wall, near the check-in point.
5 points

Clue 121: Now find a similar Hidden Mickey on a wall in the *Congress Park* section near the Disney Springs lagoon.
5 points

Clue 122: Check for a Hidden Mickey inside the Aquatic Play Area at *The Paddock Villas* pool.
4 points

Clue 123: Look around for Hidden Mickeys on outdoor wall lights.
4 points for one or more

Clue 124: Find classic Mickeys in the various Villa courtyards.
3 points for one or more

Clue 125: Smile at Hidden Mickeys on a gazebo at the *Carousel Villas*.
2 points

Clue 126: Locate Mickey in a gate near the *Grandstand Pool*.
3 points

Clue 127: Search near the *Backstretch Bar* for Mickey.
5 points

Chapter 6: Resort Hotel Scavenger Hunt

Epcot Area Resorts

You'll find Hidden Mickeys in *Disney's BoardWalk*, *Beach Club*, and *Yacht Club* Resorts. To explore them, stop at one and walk around Crescent Lake to the others.

Disney's BoardWalk Resort (39 points)
[bus, boat, or Disney Skyliner]

Clue 128: Spot two classic Mickeys on a horse in the main lobby.
3 points for both

Clue 129: Search for a classic Mickey on a lobby wall.
4 points

Clue 130: Squint to spot some classic Mickeys above an elephant.
4 points for one or more

Clue 131: Look for Mickey near the *Villa* elevators.
4 points for one or more

Clue 132: Look down as you wander around the guestroom and elevator hallways in both the *BoardWalk Inn* and the *BoardWalk Villas*.
8 points for four or more different Mickey images

Clue 133: Study a *BoardWalk* surrey bike for a Hidden Mickey.
3 points

Clue 134: Admire the decor inside *AbracadaBar* to discover a Hidden Walt Disney with a rabbit.
4 points

Clue 135: Search inside *AbracadaBar* for a Hidden Mickey on a playing card.
4 points

Clue 136: Walk into the waiting lobby for *Trattoria al Forno Restaurant*. Scan the walls of the lobby for a tiny Hidden Mickey.
5 points

Walt Disney World's Hidden Mickeys

Disney's Beach Club Resort (59 points)
[bus, boat, or Disney Skyliner]

Clue 137: Look around just inside the entrance to *Cape May Cafe* for Mickey on a plate.
4 points

Clue 138: Search for Mickey Mouse along the inside walkway in front of the *Cape May Cafe*.
3 points

Clue 139: Visit *Martha's Vineyard* for Hidden Mickeys on the wall.
4 points for both

Clue 140: Search for Mickey in the tile floor in the hallway across the main lobby from *Cape May Cafe*. (Psst! Look near the luggage room door.)
4 points

* Walk to the *Beach Club Solarium* to find more Hidden Mickeys. (Psst! Check the walls.)

Clue 141: Spot some car tires with Mickey's full face.
3 points

Clue 142: Now look for classic Mickeys in the same general area.
2 points

Clue 143: Gaze at Mickey's face in the sky.
3 points

Clue 144: Search for Mickey on the sand.
4 points

Clue 145: Now find classic Mickeys in the water.
2 points

Clue 146: Do you see other classic Mickeys floating in the air?
2 points

Chapter 6: Resort Hotel Scavenger Hunt

Clue 147: Squint for a Hidden Mickey atop a building.
5 points

Clue 148: Walk to a guestroom hallway to find classic Mickeys under your feet.
2 points for one or more

Clue 149: Study the area near the entrance to the *Beach Club Villas* for a classic Mickey.
4 points

* Clue 150: Enter the *Breezeway* in the Beach Club Villas and locate three different Hidden Mickey images.
5 points for all three

Clue 151: Walk toward the nearby restrooms inside and find Mickey in a painting.
5 points

Clue 152: Wander into the *Beaches & Cream Soda Shop* to spot a tasty Hidden Mickey on the wall.
4 points

Clue 153: Now watch hamburger preparation on the *Beaches & Cream* grill for a classic Mickey.
3 points

Disney's Yacht Club Resort (14 points)
[bus, boat, or Disney Skyliner]

Clue 154: Study the globe in the main lobby.
5 points

Clue 155: Search resort carpets for Mickeys.
4 points for two or more

Clue 156: In the *Yachtsman Steakhouse*, look for the photograph of (now deceased) Minnie Moo, a cow born with a black classic Mickey on her side. (You may have to ask a Cast Member where the photo is located. It's sometimes not on public display.)
5 points

Walt Disney World's Hidden Mickeys

Magic Kingdom Area Resorts

This area is home to resorts and to *Disney's Fairytale Wedding Pavilion*. The resorts with Hidden Mickeys include *Disney's Fort Wilderness*, *Wilderness Lodge and Villas*, *Shades of Green*, and the three monorail resorts (*Polynesian Village*, *Grand Floridian*, and *Contemporary*), so-called because they are all connected to one another and to the Magic Kingdom by monorail.

Tip: To explore *Disney's Fort Wilderness* and *Wilderness Lodge*, take a boat from the Magic Kingdom or from the *Contemporary Resort* to their respective marinas, or hop on a Disney bus for transportation to their front entrances.

Disney's Fort Wilderness Resort
(21 points) [bus or boat]

If you drive to *Fort Wilderness*, swing by the entrance to the *Golden Oak* community at the intersection of Vista Boulevard and Bonnet Creek Parkway (not far from *Port Orleans Resort—Riverside*) to spot another Hidden Mickey.

Clue 157: Look for a Hidden Mickey on a sign.
3 bonus points

At *Fort Wilderness*, you'll need to ride an internal bus between the Hidden Mickeys at the rear near the lake (where your hunt begins) and the Hidden Mickeys near the front parking area.

Clue 158: Stroll into the *Tri-Circle-D Ranch Horse Barn* and admire Hidden Mickeys in a display.
3 points

Clue 159: While you're in the *Horse Barn*, search for Hidden Mickeys near the horse stalls.
3 points

Chapter 6: Resort Hotel Scavenger Hunt

Clue 160: Visit the *Blacksmith* (near the *Horse Barn*) and find a Hidden Mickey.
3 points

Clue 161: Check inside *Trail's End Restaurant* for a classic Mickey.
3 points

Clue 162: Stop by the *Meadow Depot* area and search near the *Bike Barn* for a Hidden Mickey.
3 points

Clue 163: Go to the *Trail Ride Check-In* building near the front parking area to find two Hidden Mickeys.
3 points for both

Clue 164: Stroll over to the Fort Wilderness registration building *("Reception Outpost")* at the far side of the front parking area and look for Mickey.
3 points

Disney's Wilderness Lodge (132 points*)
* includes *Boulder Ridge Villas* points [bus or boat]
Clue 165: Check out the signs on the right side of the entrance drive.
2 points

Clue 166: Search out a classic Mickey on the guard gate kiosk.
3 points

Clue 167: Near the car unloading area, search high for a classic Mickey etched in a support pole and partially hidden under a black metal band.
4 points

Clue 168: Glance down for a tiny classic Mickey traced in the cement on a black stripe.
5 points

Clue 169: Look up again for a classic Mickey etched on a side support pole.
4 points

Clue 170: Find a classic Mickey on a large key in the registration area.
1 point

Clue 171: Look overhead for Mickey driving a bus.
2 points

Clue 172: Find a classic Mickey on the rock of the main lobby fireplace.
5 points

Clue 173: Peek at a fireplace inside the *Whispering Canyon Cafe* for a classic Mickey. (Ask a Cast Member to let you into the rear of the cafe.)
4 points

Clue 174: Search around the bubbling spring in the lobby for a classic Mickey.
4 points

Clue 175: Look for a classic Mickey on a wall map at the entrance stairs to the *Territory Lounge*.
3 points

Clue 176: Now go inside and spot a classic Mickey on a ceiling mural above the bar.
4 points

Clue 177: Inside the *Artist Point restaurant*, spot a classic Mickey in a large mural above the entrance to the rear left dining area.
4 points

Clue 178: Now scan another mural for a classic Mickey near the restaurant's ceiling. (Psst! Turn back toward the entrance.)
5 points

Clue 179: Next, scan the walls of the restaurant for Winnie the Pooh.
3 points

Clue 180: Search inside the *Roaring Fork snack bar* for a Hidden Mickey in a display case.
3 points

Chapter 6: Resort Hotel Scavenger Hunt

Clue 181: Find a classic Mickey in one or more lights near the elevators close to the snack bar.
3 points

Clue 182: Look down in the hallways for more Mickeys.
2 points

Clue 183: Locate a classic Mickey near *Room 6106*.
3 points

Clue 184: Explore one floor down for a classic Mickey near *Room 5066*.
3 points

Clue 185: Find another classic near *Room 4035*.
3 points

Clue 186: Search for a classic Mickey in the rock outside at *Fire Rock Geyser*.
4 points

Clue 187: Find stairs outside an exit door from the main building (on the side toward the *Boat and Bike Rental*) and look up for a classic Mickey.
4 points

Clue 188: Locate a rope Hidden Mickey near the *Boat and Bike Rental* cabin.
4 points

- *Boulder Ridge Villas* (50 points)

Clue 189: Just inside the main entrance to the *Villas*, stop before you get to the elevators on your left. Check out the rock pillar to your right for a Hidden Mickey.
5 points

Clue 190: Search for four classic Mickeys near the elevators. (Psst! Look behind some fabric for one of the four.)
5 points for all finding all four

235

Clue 191: Look around the rock pillars near the *Villas* lobby for a classic Mickey in the rock.
5 points

Clue 192: Smile back at Mickey hiding in a hole in a beam in the lobby.
5 points

Clue 193: Locate a side profile of Mickey on a wall in the lobby.
4 points

Clue 194: Try to make out a classic Hidden Mickey above the fireplace in the main lobby.
5 points

Clue 195: Admire a classic Mickey inside the small telephone alcove near the lobby.
5 points

Clue 196: Check out a painting frame in the main lobby.
2 points

Clue 197: Spot Mickeys around a painting in a room near the lobby.
2 points

Clue 198: Find Mickey in the rock in the *Carolwood Pacific Railroad Room* near the lobby.
5 points

Clue 199: Look up to spot Mickey in the hallways of the *Boulder Ridge Villas*.
2 points

Clue 200: Search for Mickey on a hallway wall near *Room 1507*.
5 points

Chapter 6: Resort Hotel Scavenger Hunt

Magic Kingdom Monorail Resorts

* includes *Disney's Fairytale Wedding Pavilion* points

To find the Hidden Mickeys in these resorts and the nearby *Fairytale Wedding Pavilion*, stop at the *Polynesian Village* or the *Grand Floridian* and ride the monorail to the other two resorts and past the Wedding Pavilion. (Note: *Polynesian Village* has the larger parking lot.)

Disney's Polynesian Village Resort (37 points) [bus, boat, or monorail]

Clue 201: On the lower level, look for a classic Mickey on the floor near the main entrance.
4 points

Clue 202: Find Mickey overhead in the lobby.
4 points

Clue 203: Spot three Hidden Mickeys in the *Tiki Boutique store*.
4 points for finding all three

Clue 204: Study the bamboo-ring wall decorations by the corner staircase.
3 points

Find a Hidden Mickey in the *Moana Mercantile shop*.

Clue 205: Look along a wall.
3 points

Clue 206: Admire three Hidden Mickeys near the second-floor elevators.
4 points for all three

Clue 207: At the *Kona Island coffee and sushi bar*, search for a small classic Mickey.
5 points

Clue 208: Look down for Hidden Mickeys in hallways and elevators.
3 points for spotting them in both places

Clue 209: Wander to the marina area and admire a Sea Raycer for a Hidden Mickey.
2 points

Clue 210: Stroll along the lagoon walkway toward *Disney's Wedding Pavilion* and spot small, white Hidden Mickeys near your feet. (Hurry and find them; they're fading with time!)
5 points for one or more

Disney's Fairytale Wedding Pavilion
(3 points)

Clue 211: As your monorail car passes by the pavilion buildings, observe the weathervane.
3 points

(Note: A Hidden Mickey may be lurking inside, but the Wedding Pavilion isn't open to the general public.)

Disney's Grand Floridian Resort & Spa
(51 points) [bus, boat, or monorail]

Clue 212: Take a good look at the weathervanes on the roofs.
3 points for one or more

Clue 213: Check the large trolley carts outside the hotel.
1 point

Clue 214: Study the lobby carpet.
2 points

Clue 215: Look at the floor tile for a classic Mickey.
2 points

Clue 216: While you're at it, check the tile for the Fab Five.
5 points for five characters

Chapter 6: Resort Hotel Scavenger Hunt

Clue 217: Look near *1900 Park Fare restaurant* for a Mickey hat.
3 points

Clue 218: Also near *1900 Park Fare*, find Mickey and Minnie below your feet.
2 points for both

Clue 219: Now look for other Disney movie characters, as well as Mickey and Minnie, in the floor encircling the main lobby and in front of the *Grand Floridian Cafe*.
5 points for five or more characters

Clue 220: Search a wall map for a Hidden Mickey.
4 points

Clue 221: Spot Mickey on the outside of the ornate lobby elevator by the stairs.
4 points

Clue 222: Look up high for Mickey on the ceiling above the main lobby.
4 points

Clue 223: Check out the classic Mickey in front of the *M. Mouse Mercantile shop*.
1 point

Clue 224: Locate a Hidden Mickey while walking outside toward the *Grand Floridian Villas*.
3 points

Clue 225: Study the area around the main pool near the *Villas* for a Hidden Mickey in rock.
5 points

Clue 226: Stroll into *Gasparilla Island Grill* and search for Mickey.
3 points

Clue 227: Wander to the marina area and admire a Sea Raycer for a Hidden Mickey.
2 points

Clue 228: Walk into the Grand Floridian *Convention Center's* main entrance and look around for Mickey.
2 points

Disney's Contemporary Resort (59 points*)
* includes some Bay Lake Tower points [bus, boat, or monorail]

Clue 229: From the window of the *California Grill restaurant*, on the top floor, spot a stretched-out Mickey watchband on the ground in front of the hotel.
4 points

Clue 230: Go to the *sixth floor* and walk in the direction of the *Transportation and Ticket Center* to an outside balcony to spot this amazing Hidden Mickey.
5 points
Caution: Be sure to prop the hallway door open, as it may lock upon closing.

Tip: This Mickey can also be seen from the resort and express monorails.

Clue 231: Look for Mickey's profile inside *Chef Mickey's restaurant*. (You'll also encounter many decor—not Hidden—Mickey images inside the restaurant.)
1 point

Clue 232: Don't miss Mickey's ears at the rear of *Chef Mickey's*!
3 points

Clue 233: Find Mickey low on a wall near the *Contempo Cafe*.
3 points

Clue 234: Now study this mural higher up for a classic Mickey in a basket.
4 points

Clue 235: Look high for a classic Mickey on an animal in the next mural to the right.
4 points

Chapter 6: Resort Hotel Scavenger Hunt

Clue 236: Search around for a stick-figure Mickey near the shops.
3 points

Clue 237: Look for classic Mickeys in *The Game Station Arcade*.
3 points for all

Clue 238: Walk to the *Market shop* for a Hidden Mickey right at the entrance.
3 points

Clue 239: Ride up the monorail escalator to spot a classic Mickey on the wall. (Enjoy the five-legged goat while you're up there!)
4 points

Clue 240: Find a classic Mickey silhouette in the bricks behind the main hotel. (Psst! It's near Mickey Mouse himself.)
2 points

Clue 241: Scan the marina dock for a Hidden Mickey.
3 points

Clue 242: Stare at the nautical flags on the glass front of *The Sand Bar*. Can you guess what they spell?
3 points

Clue 243: Locate a classic Hidden Mickey in *The Sand Bar*.
3 points

Clue 244: Spot Mickey in the tile at the exit from the Garden Building to the parking lot.
5 points

Clue 245: Look up for Mickey at the hotel entrance.
2 points

- *Bay Lake Tower* (4 points)

Clue 246: Walk to *Bay Lake Tower* and locate Mickey from the outside. (Psst! Look high!)
4 points

Shades of Green Resort (9 points)
(Only folks with military connections are allowed into this resort.) [bus]

Clue 247: Search for four classic Mickeys in the lobby.
5 points for finding all four

Clue 248: Find a large classic Mickey outside (or on a map of the resort).
4 points

It's time to tally your score.

A perfect score for this scavenger hunt is 857. You may have done even better if you earned bonus points in the **All-Star Sports** and/or **Pop Century** food court(s), by finding the Hidden Mickey in the entrance sign to the **Golden Oak** community, and/or by spotting Hidden Characters on the **WDW buses**.

Total Points for Hotel Hunt =

_____

How'd you do?

Give yourself Gold if you scored at least 80% of the points available for the places you've searched, Bronze if you scored at least 40%.

Here is a point breakdown by resort (they're grouped by area), so that you can compare your score with the perfect score for the areas you've covered.

Chapter 6: Resort Hotel Scavenger Hunt

Animal Kingdom Lodge (104 points)
Disney's All-Star Resorts (19)
Coronado Springs Resort (52)
Art of Animation Resort (45)
Pop Century Resort (48)

Caribbean Beach Resort (15)
Riviera Resort (40)
Old Key West Resort (14)
Port Orleans Resort-French Quarter (5)
Port Orleans Resort-Riverside (13)
Saratoga Springs Resort & Spa (78)

BoardWalk Resort (39)
Beach Club Resort (59)
Yacht Club Resort (14)

Fort Wilderness Resort (21)
Wilderness Lodge (132)
Polynesian Village Resort (37)
Disney's Fairytale Wedding Pavilion (3)
Grand Floridian Resort & Spa (51)
Contemporary Resort (59)
Shades of Green Resort (9)

Chapter 6: Resort Hotel Scavenger Hunt

Animal Kingdom Area Resorts

Disney's Animal Kingdom Lodge

Hint 1: Outside, above the lower roof, the second tall figure to the left of the car baggage drop-off area has a classic Mickey in its mouth.

Hint 2: On the right wall mural between the outer and inner entrance doors to the main lobby, an orange and brown creature sports a classic Mickey in a circle on its mid back.

Hint 3: Inside the main lobby, you can find a classic Mickey near the bottom of the second chandelier on the right (as you face in from the front entrance). The Hidden Mickey is near the bottom of one of the shields.

Hint 4: Around the main lobby, classic Mickeys are formed by logs banded to wood supports. One of the best is the second support on the right (as you enter the lobby from the front doors). It's on the second level, on the side away from the main lobby entrance.

Hint 5: On the right side of the main lobby (as you face in from the front entrance), a short bridge crosses a rockbound pool of water. A classic Mickey is visible on the rock from the side of the bridge nearest the lobby. It's toward the rear on the right side. To spot it, look for the first recess in the rock from the right side of the pool. Mickey is on the rear big rock at the back of this recess, above the water line.

Hint 6: Go down the staircase at the rear of the lobby. Turn left and walk down the *Kudu Trail* hallway. In the first small lobby, near the elevator, a classic Mickey is on the top end of a piece of wood that's roped to two giant "log" supports that are closest to the elevator. Mickey is above the second rope binding, near the ceiling.

Hint 7: Outside the rear doors of the main lobby, a green Mickey in side profile hides in the decorative vines to the right as you exit. He is about two-thirds of the way up the side of the vine-covered column, above the middle horizontal brace, at the top of an open space in the vines. He's looking into the lobby.

Hint 8: Outside the rear exit from the main lobby, on the left side of the trail to *Arusha Rock Overlook*, check the rock wall for a decorative relief of a group of giraffes. You'll find a classic Mickey among the spots on the middle of the large giraffe in the center, above its inner front leg.

Hint 9: Along the walkway in *Arusha Rock Overlook*, a rock sports a classic Mickey. Look for it where the trail first turns left between rock walls. It's on the right side in the

Chapter 6: Resort Hotel Scavenger Hunt

first small alcove, about six feet up from the path and under a large overhanging rock.

Hint 10: Toward the bottom of the staircase that winds from the right side of the main lobby to *Boma restaurant*, there's a classic Mickey on the rock wall.

Hint 11: Inside *Jiko restaurant*, a classic Mickey is formed on the ceiling above the two large orange oven exhausts and the white column behind them.

Hint 12: From the entrance to *Jiko*, walk to the third table on your left, next to the glass windows. Outside in the shallow pool area, a classic Mickey is sculpted on the first rock island from the left that has a pillar jutting out of it.

Hint 13: Outside the exit from the restaurants, a large rock on the left side of the path behind the water slide has a classic Mickey impressed on its lower half near the ground. The rock is behind a fence and about three-quarters of the way along the walkway to the water slide. A small light pole juts out of the top of this rock.

Hint 14: A classic Mickey is cut into a rock wall behind the swimming pool. The wall forms the back of the pool's water slide. The Mickey is several feet above the walkway, below a gazebo that marks the starting point for the water slide.

Hint 15: Walk behind the pool to the bird and flamingo overlook and look to your right to the opposite fence. About two-thirds of the distance along this fence away from the main trail, a classic Mickey is impressed in the rock about one foot down from the top of the rock.

Hint 16: A classic stone Mickey is on the rear of the short wall behind *The Mara* seating area. It's about three feet up from the ground, behind an emergency phone and a tall brown pole.

Hint 17: In the food area of *The Mara*, a classic Mickey is on the upper left wall in the second leaf from the left tree (in the mural of falling leaves).

Hint 18: Also in the food area, a classic Mickey, sideways to the left, hides in a leaf in the middle of the upper right mural of falling leaves.

Hint 19: As you enter the elevator to the *Fitness Center*, you can spot a classic Mickey on the lower left panel (as you face the rear of the elevator).

Hint 20: Many small classic Mickeys can be found in the carpet in the hallways in front of guestrooms. Classic Mickey images in the carpets below the fifth floor may differ from those on and above the fifth floor.

Hint 21: On the second floor of the *Zebra Trail*, near a mask display and the elevators to *Simba's Cubhouse*, look up for a classic Mickey that's etched at the bottom end of a piece of wood that's roped to two giant "log" supports. Mickey is below the upper rope binding. (Note: these images change or disappear from time to time.)

- *Kidani Village*

Hint 22: A classic Mickey is at the 6:30 position on a large decorative gold clock on a table just inside the entrance to the lobby.

Hint 23: A white classic Mickey is on a ladybug on the middle level of the closest chandelier to the front lobby entrance.

Hint 24: At the entrance to *Sanaa* restaurant downstairs, a classic Mickey made of dark brown baskets is on the far left of the wall behind the check-in desk. It's tilted slightly to the left.

Hint 25: Inside *Sanaa*, a classic Mickey is above a booth on a white wall. It is to the left as you enter.

Chapter 6: Resort Hotel Scavenger Hunt

Hint 26: Classic Mickeys hide in the woodwork in the middle of some of *Sanaa's* square dining tables.

Hint 27: Outside *Sanaa*, a classic Mickey is etched on the rockwork at the rear of the lobby stairs near the exit doors. It's about halfway up the wall from the floor.

Hint 28: A variety of small classic Mickeys can be found in the carpet in the hallways in front of guestrooms.

Hint 29: A classic Mickey is lightly traced in cement in the walkway from the *Kidani Village* main lobby to the *Samawati Springs Pool*. It's near the curb and about 25-30 feet before the parking directions sign.

(Other Hidden Mickeys are in the *Samawati Springs Pool* area, but sometimes only *Kidani Village* guests are allowed to enter there.)

Disney's All-Star Resorts

- All-Star Sports Resort

Hint 30: Inside a display case on the wall to the right of the entrance to the *Sport Goofy* gift shop, some Mickey images are drawn on the front of a cereal box. An obvious classic Mickey is above the "S" in "CHAMPS," but notice the small white Mickey shapes at the bottom of circles above the "CH."

Hint 31: Midway along the left wall of the *End Zone* food court seating area, one painting shows Mickey after he's hit in the head with a basketball. Some of the "stars" he sees are yellow classic Mickeys.

Hint 32: In the food court, an image of me (Hidden Mickey Guy, Steve Barrett) is on the last decorative pane near the rear exit from the *End Zone* food court seating area. I'm sitting in the stands behind hockey player Minnie Mouse, and you can find me on both sides of the pane. I'm holding a yellow *Hidden Mickeys* book with a magnifying glass on the cover, and a tiny classic Mickey is on my shirt! Needless to say, I'm incredibly honored by this!

Hint 33: Outside, behind and to the right of the registration building, and past the buildings with surfboards, a large Mickey statue stands directly over a classic Mickey (white head and black ears) in the cement.

- *All-Star Music Resort*

Hint 34: A painting of an animal orchestra, conducted by Mickey Mouse, is on the right wall as you enter the *Intermission Food Court* order area. In the painting are three black classic Mickey notes, each on a different music sheet.

Hint 35: At the rear of the *Intermission Food Court* seating area, a classic Mickey atop a cactus is in a decorative pane perched on a seating partition. Find the Hidden Mickey cactus directly above the banjo. You can spot it from both sides of the pane.

Hint 36: In the *Jazz Inn* courtyard, classic Mickey ears top the display cymbal stands. Each is a winged nut that holds a cymbal in place. (These nuts come and go.)

Hint 37: In the *Country Fair* area, you'll find classic Mickeys on the front and back of the huge boots.

- *All-Star Movies Resort*

Hint 38: In Andy's Room in the *Toy Story* section, classic Mickeys are on the large checkers.

Disney's Coronado Springs Resort

Hint 39: At the front entrance to the main lobby, a medallion in the upper left rectangle of the left large, open wooden door is a three-dimensional relief of Mickey's face.

Chapter 6: Resort Hotel Scavenger Hunt

Hint 40: On the far wall opposite the main entrance to the registration area, three spotlights sometimes create a classic Mickey image. The light circles change size from time to time.

Hint 41: At the far end of the registration lobby, a statue of an eagle stands on the left side. Circles on an emblem on its chest form a classic Hidden Mickey.

Hint 42: A three-dimensional Mickey face is in an upper rectangle on the large right wooden door (as you face the doors from outside) at the exit labeled "El Centro."

Hint 43: Subtle circles form classic Mickeys in the ornate design of the outside black glass walls of *Rix Lounge*. They're on the walls that face *El Mercado de Coronado*.

Hint 44: In the hallway outside the *Veracruz Exhibit Hall* in the Convention Center, a black classic Mickey pattern repeats along the sides of some of the ceiling chandeliers. Nearby, a similar Mickey pattern can be spotted on rectangular light covers that are flush with the ceiling.

Hint 45: A classic Mickey is chipped into the cement next to the lamppost and flagpole that are near the sales/merchandise gazebo.

Hint 46: At the *Dig Site* swimming pool's main entrance (closest to the lake), a classic Mickey hides on a wall to your right. To spot it, check out the upper middle part of the wall facing the lake before you enter the *Dig Site*.

Hint 47: After you enter the *Dig Site*, examine the wall to your left (as you enter) that faces the pool. A classic Mickey is on the upper left side.

Hint 48: Also at the *Dig Site*, you'll find a whitish, somewhat distorted classic Mickey near the very top of the Mayan pyramid, on the side facing the pool. It's on the second stone block from the left, fourth row from the top.

Hint 49: To the left of the restrooms at the *Dig Site*, a circular stone tablet with relief images is hanging on the wall. A somewhat distorted sideways classic Mickey hides at the lower right.

Hint 50: A section of the walkway in front of *Ranchos Building 6A* is made of circular flat gray rocks. Some of these rocks form classic Mickeys. As you approach the *Ranchos buildings*, you'll find an upside-down Hidden Mickey in the mid left part of the rock section and another upside-down Mickey near the far end—right side—of the rock section.

Hint 51: Mickey is hiding throughout the *Gran Destino Tower*! In the main lobby, small black classic Mickeys are in the design of panels behind the registration counters and along the lobby wall; small white classic Mickeys are in the design on the lobby columns; small classic Mickeys are along the top and bottom of wall and column lamp covers (and they cast classic Mickey shadows on the wall behind them!); and classic Mickeys are part of the design of lamp covers on lobby tables. (Find other Hidden Mickeys throughout the Tower).

Hint 52: One floor down from the *Gran Destino Tower* lobby, a large subtle classic Mickey hat ("ears" and upper half of "head") is in the middle of the stained-glass design on the curved wall behind the bar counter of the Barcelona Lounge.

Hint 53: Mickey Mouse (side profile) is sitting in a bus on some of the bus stop signs located around the periphery of the resort (such as at Bus Stops No. 2, No. 3, and No. 4).

Chapter 6: Resort Hotel Scavenger Hunt

Disney's Art of Animation Resort

Hint 54: In the *Landscape of Flavors* food court seating area, one of the hanging paintings shows bubbles and jellyfish. At the lower middle of the painting, the head of a small orange jellyfish forms a classic Mickey with two bubbles above it.

Hint 55: In the *Landscape of Flavors* food court seating area, at the far right as you enter, an image of Lightning McQueen is in the clouds on the side of a large circular light fixture hanging from the ceiling.

Hint 56: At the rear of the same food court seating area, the painting on the bottom of another large circular light fixture includes a faint fullbody image of Mickey Mouse. Look for Mickey near the bright light at the center of the overhead fixture. The image is in what appears to be a framed photo that is sitting on a shelf above some books.

Hint 57: Behind *The Big Blue Pool* is a play area for kids formed by a blue coral reef rising from the ground. Walk to the left of the slide exit and duck your head as you enter a small passageway through the coral. Halfway along the passageway, about three-quarters of the way up on the right wall, depressions in the rock form a classic Mickey.

Hint 58: Behind the blue coral reef kids' play area, on the side away from *The Big Blue Pool*, colorful standing corals line the steps and blue handrails. On the right side (as you face the steps), three corals—a pink "head," a light purple right "ear" and a green left "ear"—come together as a classic Mickey. It's across from the third step from the bottom, and it's tilted to the right.

Hint 59: Face Animation Hall and walk on the sidewalk next to *Finding Nemo Building #5*. This sidewalk is to your right and follows the fence encircling the *Big Blue Pool*. As you walk, look for a green fish perched in the grass near the fence. You'll find the fish after you pass the end of the *Finding Nemo Guest Room Building* on your right. A decent sideways classic Hidden Mickey is on each side of the fish, below each eye and near both corners of the mouth.

Hint 60: Approaching the resort's *Lion King* section, you'll be greeted by a statue of Rafiki. Gourds hang from the top of his staff. When viewed from the right angle, three of the gourds—a striped one for the "head," a small brown one for the left "ear," and a small yellow one for the right "ear"—simulate an almost sideways classic Mickey.

Hint 61: Outdoors in the resort's *Lion King* section, there is a cave in the *Boneyard* play area. Walk under the elephant ribs to enter the cave on the right side and then keep your eyes peeled. About halfway through the cave, depressions in the rock form a classic Mickey—sideways to the left—on the right wall.

Hint 62: In *The Little Mermaid* section, three orange spots on green seaweed under a clam design form a classic Hidden Mickey. You can find this image repeated in several of the clam designs on handrails along the inner perimeter of the guest room buildings.

Hint 63: A variety of classic Mickeys hide in the hallway carpets of the resort's various sections. Each carpet design is consistent with the decor of the specific section, so these carpet Hidden Mickeys vary, too.

Hint 64: Poster ads for pizza delivery are inside the guest building elevators. Check out the upside-down classic Hidden Mickeys formed by pepperoni pizza toppings on each slice. (These ads have been in place for a while).

Chapter 6: Resort Hotel Scavenger Hunt

Disney's Pop Century Resort

Hint 65: In a small TV room near the check-in area, classic Mickey bubbles rise under a fish in a fishbowl painted on the wall.

Hint 66: In a photograph on the wall behind the middle of the long registration counter, two Hidden Mickeys formed of craters and shadows lie on the moon. Look at the lower right of the television screen and below the word "moon" for a small sideways classic Mickey and above the same word for a large upright classic Mickey.

Hint 67: Three classic Mickeys are hiding on the tile floor of the Everything Pop Food Court order area. One is on the left side of the order area (as you enter), in the outer part of the winding queue for the leftmost food serving station. Another is in the center of the order and pay area, halfway between the colored rectangle tiles and the zigzag green tiles. A third classic Mickey is in front of the middle cash register, in front of a beverage cooler cabinet.

Hint 68: A tiny black classic Mickey is inside one or more round lights suspended from the ceiling in the food court order area. (Note: These images change or even disappear at times.)

Hint 69: Inside the food court seating area, classic Mickeys made of circles can be found on the undulating purple, brown, blue, and green divider walls.

Hint 70: In the shop near the food court, classic Mickey holes are in poles that hold merchandise racks.

Hint 71: Inside the gift shop, near the exit to the bus stop, check the wall behind the cash registers to spot round gift boxes that form a classic Mickey. The image appears twice in faux package-locker windows. One image is in the second window from the top of the second column of windows from the right side. The other is in the third window from the left along the top row.

Hint 72: On the map/directory signs standing at different spots along the walkways to the guest room buildings, a classic Hidden Mickey symbol sits in the collection of symbols for the Lobby in the enlarged map for Classic Hall. This classic Mickey is the symbol for the Disney Vacation Club Information Center.

Hint 73: Poster ads for pizza delivery are inside the guest building elevators. Check out the upside-down classic Hidden Mickeys formed by pepperoni pizza toppings on each slice.

Hint 74: Behind Roger Rabbit, in a mural on one of the *'80s buildings* near the *Computer Pool*, a classic Mickey hides at the top of a bush beside a building. The bush's topmost leaf is just above Mickey's head and ears, and one hand of a traffic signal points to Mickey!

Hint 75: Two black classic Mickeys are on the keyboard of the huge computer near the *Computer Pool*. Both are on the lower row of keys. One is on the second key from the left and the other is on the second key from the right. (More obvious decorative classic Mickeys are in the computer monitor's screensaver.)

Hint 76: Look sharp for a faint classic Mickey in green paint on an outside wall of the *'60s building*, behind the Mowgli figure near the *Hippy Dippy Pool*. It's on the left side of the wall with green plants at about eye level, between two complete vertical leaves, and near the wall's left border.

Hint 77: "Mickey Mouse Club March" is choice "C2" on the giant jukebox near the *Bowling Pool*. ("I've Got a Date at Disneyland" is choice "F10.")

Hint 78: Outside the main lobby, classic Mickeys are at the ends of the guardrails near the bus stops.

Chapter 6: Resort Hotel Scavenger Hunt

Disney Springs Area Resorts

Disney's Caribbean Beach Resort

Hint 79: A group of three logs stuck in the ground forms a classic Mickey. Find the image in a border of logs along the lakeside promenade and between *Martinique Buildings 24 and 25*. The Hidden Mickey is next to a recessed drain that faces and is adjacent to the lakeside promenade. To find it, turn right from the sidewalk between *Buildings 24 and 25* onto the lakeside promenade.

Hint 80: Behind *Old Port Royale*, a classic Mickey appears in the "Barefoot Bay Boat Yard" sign on the side of the lighthouse near the bike racks.

Hint 81: In the child's aquatic play area near the main pool, a classic Mickey is on the helm near the wheel of the wrecked pirate ship.

Hint 82: Where the sidewalk from *Barbados* meets the sidewalk outside the main *(Old Port Royale)* pool, they are joined by a short sidewalk that takes you to the right toward the main resort parking area. As you face the parking area from this intersection, look down at the lower right corner of the first white cement middle section of the short sidewalk. A small classic Mickey is etched in the pavement not far from a green lamppost.

Disney's Riviera Resort (All new Hidden Mickeys!)

Hint 83: As you walk toward the Resort from the Disney Skyliner, you'll pass by colorful murals that arch over you. One mural shows a scene from Disney's *Tangled* movie. At the middle of the left corner (as you face the Resort) of the arch above you, look for small yellow-orange circles that come together as a classic Hidden Mickey. It's not far above the tallest spire of the castle.

Hint 84: Further along the *Tangled* mural above you, search for another yellow-orange circle classic Hidden Mickey in the middle of the mural, not far from a red cloud.

Hint 85: Stroll outside through the Resort and study the guest room window railings. In the middle of some of the railings is a large classic Mickey design, and next to Mickey is Minnie Mouse with her bow!

Hint 86: Classic Mickeys can be seen in the design along the top of some fences, railings, and gates.

Hint 87: Find swirly classic Mickey designs on some of the outside lampposts, like ones that hold signs pointing to various areas.

Hint 88: At *Bar Riva*, admire the mural on the inside left wall and spot classic Hidden Mickeys on the bow and on the smokestacks of a Disney ship.

Hint 89: On the right side wall of the resort lobby (as you walk through the main entrance), look for a mural on the rear right wall. The mural shows a colorful village with houses, garden terraces, and a cruise ship on the sea. At the bottom left of the mural is a group of red round plants, and several of the plant circles come together as classic Hidden Mickeys.

Hint 90: Inside the Resort, walk to the carpet in front of upper floor elevators and say hello to the Fab Five, who are traced along the outer rim of the circular carpet.

Hint 91: Look down at classic Hidden Mickeys in the corners of the design of the guest hallway carpets.

Hint 92: A large classic Mickey sits at the top middle of the sign above the entrance to *Topolino's Terrace Restaurant*.

Hint 93: Outside the Resort's main entrance doors, under the roof of the car unloading

Chapter 6: Resort Hotel Scavenger Hunt

area, the overhead lighting fixture forms a classic Hidden Mickey when viewed from a certain angle. Get the best perspective by standing at a corner of the overhead structure across the driveway from the Resort entrance doors.

Hint 94: Spot classic Mickeys in the outside ornate swirly design work in various areas around the Resort.

Hint 95: Outside behind the Resort, find a Running Trail Map posted along the waterfront walkway. At least three clusters of green bushes on the map - one at the top middle and two on the lower left side of the map - make classic Hidden Mickeys.

Disney's Old Key West Resort

Hint 96: Throughout *Conch Flats General Store*, the design in the fence woodwork and in the merchandise poles includes classic Mickeys.

Hint 97: Classic Mickeys are worked into the design of the fence railings behind the check-in counter in the registration area.

Hint 98: At the main pool (behind the registration building), the water slide (hidden in the rock) opens into the pool through the head of a classic Mickey.

Hint 99: At the upper right of the entrance to the steps to the water slide, a classic Mickey is impressed in the white rock, above a space in the wall.

Hint 100: You'll see classic Mickeys in the outdoor railings around the guest buildings.

Disney's Port Orleans Resort - French Quarter

Hint 101: On the third painting from the left behind the registration counter, an upside-down classic Mickey is on a man's crown.

Hint 102: Upside-down classic Mickeys made of blue and white gemstones adorn the top of a crown that sits on a shelf at the left side of the food court seating area.

Disney's Port Orleans Resort - Riverside

Hint 103: Above the registration area, classic Mickeys are repeated in the wooden latticework circling the central lobby.

Hint 104: In the registration area, classic Mickeys decorate the sides of the brackets that hold the giant fans hanging from the ceiling above the center of the lobby.

Hint 105: Classic Mickeys are at the base of the strapping on the big ceiling fans.

Hint 106: Three circles make a classic Hidden Mickey in each of the small round headlights on some of the surrey bikes available to rent. (Some of the surrey bikes have headlights with three same-size circles—not a properly proportioned classic Hidden Mickey).

Hint 107: Small classic Mickeys are in the lower middle of handrail poles at *Parterre Place*.

Disney's Saratoga Springs Resort & Spa

Hint 108: A carriage sits just outside the registration lobby. Classic Hidden Mickeys can be found above the front and rear wheels in the exterior design on the carriage.

Hint 109: In the main registration lobby, red swirls in the center carpet form a series of classic Hidden Mickeys.

Hint 110: Halfway down the hallway behind *The Artist's Palette* shop (turn right as you enter the shop from the main lobby), a full-body impression of Mickey Mouse swinging a golf club is on a handle on the left door.

Chapter 6: Resort Hotel Scavenger Hunt

Hint 111: A large framed photo of a side-profile Mickey golf green hangs on a wall in a sitting room at the end of the hallway behind *The Artist's Palette* shop.

Hint 112: In the hallway leading to *The Turf Club Bar and Grill*, the jacket in a display on the left wall sports block classic Mickeys.

Hint 113: On a wall inside the lounge in front of *The Turf Club*, Mickey and other Disney characters decorate billiard balls. They are in the first display to the left as you enter from the hallway.

Hint 114: Just inside the dining area of *The Turf Club*, three circles on equestrian equipment in the upper right section of a wall display form an upside-down classic Mickey. The display is on the left wall (as you enter).

Hint 115: On a statue of a horse and rider outside the main lobby, the rings attaching the bridle to the reins and bit on both sides of the horse's mouth form classic Mickeys. Tiny classic Mickeys are also hidden in the roses on both sides of the horse's winner's blanket. You'll find them in the middle of the blanket in about the third or fourth row down. Finally, large blue classic Mickeys decorate the back and front of the jockey's jersey. (In addition, a blanket on the horse includes a yellow decor Mickey.)

Hint 116: As you walk away from *The Artist's Palette*, look for depressions in the left rock wall at the top of the stairs to the *High Rock Spring Pool*. One classic Mickey is in the middle of the top horizontal rock of the wall, and a second classic Mickey is below the first one—near the handrail post on the lower horizontal rock.

Hint 117: Behind Donald Duck in the children's water play area at *High Rock Spring Pool*, a classic Mickey, about six feet tall and tilted to the left, is made of three depressions in the rock wall behind the waterfall. As

261

you face the rock wall, the Hidden Mickey is at the left side. It's easier to see when the waterfall is turned off.

Hint 118: At the left side of the *High Rock Spring Pool* (as you face it from the main building), impressions in the rock wall that borders the zero-grade entrance to the pool form three classic Mickeys. Three large circles on the middle of the rock face form an upright classic Mickey, while three smaller circles at the right middle tilt to make a sideways classic Mickey. Behind the layered stone wall, three more circles on the end of the gray rock form another upright classic Mickey.

Hint 119: Some balcony railings on the guest buildings have classic Mickey holes.

Hint 120: In the resort's *Springs section (Villas 4101 to 4436)*, across from the check-in parking lot, a large faint classic Mickey is on an outdoor red wall.

Hint 121: In the resort's *Congress Park section (Villas 1501 to 1836)*, near the lagoon over which you can see *Disney Springs*, another large faint classic Mickey is on an outdoor red wall. I stood near this red wall and could spot the *Rainforest Cafe* across the lagoon.

Hint 122: A classic Mickey is inside the Aquatic Play Area at *The Paddock* pool. This Hidden Mickey is formed by three stones in the middle front of a pillar that is on your right after you pass through the entrance gate.

Hint 123: Classic Mickeys can be found in the upper corners of some of the outside lights on the guest buildings, such as on the exterior of the enclosed stairways.

Hint 124: Classic Mickeys are at the bottom of obelisks in the various Villa courtyards.

Chapter 6: Resort Hotel Scavenger Hunt

Hint 125: Classic Hidden Mickey holes are in the corners of the decorative design work along the ceiling perimeter of the carousel-themed gazebo at the *Carousel Villas*.

Hint 126: Partial classic Mickeys hide in the left side of the gate to the *Grandstand Pool* and on the back gate next to the restrooms.

Hint 127: At the Grandstand Pool's *Backstretch Pool Bar*, a classic Mickey hides at the top of the green trees painted on the lower front wall below the bar counter.

Epcot Area Resorts

Disney's BoardWalk Resort

Hint 128: In the main lobby, a horse on the outer ring of the small carousel has brown spots that form two classic Mickeys, one on the neck and one on the thigh.

Hint 129: In the middle painting on the wall above the middle registration counter in the main lobby, a classic Mickey is formed by the second small group of trees from the right.

Hint 130: Along a side wall inside the lobby, tiny classic Mickey holes are at the very tops of the red latticework designs on all sides of the canopied seat (called a "howdah") atop the elephant.

Hint 131: On the first to the fifth floors of the *BoardWalk Villas*, a classic Mickey sits atop light fixtures alongside the elevators.

Hint 132: Classic Mickeys hide in the carpet in front of some elevators and also appear in the lobby carpets and the guestroom hallway carpets in both the *BoardWalk Inn* and *BoardWalk Villas*. (Note: The images in these areas change or disappear from time to time.)

Hint 133: Three circles make a classic Hidden Mickey in each of the small round

263

headlights on some of the BoardWalk surrey bikes available to rent. (Other surrey bikes have headlights with three same-size circles—not a properly proportioned classic Hidden Mickey).

Hint 134: Look in the room to your right as you enter *AbracadaBar* from the outside promenade. A photo of Walt is in the right lower corner of a huge display case next to an exit door at the opposite side of the room. Walt is pulling a rabbit out of a hat!

Hint 135: Inside *AbracadaBar*, a club suit in a framed Ace of Clubs is altered to form a classic Mickey. This frame hangs in the hallway leading to the restrooms, on the right wall. It is next to the magical mirror.

Hint 136: The words "Trattoria al Forno" are etched in the wall behind the check-in counter for the restaurant. A tiny classic Mickey is impressed in the lower right leg of the first "A" in "Trattoria."

Disney's Beach Club Resort

Hint 137: A classic Mickey is on a blue plate inside *Cape May Cafe*. The plate is perched on a small shelf on the right wall just past the check-in podium at the restaurant's entrance. Mickey is on the inside of the plate and has a red circle for the "head" and two black circles for the "ears."

Hint 138: Along the inside walkway in front of the *Cape May Cafe*, a full-length Mickey Mouse is standing in a sandcastle. It's the sculpture farthest to the left, on the wall facing the pool. (This image disappears at times.)

Hint 139: In *Martha's Vineyard* lounge, two dark green classic Mickeys appear on the ground at the left lower section of a framed painting on the wall to the immediate left of the bar. One image is at the lower left corner and the other is nearby to the right (and a partial classic Mickey is at the middle bottom edge of the painting).

Chapter 6: Resort Hotel Scavenger Hunt

Hint 140: In the Beach Club lobby, on the left as you walk toward the *Marketplace* shop, a white classic Mickey surrounded by a white circle is inlaid in a floor tile. Look for it under a light fixture and in front of the luggage room door.

Hint 141: Enter the *Solarium* from the Beach Club main lobby. The first painting on the wall to your left has Mickey's face on spare tires on the backs of the yellow car (left side) and the blue car (right side).

Hint 142: Classic Mickey hood ornaments adorn the blue and red cars on the right of this painting.

Hint 143: In the second painting on the left wall, you can see Mickey's face looking out at you from the clouds at the upper right.

Hint 144: In this second painting, a lady on the beach is sitting on a Mickey Mouse towel.

Hint 145: The cruise ship smokestacks in this second painting have classic Mickey decals.

Hint 146: Mickey balloons are on the right side of the third painting to your left.

Hint 147: Also on the right side of this third painting is a tiny white classic Mickey atop the front post of a small building with a brown roof.

Hint 148: The guestroom hallways have carpet segments with classic Mickeys.

Hint 149: Under the Ariel statue in front of the entrance to the *Beach Club Villas*, three seashells (a larger one for the "head") in the middle front of the base of the statue come together as a small classic Mickey, sideways to the left.

Hint 150: In *The Breezeway* at the Beach Club Villas, three different Mickey images hide in a painting on the left wall (as you enter *The Breezeway* from the front doors):

- Classic Mickeys are on a fence in the lower part of the painting.
- A full-body shadow of Mickey Mouse is in a bottom-floor hotel window in the middle of the painting.
- A subtle dark smiling Mickey face drawn in the sand lies to the right of the two people standing closest to the water.

Hint 151: Near the restrooms off the lobby inside the entrance doors to the *Beach Club Villas*, a colorful picture entitled "Cape May" is on the left wall in the short hallway to the left of *The Breezeway*. Look at the top border and you'll spot a train just to the left of center. A classic Mickey is formed by the coal in the car behind the engine.

Hint 152: Onion rings form a classic Mickey in one of the food images decorating the *Beaches & Cream Soda Shop*. The image is on the left wall as you enter, on the second panel back from the rear wall.

Hint 153: You can spot classic Mickey holes in the hamburger press used at the *Beaches & Cream Soda Shop* to hold the burgers on the hot griddle.

Disney's Yacht Club Resort

Hint 154: On the globe in the main lobby, a blue classic Mickey is at the bottom near a sea monster, under the sea monster's head and below the island of Madagascar.

Hint 155: Various other classic Mickey images can be found in other carpets around the resort, especially near elevators, in the guest hallways, and in the phone bank area.

Hint 156: A photo of (now deceased) Minnie Moo, a cow born with a black classic Mickey on her side, often hangs in the *Yachtsman Steakhouse*. Examine the left wall just past the entrance podium. Minnie Moo once resided at *Fort Wilderness*.

Chapter 6: Resort Hotel Scavenger Hunt

Magic Kingdom Area Resorts

Disney's Fort Wilderness Resort

Hint 157: On the sign at the entrance to the *Golden Oak* community on Vista Boulevard near the *Fort Wilderness Resort*, a classic Mickey is hidden in the tree of Golden Oak's logo.

Hint 158: In the room to the right as you enter the *Tri-Circle-D Ranch Horse Barn*, classic Mickeys decorate the horse bridle gear hanging in a display.

Hint 159: Inside the *Tri-Circle-D Ranch Horse Barn*, horse stalls are identified by numbers, which are posted on Mickeyshaped labels above the stall gates.

Hint 160: A classic Mickey brand is on the left side of the *Blacksmith* sign near the *Horse Barn*.

Hint 161: Inside *Trail's End Restaurant*, a classic Mickey is formed by frying pans hanging from hooks on the wall behind the food serving station.

Hint 162: Several white classic Mickeys are on a rock across the walkway in front of the *Bike Barn*.

Hint 163: At the front parking lot, two Hidden Mickeys are on the Tri-Circle-D Ranch sign on the small *Trail Ride Check-In* building. They are in the middle of the scrollwork at both sides of the sign.

Hint 164: Inside the *Fort Wilderness* registration building *("Reception Outpost")* at the far side of the main parking lot, a plush Mickey Mouse stands in a metal jug at the far left of a shelf directly over the registration counter.

Disney's Wilderness Lodge Resort

Hint 165: On the right side of the entrance drive to the hotel, a full-length Mickey Mouse is walking on top of the "Bear Crossing" sign.

Hint 166: A classic Mickey is on the slanted end of the first horizontal log beam (perpendicular to the road) of the guard gate kiosk as your car approaches the entrance gate.

Hint 167: As you approach the center steps to the car unloading area from the parking lot, you'll see that the roof of the covered area in front of the hotel entrance is supported by huge wooden logs, banded together (four to a set) by black metal strips. In the set of support poles on the left after you walk up the center steps, the pole in the corner closest to you and the hotel entrance has a classic Mickey etched in the wood. This Mickey faces the steps and is partially covered by the upper black metal band; only his head and part of his right ear are visible.

Hint 168: In the cement of the car entrance drive-through, the black stripe nearest the center steps from the parking lot hides a tiny classic Mickey. From the red rectangle in the cement, follow the right (as you face the hotel entrance) diagonal crack to the black stripe. The tiny classic Mickey is traced in the cement about six inches to the right of the intersection of the crack and the stripe.

Hint 169: As you face the hotel entrance, the left rear support pole of the far left set of poles closest to the parking lot has a classic Mickey etched in the wood. It's above the lateral crossbeam on the lower part of the pole.

Hint 170: A classic Mickey hides on the left side of a large key in a wall display behind the registration counter. Look near the entrance to the *Mercantile* shop.

Hint 171: A sign that says "Walt Disney World Transportation" hangs from the

Chapter 6: Resort Hotel Scavenger Hunt

ceiling near the *Mercantile* shop. Mickey (in side profile) is driving the bus at the top of the sign.

Hint 172: In the lobby, you'll find a classic Mickey etched on the rock in the corner at the upper right of the fireplace. Search at the level of and near the lower round wooden horizontal beam that juts toward the lobby.

Hint 173: The outer grillwork of a fireplace in the rear room of the *Whispering Canyon Cafe* is adorned with decorative cutouts. Bend down low and look for a classic Mickey on the bottom row. It is the third cutout from the left corner.

Hint 174: A small classic Mickey lies on the floor at the left front corner (as you face the rear of the lobby) of the rectangle of dark hardwood slats that surround the bubbling source of the water spring. The "head" is formed by a circle in the wood with small indentations in the wood for "ears." You may need to lift the corner of the rug to spot it.

Hint 175: At the entrance stairs to the *Territory Lounge*, a classic Mickey decorates a pot in the right lower section of a wall map.

Hint 176: Inside the *Territory Lounge*, a classic Mickey rests on the rear of a beige mule in a ceiling mural. Look above the center of the bar.

Hint 177: Inside the *Artist Point restaurant*, examine the large mural above the entrance to the rear left dining area. You can spot a classic Mickey in the upper part of the lowest tree on the right if you look between the third and fourth lights (counting from the left) illuminating the mural. The Hidden Mickey is tilted to the right.

Hint 178: Turn left toward the *Artist Point* entrance and study the large mural near the ceiling and between the two front sections of the restaurant. On the clothing at the lower back of the leftmost of four horsemen is a light brown classic Mickey, tilted slightly to the right.

Hint 179: Inside the rear left dining area, the top middle part of a dark cloud in a painting on the left wall is shaped like a side profile of Winnie the Pooh. He's looking to the right.

Hint 180: A display case on an inside wall facing the entrance to the *Roaring Fork snack bar* contains three chestnuts arranged to form a classic Mickey.

Hint 181: You'll find classic Mickey images on a few of the wall-light covers, most often as a sideways image at the lower center of the light cover. Some of these covers are near the elevators just past *Roaring Fork snack area*. One or more can be found elsewhere around the hotel.

Hint 182: Segments of the guest hallway carpets contain tiny blue classic Mickeys.

Hint 183: A classic Mickey is etched near the bottom of a flat vertical wooden post around the corner from *Room 6106* and near a green EXIT sign.

Hint 184: Near *Room 5066*, a classic Mickey is etched on a flat vertical wooden post about five and a half feet from the floor. It's across from an ice machine.

Hint 185: A classic Mickey is etched on a vertical wooden post about six feet up from the floor across from *Room 4035*.

Hint 186: Outside, from the walkway next to *Fire Rock Geyser*, scan the shallow stream running down from the small pool by the geyser. You'll find a slightly distorted classic Mickey with white rocks for ears in the rock of the streambed about a third of the way up to the geyser.

Hint 187: Walk toward the *Teton Boat and Bike Rental* cabin and locate stairs to an exit door in the corner of the main building.

Chapter 6: Resort Hotel Scavenger Hunt

A classic Mickey is impressed in a vertical wooden beam at the left side of the exit door (as you face the door) across from the fourth-floor balcony. Mickey is on the right side of the beam, just below the log that juts out to the right.

Hint 188: At the marina, to the left of the *Boat and Bike Rental* cabin, the Cast Members usually maintain a classic Hidden Mickey made of coiled rope. Look for it on the front of a display boat that sits on the marina pier. (Note: The Disney Navy decorates the front of some of the Sea Raycer display boats with classic Mickey coils of rope. You can often spot this Hidden Mickey at the marinas of various WDW Resorts.)

- *Boulder Ridge Villas*

Hint 189: Turn left toward the elevators after you enter the *Villas'* main entrance. On the rock pillar to your right as you walk toward the elevators, an almost upside-down classic Hidden Mickey is etched in a square, dark gray rock. Find it on the second rock from the floor, about two and one-half feet up.

Hint 190: Near the lobby elevators to the left of the entrance to the *Villas*, four classic Mickeys hide on the wall. One is to the right of the elevators near the lower left corner of a picture frame. Two more are part of the wall decoration between the elevators, and a fourth can be found to the left of the leftmost elevator. This last Mickey is hiding behind the red tapestry.

Hint 191: A classic Mickey made of depressions in the rock is tilted to the right on the last stone pillar to your left as you walk to the lobby from the elevators. You can spot this image just before you step into the lobby. It is about three feet from the floor and folded across the corner (that faces the entrance) of the second rock from the floor.

Hint 192: Mickey Mouse is peeking out of a hole on the outer side of the first overhead beam to your right as you enter the lobby of the *Boulder Ridge Villas*. The beam is jutting out into the lobby and has a rattlesnake on top.

Hint 193: A side profile of Mickey Mouse is on the upper part of a wall, between two moons, in the lobby of the *Boulder Ridge Villas* (and to the right as you face the lobby).

Hint 194: Above the inner section of the fireplace on the right side of the Villas lobby, a classic Hidden Mickey is etched in a horizontal rectangular stone, in the center of the second row of stones down from the ceiling. The classic Mickey is sideways to the right, with an incomplete lower "ear."

Hint 195: Looking out from inside the small telephone alcove near the lobby, a sideways (to the right) classic Hidden Mickey is impressed in the rock on the right near the floor.

Hint 196: Classic Hidden Mickeys are in the corners of a painting frame on the rear wall of the Villas lobby.

Hint 197: Examine the art hanging in the first room to the right after you pass through the *Villas'* lobby entrance doors. A painting that's hanging on the room's right wall has a frame with classic Mickeys in the corners.

Hint 198: Walk to your right (as you face the Villas lobby) to the *Carolwood Pacific Railroad Room*. On the left side of the fireplace, a classic Mickey—tilted right—is embedded in the stonework at about the height of the fireplace mantel.

Hint 199: High along the hallways of the *Villas*, you'll find classic Mickey corner brackets.

Hint 200: To the left of the entrance doors to the *Villas*, in a hallway on the left past the elevators, a dark classic Mickey appears on

Chapter 6: Resort Hotel Scavenger Hunt

the baseboard near the hall carpet. It's down the hallway on your right, about eight to ten feet before you reach *Room 1507*.

Magic Kingdom Monorail Resorts

Disney's Polynesian Village Resort

Hint 201: On the lower level, just inside the main lobby entrance, there's a classic Mickey design in the flagstone tiles of the lobby floor.

Hint 202: Overhead in the lobby, some rope knots securing the round lights resemble Hidden Mickeys.

Hint 203: Inside the *BouTiki store* on the first floor and near the various entrances, three wooden statues holding merchandise are adorned with classic Mickeys. Two of the Mickeys are blue and white while the third is red.

Hint 204: Along the right rear corner staircase from the lobby, bamboo wall decorations are composed of rings. Seen end on, some of the lower bamboo rings in the decoration on the right side form classic Mickeys.

Hint 205: Inside *Moana Mercantile Shop* upstairs, a classic Mickey is formed of blue and green balls hanging in knotted ropes high along the middle of the rear wall, above the merchandise shelves.

Hint 206: Two paintings with Hidden Mickeys hang on the wall across from the second-floor elevators near the main lobby. In the painting on the right (near the fire extinguisher), two classic Mickeys in the middle left are made of brown rocks—one upright and one (at the far left) upside down. In the painting on the left, circles in the foamy water on the shore make a classic Mickey in the lower middle of the painting.

Hint 207: At the *Kona Island coffee and sushi bar*, in front of the Kona Cafe, small purple tiles on top of the mosaic tile counter form a classic Mickey. You'll spot it to the left of the glass case.

Hint 208: The carpet in some of the hallways and elevators sports classic Mickeys.

Hint 209: On the display Sea Raycer boat outside by the marina, three dials at the left side of the dashboard form a classic Mickey. (You can see other Sea Raycers with this dashboard classic Hidden Mickey on display at other Walt Disney World Resorts.)

Hint 210: Four sets of tiny, white classic Mickeys in pairs lie along the lagoon walkway, about halfway between the *Polynesian Village Resort* and *Disney's Fairytale Wedding Pavilion*. Look for them in the area where you see a wooden wall a few feet to the side of the walkway and opposite the lagoon. The Hidden Mickey pairs appear every few feet along the length of the wall. One is on the walkway itself and the other on the curb just above it. (They're fading over time!)

Disney's Fairytale Wedding Pavilion

Hint 211: The weathervane on top of the building closest to the monorail has a full-length side profile of Mickey Mouse.

Disney's Grand Floridian Resort & Spa

Hint 212: Weathervanes on various roofs at the front of the resort sport classic Mickeys.

Hint 213: The large trolley carts outside the hotel have classic Mickeys in the woodwork around the luggage storage areas at the back of the carts.

Hint 214: In the main lobby, gold classic Mickeys are in the middle of the carpet.

Hint 215: Green classic Mickeys are in the corners of the marble tile designs on the floors of the first and second levels of the main building.

Chapter 6: Resort Hotel Scavenger Hunt

Hint 216: You'll find the Fab Five Disney characters (Mickey, Minnie, Pluto, Donald, and Goofy) in the tile floor near the main lobby's front entrance—and directly above in the tile on the second-floor entrance from the monorail.

Hint 217: Along the entrance hall to *1900 Park Fare restaurant*, a Mickey-hat image is at the left lower corner of the left lower picture in a group of carousel pictures on the wall.

Hint 218: Minnie is here with Mickey (green full-body images) on the tile floor of the foyer in front of the dining area of the *1900 Park Fare restaurant*.

Hint 219: Other Disney movie characters are in the tile floor encircling the main lobby and in front of the Grand Floridian Cafe. They include Tinker Bell, Cinderella and Prince Charming, Peter Pan and friends, Mrs. Potts and Chip, and of course Mickey and Minnie.

Hint 220: Wall maps of the *Grand Floridian Resort* are on the first and second floors, toward the front of the building. A small sideways classic Mickey is formed by bushes at the upper right of the Sago Cay building, located at the left middle of the map.

Hint 221: Ornate ironwork encloses the elevator out in the lobby, and the decorative sections between the floors host multiple classic Mickeys. You'll find four classic Mickeys in each ironwork panel at the intersection of the diagonal spokes and the large circle. The ears are oriented toward the center. (Tip: Stand inside the main lobby elevator for the best view of these classic Mickeys.)

Hint 222: A classic Mickey design is at the bottom of each of the four tall blue flowers in the stained-glass dome above the main lobby of the *Grand Floridian*.

Hint 223: On the second floor, a classic Mickey hides on the top of a pole on the *M. Mouse Mercantile* sign in front of the shop.

Hint 224: Along the covered walkways outside the *Grand Floridian Villas*, look up for classic Hidden Mickeys in the latticework design. They occur only at certain points along the walkways.

Hint 225: A classic Mickey is two-thirds of the way up the huge rock wall at the side of the main pool near the *Grand Floridian Villas*. The Hidden Mickey, made of circular depressions in the rock, is behind the waterfall and is sometimes difficult to make out if the water flow is heavy and obscures the image.

Hint 226: Inside *Gasparilla Island Grill*, classic Mickeys are in the metalwork above the individual lights on the ceiling light fixtures.

Hint 227: On the display Sea Raycer boat outside by the marina, three dials at the left side of the dashboard form a classic Mickey. (You can see other Sea Raycers with this dashboard classic Hidden Mickey on display at other Walt Disney World Resorts.)

Hint 228: Step into the main entrance area of the *Grand Floridian Convention Center* and look up for a hot air Mickey balloon painted on the ceiling.

Disney's Contemporary Resort

Hint 229: From the window of the *California Grill restaurant* on the hotel's top floor, you can see a stretched-out Mickey watchband on the ground in front of the building. It's among the conicalshaped trees. (You can see part of this watchband from the monorail.)

Hint 230: *(Caution: Prop the hallway door open before you step out onto the balcony to look for Mickey.)*

Chapter 6: Resort Hotel Scavenger Hunt

From the *sixth-floor* outdoor balcony closest to the front of the hotel, look left to see Mickey sitting on the edge of a roof below! This Mickey can also be spotted from either monorail just outside the hotel (the opening nearest the *Transportation and Ticket Center*). If you're on the resort monorail, you have to bend down to view Mickey through the lower part of the window (to the left of forward motion) and below the express monorail track next to you. On the express monorail, look to the right of forward motion.

Hint 231: Inside *Chef Mickey's restaurant*, a large side-profile Mickey decorates both sides of the large black, white, and red tile divider.

Hint 232: Mickey ears are atop posts at the rear of *Chef Mickey's restaurant*.

Hint 233: On the lower part of the wall mural facing *Contempo Cafe*, the fourth girl from the right corner of the wall has a classic Mickey on her dress.

Hint 234: At the upper middle of this wall mural facing *Contempo Cafe*, a girl in a blue and white dress is carrying orange and light purple round fruits in a basket on her head. In the right side of the basket, a light purple "head" and two smaller orange "ears" form a classic Mickey tilted to the left.

Hint 235: High on the wall mural facing *Bay Lake*, a black classic Mickey is on an owl perched on a girl's head. It's on the red right wing (as you face the mural).

Hint 236: On the fourth floor, a stick-figure Mickey is in an artwork display on the side of the *Bayview Gifts store* facing the monorail.

Hint 237: On the fourth floor, classic Mickeys are in the carpet inside *The Game Station Arcade*.

Hint 238: Large but faint classic Mickeys are in the carpet in the *Market shop*. You can spot one just inside the entrance to the shop.

Hint 239: On the wall mural facing the monorail, an upside-down classic Mickey has a blue circle for a "head" and yellow circles for "ears." It's at the top of a tree that is positioned to the lower left of the five-legged goat.

Hint 240: Behind the main hotel, a classic Mickey silhouette can be found in the bricks under the metal Mickey Mouse sculpture. (The sculpture itself is a decorative Mickey, not a Hidden Mickey.)

Hint 241: At the *marina*, a classic Mickey is on the dashboard of the display speedboat on the dock. It's made of the faint white circles surrounding the dials.

Hint 242: Also at the *marina* by the pool, the marine alphabet letter flags on the glass front of the *Sand Bar* spell "MICKEY."

Hint 243: Inside the *Sand Bar*, near the middle of the upper left wall border, one of the semaphore figures is wearing Mickey ears.

Hint 244: At the exit from the *Garden Building* to the parking lot (facing the monorail), a huge classic Mickey is traced in the tile under the exit canopy between the benches.

Hint 245: Subtle, large white classic Mickeys are frosted into glass partitions that support the curved roof covering the vehicle drive-through entrance area to the hotel.

- *Bay Lake Tower*

Hint 246: Classic Mickeys are at the top of both elevator towers at the sides of the hotel. (Ceiling lights hang from these Mickey-shaped metal plates.) You can spot one of them from the monorail and either or both from the ground.

Chapter 6: Resort Hotel Scavenger Hunt

Disney's Shades of Green Resort

Hint 247: In the lobby, a Mickey statue stands in front of a framed picture of a blue sky with puffy clouds. Three classic Mickeys are in the clouds and another, made of fireworks, decorates the statue Mickey's right ear.

Hint 248: The *Millpond pool* is shaped as a classic Mickey. You can visit this pool outside or spot it on a resort map posted on hallway walls.

Chapter 7

Hither, Thither & Yon Scavenger Hunt

• • • • • •

A car is the most efficient method for hunting the following areas. You'll need admission tickets for all destination areas except for Disney Springs. I've planned the hunt taking time of day and location into consideration. However, some backtracking will help keep you ahead of the crowds. Don't forget to be courteous to the shoppers, diners, golfers, swimmers, other guests and Cast Members you encounter during your hunt. (Note: Because you may want to hunt only one area at a time, I've listed the perfect score for each area in parentheses after its name in the Clues section.)

Try to park in the *Lime Garage* for the Hidden Mickeys Hunt in Disney Springs.

Bonus Points Opportunity. As I advised in Chapter Six, pay attention to the ***Disney buses*** during your Hidden Mickey hunt around WDW property. You may get lucky! The ***Disney Cruise Line bus*** has a Hidden Pluto on each side of the gold scrollwork on the front of the bus between the headlights. Look for a green classic Mickey on the back of many buses that are diesel. Some general ***Disney transport buses*** sport a classic Mickey on the rear of the vehicle, usually related to rear upper or lower lights. Even more subtle are the faint classic Mickey images in the windows of some buses, only visible when the lighting is just right! If you spot one or more of these images, give yourself 5 bonus points for each one you find.

Walt Disney World's Hidden Mickeys

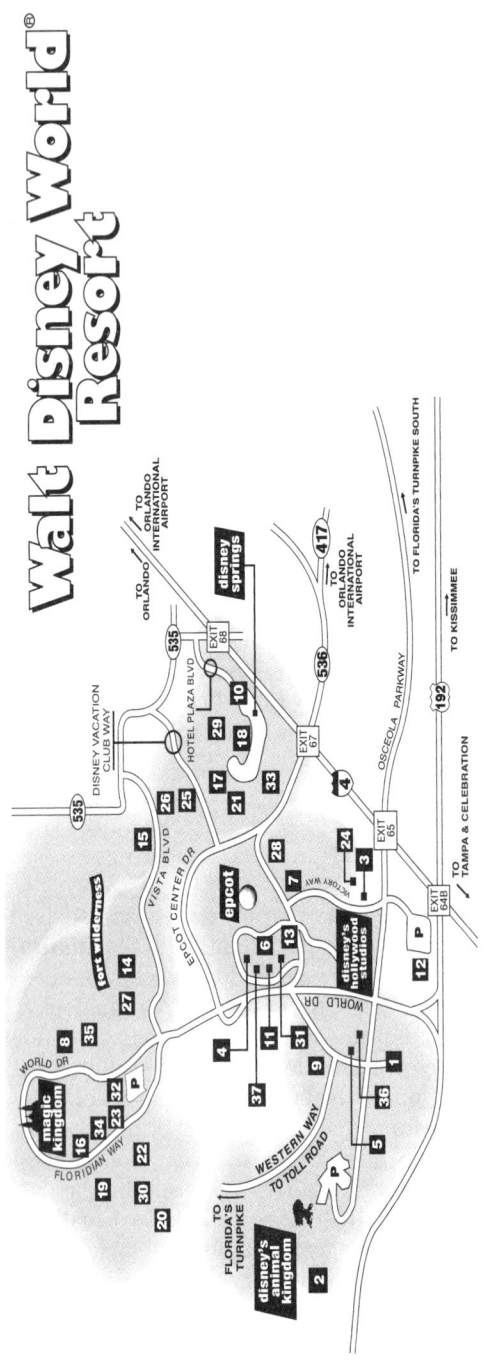

282

Chapter 7: HTYon Scavenger Hunt

Walt Disney World Resort®

1. All-Star Resorts
2. Animal Kingdom Lodge
3. Art of Animation
4. Beach Club
5. Blizzard Beach
6. BoardWalk
7. Caribbean Beach
8. Contemporary
9. Coronado Springs
10. Disney Springs
11. Dolphin
12. ESPN Wide World of Sports Complex
13. Fantasia Gardens Mini Golf
14. Fort Wilderness
15. Golden Oak
16. Grand Floridian
17. Lake Buena Vista Golf Course
18. The Landing, in Disney Springs
19. Magnolia Golf Course
20. Oak Trail Golf Course
21. Old Key West
22. Palm Golf Course
23. Polynesian Village
24. Pop Century
25. Port Orleans – French Quarter
26. Port Orleans – Riverside
27. Reflections – A Disney Lakeside Lodge
28. Riviera
29. Saratoga Springs
30. Shades of Green
31. Swan
32. Transportation and Ticket Center
33. Typhoon Lagoon
34. Wedding Pavilion, Disney's Fairytale
35. Wilderness Lodge
36. Winter Summerland Mini Golf
37. Yacht Club
P. Parking

Disney's Magnolia Golf Course

Clue 1: If you're a golfer, look around you for a classic Mickey sand trap.
5 points

Vista Boulevard

Clue 2: Drive east along Vista Boulevard away from *Fort Wilderness* and stay alert for a classic Mickey on a sign to your left.
3 points

ESPN Wide World of Sports
(10 points)

Clue 3: Search hard for a three-dimensional Mickey Mouse head near the high central ceiling of *The Milk House* (the Field House). He's on an upper rafter opposite the main entrance.
5 points

Clue 4: Now head for the *softball fields* and check out the pitcher's mounds for possible bonus points.
5 bonus points for one or more

Clue 5: Stroll around the *Sports Fields* to locate a Hidden Mickey on the discus field.
5 points

WDW Water Parks (46 points)

- *Disney's Blizzard Beach* (15 points)

Clue 6: Take a close look at the *Beach Haus* store's right rear wall near the dressing rooms.
3 points

Clue 7: Inside the *Beach Haus*, spot Hidden Mickeys near the merchandise.
2 points

Clue 8: Hop on the *Chairlift* to spot a classic Mickey formed by three round rocks on the

Chapter 7: HTYon Scavenger Hunt

ground near one of the support poles for the ride.
5 points
(Tip: The Singles line for the *Chairlift* is usually shorter than the Standby line.)

Clue 9: Go to the rear of the park (by tube or on foot) to find a classic Mickey with a sorcerer's hat that's formed by three stones topped by a small triangular rock. (Psst! He's near the center of the side of a stone bridge that crosses over *Cross Country Creek*.)
5 points

En Route to Typhoon Lagoon (4 points)

Clue 10: On your way to *Typhoon Lagoon* from *Blizzard Beach*, spot Mickey on the Disney Vacation Club white tower, which will appear on your left at the intersection of Buena Vista Drive and Bonnet Creek Parkway.
4 points

- Disney's Typhoon Lagoon (27 points)

Clue 11: Check out a Tip Board for a Hidden Mickey. (Note: These images come and go.)
3 bonus points

Clue 12: At the front of the surfing lagoon, scan inside the *Board Room* for a Hidden Mickey.
3 points

Clue 13: Look around the *Crush 'n' Gusher* elevator for a Hidden Mickey.
4 points

Clue 14: Search for Mickey on a bridge over *Castaway Creek*, near *Typhoon Tilly's*.
4 points

Clue 15: Don't pass by Mickey on the steps up to the *Storm Slides*.
4 points

Clue 16: Climb the trail up to *Humunga Kowabunga* and locate a classic Mickey

along the way.
4 points

Clue 17: Spot the Main Mouse hiding under a cannon along *Castaway Creek* at the rear of the park.
4 points

Clue 18: Squint for Mickey in the wall of a cave at *Ketchakiddee Creek*.
4 points

The Landing in Disney Springs (20 points)

- Near Erin McKenna's Bakery NYC

Clue 19: Locate a Hidden Mickey on an outside wall.
2 points

- Morimoto Asia Restaurant

Clue 20: Check out the walls (outside and inside) for Hidden Mickeys.
3 points

- Chef Art Smith's Homecomin'

Clue 21: Study a mural on an outside wall of the restaurant for a Hidden Mickey.
5 points

- Enzo's Hideaway Tunnel Bar and Restaurant

Clue 22: After walking down the stairs, explore the tunnel approaching *Enzo's Hideaway* for a Hidden Mickey.
5 points

- Maria and Enzo's Restaurant

Clue 23: In a hallway near the lower-level seating area for *Maria and Enzo's Restaurant*, examine displays behind glass for a small Hidden Mickey.
5 points

Chapter 7: HTYon Scavenger Hunt

Disney Springs West Side (38 points)

- Cirque du Soleil

Clue 24: Look down for a Hidden Mickey in the sidewalk near the *Strawberry Parking Lot*.
5 points

Clue 25: Don't step on another sidewalk Mickey between *Cirque du Soleil* and *City Works Eatery & Pour House*!
5 points

- House of Blues

Clue 26: Search for a classic Mickey on the ceiling.
3 points

- Splitsville Luxury Lanes

Clue 27: Admire the mural inside on the lower level for Hidden Mickeys.
5 points for three different kinds of Mickey images

Clue 28: Find Mickey on a huge orange on the upper level.
3 points

Clue 29: Search the orange trees on the upper level.
4 points

- Disney's Candy Cauldron

Clue 30: Go inside to find a classic Mickey marking on a stone.
4 points

- Starbucks

Clue 31: Locate a Hidden Mickey on a wall in the seating area. (Tip: You may need to wait a few minutes for it to appear!)
4 points

- DisneyStyle Store

Clue 32: Look for a Hidden Mickey in the cement walkway near the *DisneyStyle* store.
5 points

Disney Springs Marketplace (94 points)

Entrance to the Marketplace

Clue 33: Study the green benches for Hidden Mickeys at the entrance and elsewhere around *Disney Springs Marketplace*.
2 points

- Disney's Wonderful World of Memories

Clue 34: Search for Mickey outside the store.
3 points

- Disney's Days of Christmas

Clue 35: Step inside and search for a Mickey made of rocks.
3 points

Clue 36: Find at least one classic Mickey on each of three large trees.
4 points total for at least one on each tree

Clue 37: Study the walls and carpet for classic Hidden Mickeys.
3 points for two or more

Clue 38: Take a good look at the ceiling in the rear room of the shop.
2 points

Clue 39: Admire an outside window of the store for subtle Hidden Mickeys.
3 points

Chapter 7: HTYon Scavenger Hunt

- *Goofy's Candy Co.*

Clue 40: Find Goofy and other characters on the wall.
4 points for three or more characters

- *Rainforest Cafe*

Clue 41: Look for Hidden Mickeys on the outdoor signs.
4 points for both

- *Sassagoula River Cruise ferry*

Clue 42: If you have time, take the *Sassagoula River Cruise* ferryboat to *Port Orleans—French Quarter*, disembark, and then ride the next boat back to *Disney Springs Marketplace*. During both your crossings, study the *Treehouse Villas* for Hidden Mickeys.
5 points for one or more

- *Marketplace Carousel*

Clue 43: Study the decorative inner and outer panels on the Carousel for four classic Mickeys.
5 points for spotting all four

- *Once Upon a Toy*
Note: This store sports numerous Mickeys and other Disney characters in the decor in addition to the Hidden Mickeys below.

Clue 44: Examine the interactive fountain near the store.
(Note: Two Hidden Mickeys are there all the time, a third appears only when the water is on.)
4 points for two, 5 points for spotting all three

Clue 45: Outside the main entrance, look for classic Mickeys with tires for ears.
2 points for one or more

Walt Disney World's Hidden Mickeys

Now enter the store.

Clue 46: Gaze up for classic Mickeys.
2 points for one or more

Clue 47: Check out the tops of merchandise stands. (Only some sport Hidden Mickeys.)
1 point for one or more

Clue 48: Now examine the center post of some of these stands.
1 point for one or more

Clue 49: Look at the upper beams of the wooden merchandise displays.
1 point for one or more

Clue 50: Now observe the bolts on those displays.
1 point for one or more

- *Disney's Pin Traders*

Clue 51: Spot a Hidden Mickey on a Mickey statue inside the store.
3 points

Clue 52: Find three Hidden Mickeys on Donald's statue.
5 points for all three

- *Tren-D*

Clue 53: Look around for classic Mickeys on the tops and sides of various merchandise tables in the store.
3 points for two or more

Clue 54: Spot a blue Hidden Mickey on the wall inside the store.
5 points

Clue 55: Search for a small Hidden Mickey on a door.
4 points

Clue 56: Smile at the initials of two Disney characters on a countertop!
5 points

Chapter 7: HTYon Scavenger Hunt

Clue 57: Locate Mickey circles on a countertop.
3 points

- Ghirardelli Soda Fountain & Chocolate Shop

Clue 58: Locate Mickey on a wall inside.
4 points

Near the lake

Clue 59: Spot Mickeys in the fence around the lake.
1 point

- World of Disney

Clue 60: Find light brown Mickeys outside the store.
2 points

Clue 61: Now find him on a wall near the restrooms.
3 points

- T-REX

Clue 62: Admire a classic Mickey in the bar area.
5 points

WDW Casting Center

Clue 63: Drive to the *Casting Center* building, across Buena Vista Drive from Disney Springs Marketplace, to locate more classic Mickeys. (These Hidden Mickeys can also be spotted from Interstate 4.)
3 points

Miniature Golf Courses (22 points)

You can find these Hidden Mickeys while you play the courses. Or you may be able to walk the courses without playing if it's not crowded, due to rain or luck. (Tell the attendants that you're hunting Hidden Mickeys and ask if you can take a look around.)

Walt Disney World's Hidden Mickeys

- *Fantasia Gardens* (4 points)
Clue 64: Check the tee-off areas.
1 point

Clue 65: Take a good look at the 12th hole on the *Gardens Course*.
3 points

- *Winter Summerland* (18 points)

Clue 66: Can you point to a Hidden Mickey at the check-in area?
3 points

Clue 67: Find Mickey on the 3rd hole of the *Winter Course*.
3 points

Clue 68: Now check around the 16th hole of the *Winter Course* for a Mickey Mouse gingerbread cookie.
2 points

Clue 69: Find Mickey and Minnie on the 16th hole of the *Summer Course*. (Psst! This Hidden Mickey is also visible from the 16th and 17th holes of the Winter Course.)
3 points for both

Clue 70: Look around for a gift box Hidden Mickey.
3 points

Clue 71: Wait for Mickey on the 17th hole of the *Winter Course*.
1 point

Clue 72: Study the Christmas tree on the 17th hole of the *Summer Course* for Hidden Mickeys.
3 points for three Hidden Mickeys

Near Epcot

Clue 73: You can only admire this huge classic Mickey made of *solar panels* from above with a Google Earth search. It sits near Disney's Yacht Club Resort.
5 points

Chapter 7: HTY on Scavenger Hunt

Near Celebration, Florida

Okay, I admit it, this Mickey isn't hidden. Just the opposite, in fact. But it is unique. So, I decided to include it anyway. You'll find a huge classic Mickey near Celebration, Florida, on the west side of *Interstate 4*.

Clue 74: Look for it as you get close to Exit 62.
4 points

Near the Magic Kingdom

Clue 75: From the air or with a Google Earth search, check out a lake shaped like a classic Mickey. It's south of the Transportation and Ticket Center.
5 points

Clue 76: Another classic Mickey, originally made of tree groves, can be seen from the air or with a Google Earth search. It's a few miles northwest of the Magic Kingdom. Good luck!
5 Points

**Total Points for
Hither, Thither & Yon Hunt =**

_____

How'd you do?
A perfect score for this hunt is 261. You may have done even better if you earned bonus points in ***ESPN Wide World of Sports***, ***Typhoon Lagoon***, and/or by spotting Hidden Characters on the ***Disney buses***.

You'll find a breakdown by area below, so that you can tally your score for only those places you've covered. Give yourself Gold if you scored at least 80% of available points, or Bronze if you scored at least 40%.

Magnolia Golf Course (5)

Vista Boulevard (3)

Walt Disney World's Hidden Mickeys

ESPN Wide World of Sports (10)

WDW Water Parks (46)
 - Blizzard Beach (15)
 - En route to Typhoon Lagoon (4)
 - Typhoon Lagoon (27)

The Landing in Disney Springs (20)
 - near Erin McKenna's Bakery NYC (2)
 - Morimoto Asia Restaurant (3)
 - Chef Art Smith's Homecomin' (5)
 - Enzo's Hideaway (5)
 - Maria and Enzo's Restaurant (5)

Disney Springs West Side (38)
 - Cirque du Soleil (10)
 - House of Blues (3)
 - Splitsville Luxury Lanes (12)
 - Disney's Candy Cauldron (4)
 - Starbucks (4)
 - DisneyStyle (5)

Disney Springs Marketplace (94)
 - Entrance to the Marketplace (2)
 -Disney's Wonderful World of Memories (3)
 - Disney's Days of Christmas (15)
 - Goofy's Candy Co. (4)
 - Rainforest Cafe (4)
 - Sassagoula River Cruise ferry (5)
 - Marketplace Carousel (5)
 - Once Upon a Toy (13)
 - Disney's Pin Traders (8)
 - Tren-D (20)
 -Ghirardelli Ice Cream & Chocolate Shop (4)
 - Near the lake (1)
 - World of Disney (5)
 - T-REX (5)

WDW Casting Center (3)

Miniature Golf Courses (22)
 - Fantasia Gardens (4)
 - Winter Summerland (18)

Near Epcot (5)

Near Celebration, Florida (4)

Near Magic Kingdom (10)

Chapter 7: HTYon Scavenger Hunt

Disney's Magnolia Golf Course

Hint 1: A sand trap at the sixth green is shaped like a classic Mickey.

Vista Boulevard

Hint 2: If you drive east from Fort Wilderness along Vista Boulevard, you can spot a sign for the *Golden Oak community* on your left. A classic Mickey is hidden in the tree of Golden Oak's logo.

ESPN Wide World of Sports

Hint 3: A three-dimensional Mickey Mouse looks out over the court from near the high central ceiling in *The Milk House* (the Field House). He's on an upper rafter above the sign, "The Milk House," in front of a yellow triangular wall partition that is opposite the main entrance. I spotted him to the upper left of the lower seats of section 104.

Hint 4: On some days, you may spot classic Mickey circles around the pitcher's mounds on the nearby *softball fields*.

Hint 5: Walk past Champion Baseball Stadium, the Field House, and several multi-purpose sports fields to the *Track and Field Complex* way in the back. A clever classic Mickey forms the base of the discus-throwing launch pad. (Tip: You can get a better vantage point for viewing this Mickey image by climbing up into the nearby bleachers.)

WDW Water Parks

- *Disney's Blizzard Beach*

Hint 6: Find a lighting fixture on the wall at the right rear of the *Beach Haus store* near the dressing rooms. There's a painting on the cover in which a small classic Mickey is formed by rocks at the lower center of an outdoor mountain scene.

Hint 7: As in many WDW shops, one or more of the merchandise stands has classic Mickey-shaped holes on its center pole.

Hint 8: From the *Chairlift* ride that takes you to the Mount Gushmore water slides, look to the ground on the second level of the mountain just past support pole #4 (counting from the beginning of the lift) and below the right side of your chairlift to spot a classic Mickey made of three round rocks. (Depending on the foliage, sometimes you can spot part of this rock Hidden Mickey from the left edge of the *Observation Deck* at the top of Mount Gushmore.)

Hint 9: At the rear of the park, a classic Mickey is formed by three stones jutting out from near the top edge of a stone bridge crossing *Cross Country Creek*. It's on the side of the bridge, near the center. A small triangular rock over this Hidden Mickey gives it the appearance of wearing a sorcerer's hat.
Tip: You can see this Mickey from the water

Chapter 7: HTYon Scavenger Hunt

or dry land. It's visible from the floating tubes as you approach the bridge by water. On land, you can see it through the trees (past the "*Runoff Rapids* Tube Pickup" area) either from just past the *Runoff Rapids* "Red Slope" entrance sign or from several points on the walkway on the other side of the bridge.

En Route to Typhoon Lagoon

Hint 10: Classic Mickey holes are in the railing around the white *Disney Vacation Club (DVC)* tower that stands to the left of Buena Vista Drive at its intersection with Bonnet Creek Parkway.

- *Disney's Typhoon Lagoon*

Hint 11: Tip Boards with wait times written in chalk are situated around *Typhoon Lagoon*. If there is zero wait time for an attraction, the zero is drawn in the shape of a classic Mickey. (These images come and go.)

Hint 12: The *Board Room* is a shack on a small deck at the front of the surfing lagoon. On the right wall inside the *Board Room* is a painting of an alligator holding a surfboard. In the middle of the sand dune behind the alligator, impressions in the sand come together as a classic Mickey.

Hint 13: At *Crush 'n' Gusher,* on the upper floor near the elevator, paint circles on the cement form a classic Mickey.

Hint 14: Mickey ears are at the bottom of a vertical strut in the railing of a bridge. You can see the ears if you enter *Castaway Creek* near *Typhoon Tilly's* and look behind you as you float under the first bridge. The ears are toward the right side of the bridge. You can also usually see the ears if you walk downstream on either side of the creek and look back at the bridge.

Hint 15: About halfway up the wooden steps to the *Storm Slides,* and past the stranded motorboat on the right side of the path, Mickey ears are on the left side of a walkway slat.

Hint 16: Near the end of the long trail up to *Humunga Kowabunga*, three of the last short logs in the ground under the rope fence to the left of the walkway form an upside-down classic Mickey when viewed from above. (Note: You may spot other groups of short logs in the ground along walkways that resemble classic Mickeys.)

Hint 17: You'll find a classic Mickey formed by cannonballs along *Castaway Creek*. He's on your left by the second cannon past the waterfall if you're drifting in the creek. If you're walking on the nearby trail, you'll see him just past *Forgotten Grotto* in the rear of the park as you walk alongside the drifters. (Sometimes this cannonball image is moved around in this area.)

Hint 18: In the walk-through cave at the rear of *Ketchakiddee Creek*, there is a classic Mickey impression in the rock. It's on the back wall of the cave, about one and a half feet up from the ground, and near the drain at the right side of the cave as you enter the cave from the water.

The Landing in Disney Springs

- Near *Erin McKenna's Bakery NYC*

Hint 19: Stand in front of a large wall painting advertising "Famous Florida Citrus." At the lower right section of the painting, three small oranges are close together and simulate a classic Hidden Mickey.

- *Morimoto Asia Restaurant*

Hint 20: In the metal designs on the exterior walls of *Morimoto Asia Restaurant*, Hidden Mickeys are randomly mixed in with other Japanese symbols. They light up at night! Also, as you enter the restaurant, study the walls to your left. Three dark circles are

Chapter 7: HTYon Scavenger Hunt

painted high on a wall behind the right side of the drink bar. This classic Hidden Mickey is repeated in other places on the inside walls.

- *Chef Art Smith's Homecomin' Restaurant*

Hint 21: On a rear outside wall of the restaurant is a "Jasper Family Farms" mural with a bucking horse. A faint dark marking on the horse's rear left thigh is shaped like a classic Mickey. This mural is best viewed from a nearby bridge.

- *Enzo's Hideaway*

Hint 22: High on a wall along a corridor to *Enzo's Hideaway*, a black musical note is drawn as a tiny classic Hidden Mickey!

- *Maria and Enzo's Restaurant*

Hint 23: In a display behind glass situated in a hallway near the lower-level seating area for *Maria and Enzo's Restaurant*, a white classic Hidden Mickey is stuck on the front middle of an airplane propeller. The airplane sits on the middle shelf of the display.

Disney Springs West Side

- *Cirque du Soleil*

Hint 24: A classic Mickey is etched in the sidewalk near *Cirque du Soleil,* on the second slab back from the *Strawberry Parking Lot*, just past a manhole cover and near the grass.

Hint 25: A classic Hidden Mickey made of pebbles is embedded in the cement in the middle of the main West Side promenade/walkway, between *Cirque du Soleil* and *City Works Eatery & Pour House*.

- *House of Blues*

Hint 26: Walk through the front door and

down the right-side aisle. A classic Mickey is on the ceiling past the first server's station.

- *Splitsville Luxury Lanes*

Hint 27: In the right wall mural inside the main entrance on the lower level, you can see the Mickey Earful Tower, balloons with Mickey ears, and classic Mickey holes in a red bowling ball.

Hint 28: On the upper level near the escalator, holes form a classic Mickey in a huge "orange" in the left wall mural.

Hint 29: A few classic Mickeys are formed by groups of oranges in trees in the upper-level left wall mural.

- *Disney's Candy Cauldron*

Hint 30: Inside the store, on the upper wall above the candy display, a dark marking on a stone near the ceiling forms a classic Hidden Mickey.

- *Starbucks*

Hint 31: On a wall inside the seating area, an interactive electronic screen periodically allows you to draw inside white picture frames. Classic Mickeys are in the corners of a frame at the top middle of the screen.

- *DisneyStyle Store*

Hint 32: A classic Hidden Mickey made of pebbles is embedded in the cement of the main West Side promenade/walkway in front of the *DisneyStyle* store. It's in the middle of the walkway, near the curving line of gray, rectangular cement sections.

Disney Springs Marketplace

Entrance to the Marketplace

Hint 33: Green benches with classic Mickey emblems on the top and sides are scattered

Chapter 7: HTYon Scavenger Hunt

around the *Marketplace* and the interactive fountain.

- Disney's Wonderful World of Memories

Hint 34: The sign on the store contains a full-figure Hidden Mickey on the page of a book.

- Disney's Days of Christmas

Hint 35: A large dark brown circular rock and two smaller rocks for "ears" form a classic Mickey on the middle side of the "chimney" inside the store. You'll see Dalmatians on the mantelpiece around this chimney.

Hint 36: Inside the shop, three large trees surrounded by merchandise have classic Mickeys carved in their bark near the tops of their trunks. The trees are not Christmas trees, and each of the three has one or two Mickey carvings.

Hint 37: Various sections of wallpaper and carpet often hide classic Mickeys.

Hint 38: In the rear room of the shop, classic Mickeys hide in the scrollwork on the ceiling.

Hint 39: At the corners of the store's far right outside windows that look toward the *Marketplace Carousel*, subtle classic Hidden Mickeys are in snowflakes.

- Goofy's Candy Co.

Hint 40: Goofy, Mickey Mouse, Pluto, and other characters hide in the light brown mural on the upper wall around the store.

- Rainforest Cafe

Hint 41: A green lizard on the large sign outside *Rainforest Cafe* has an upside-down classic Mickey in the middle of the circles on its neck. On the smaller sign at the left of the cafe entrance, the lizard's mid-neck classic Mickey is tilted sideways to the left.

- Sassagoula River Cruise ferry

Hint 42: From the Marketplace boat dock, take the ferryboat to *Port Orleans—French Quarter* and then back to *Disney Springs Marketplace*. Both ways, spot small white classic Mickeys in some of the *Treehouse Villas'* windows.

- Marketplace Carousel

Hint 43: At least four classic Mickeys are hiding on the inner and outer decorative panels on the *Carousel* near Disney's Days of Christmas store. (You may find more than four Mickey images, but these are the ones I like best.)
 - A blue classic Mickey is on the sign under Minnie Mouse.
 - Two light green classic Mickeys, tilted slightly to the right, hide on the dragon's nose. (For the best view of the dragon, check out an inner panel on the ceiling above the riders.)
 - Two tiny classic Mickeys hide on the pink window awnings on the right side of the panel that shows part of a store from a distance. You'll see blue umbrellas on the left side of this panel.
 - Pink classic Mickeys formed of roses hide in the upper part of the panels in the center of the Carousel.

- Once Upon a Toy

Hint 44: In the interactive flat fountain near the *Once Upon a Toy* store, water-tube heads are shaped like classic Mickeys, recessed lights in the cement are arranged in a classic Mickey shape, and the fountain water collects into a huge classic Mickey on the cement!

Hint 45: Outside the store's main entrance, classic Mickeys are formed by truck tires (the "ears") atop Lincoln Logs.

Hint 46: As you enter the store, classic Mickey pincers or clamps (holding toys) circulate on a track that hangs from the ceiling.

Chapter 7: HTYon Scavenger Hunt

Hint 47: Tinker Toys on top of merchandise stands around the store form classic Mickeys.

Hint 48: Along the center post of some of these merchandise stands, you'll find small classic Mickey holes.

Hint 49: The centers of the upper beams on wooden merchandise displays sport classic Mickey shapes.

Hint 50: On the same merchandise displays, large wing nuts on some of the bolts form Mickey ears.

- *Disney's Pin Traders*

Hint 51: On the large statue of Mickey and Minnie, Mickey wears a classic Mickey pin on his tie.

Hint 52: On Donald's statue, a red, white, and blue classic Mickey pin is on the upper right side of Donald's duffel bag. You'll find a second classic Mickey—a red one—at the front of Donald's purple suitcase, on the inside of one of the black Mickey-shaped pins spilling out of the suitcase.

-*Tren-D*

Hint 53: Look for Hidden (and decorative) classic Mickeys on the merchandise tables in the store. You can find decent Hidden Mickeys on the tops and sides of various tables.

Hint 54: A blue paint-splash classic Mickey is high on the wall inside the store near the entrance from the *Marketplace Co-Op*. If you enter the store from the main promenade, the image is on the upper wall to the right.

Hint 55: A yellow side profile of Mickey Mouse is at the top—maybe it's the clasp?—of Minnie's handbag. Minnie is painted on a "Cast Members Only" door at the rear of the store.

Hint 56: On the check-out countertop to the right as you enter from the outside promenade, smile at a reference to Mickey and Minnie. On the side closest to the main entrance, and near the angle of the countertop, "MM+ MM" is carved into the counter.

Hint 57: Near the end of the left side of the check-out countertop, circle impressions form a classic Mickey. (The circles are all the same size, but this image is accepted by guests and Cast Members as a Hidden Mickey.)

- *Ghirardelli Soda Fountain* & *Chocolate Shop*

Hint 58: A dark side-profile image of Mickey looking to the left appears as a shadow in a painting on a rear wall of the shop (to the left as you enter). Look for a streetcar in the painting. The shadow is in the streetcar's second window from the left.

Near the lake

Hint 59: Several sections of the green fence around the lake and in other areas of Disney Springs Marketplace have repeating classic Mickeys near the top of the railing.

- *World of Disney*

Hint 60: Light brown classic Mickeys can be found near the tops of the columns outside the store.

Hint 61: Near the restrooms at the far end of the store (closest to The Landing), a picture frame on the wall is lined with small classic Mickeys.

- *T-REX*

Hint 62: Just inside the entrance and over the bar, a pink classic Mickey hides on the body of an octopus across from a green praying mantis.

Chapter 7: HTYon Scavenger Hunt

WDW Casting Center

Hint 63: Classic Mickey holes can be seen in the upper outside walls of the *Casting Center* building. (These Hidden Mickeys can also be spotted from Interstate 4.)

WDW Miniature Golf Courses

- Fantasia Gardens

Hint 64: The tee-off areas on both courses are marked with classic Mickeys.

Hint 65: On the *Gardens Course*, the green at the 12th hole is shaped like a classic Mickey.

- Winter Summerland

Hint 66: Several classic Mickey ornaments hang in the decorations over both sides of the check-in area.

Hint 67: On the 3rd hole of the *Winter Course*, candy canes, milk, and gingerbread men pop out of "Defrosty" (the cooler). One is a gingerbread cookie featuring Mickey ears.

Hint 68: A Mickey Mouse gingerbread cookie pokes out from a stocking hanging on the right side of the mantelpiece on the 16th hole of the *Winter Course*.

Hint 69: On the left side of the 16th hole of the *Summer Course*, small Mickey and Minnie figurines are sitting in a sleigh on the mantelpiece, along with Pluto. Since the 16th holes of both courses are close together, this mantelpiece is also visible from the 16th and 17th holes of the *Winter Course*.

Hint 70: On the 16th (and 17th) hole of the Winter Course, you'll walk past a blue and yellow gift box. On the top of the box, a yellow candy glob in the middle and two yellow suns (for "ears") come together as a classic Mickey.

Hint 71: Mickey pops out of the present on the 17th hole of the *Winter Course* when you putt the ball under the gift box. This Mickey is big, but he is hiding most of the time!

Hint 72: At least three classic Mickey ornaments hang on the Christmas tree at the 17th hole of the *Summer Course*.

Near Epcot

Hint 73: Solar panels at the *solar panel farm* near Disney's Yacht Club Resort are arranged as a huge classic Mickey. Not visible from the ground, you can admire the image from the air or with Google Earth (28° 24" N, 81° 45" W).

Near Celebration, Florida

Hint 74: On the west side of *Interstate 4*, south of exit 62 near Celebration, you'll find a huge classic Mickey atop an electrical transmission line pole.

Near the Magic Kingdom

Hint 75: A classic Mickey lake, south of the Transportation and Ticket Center, is visible from the air or with Google Earth (28° 45" N, 81° 42" W).

Hint 76: A few miles northwest of the Magic Kingdom, a huge green classic Mickey, originally made of groves of trees, can be seen from the air with Google Earth (28° 07" N, 81° 10" W). The Hidden Mickey is in a field just off Highway 27. This Hidden Mickey may disappear.

Chapter 8

Other Mickey Appearances

• • • • • •

These Hidden Mickeys won't earn you any points, but you're bound to enjoy them if you're in the right place at the right time to see them.

* Look for holiday Hidden Mickeys if you're at WDW during the Christmas season or any major holiday.

* Other "Hidden" Mickeys-decor and deliberate-appear with some regularity throughout WDW. Notice the Mickster on popcorn buckets, WDW brochures, maps and flags, Cast Member name tags, guestroom keys, pay telephones and phone books, menus, and restaurant and store receipts. The restaurants sometimes offer classic Mickey butter and margarine pats, pancakes and waffles, pizzas and pasta, as well as Mickeys on napkins and food trays. They also arrange dishes and condiments to form classic Mickeys, and some condiment containers are shaped like Mickey. You might notice classic Mickey holes in the backs of some highchairs.

Many road signs on WDW Resort property sport Mickey ears and classic Mickey images, and WDW vehicles and monorails have Mickey Mouse images and insignia.

Cleaning personnel will often spray the ground, windows, furniture, and other items with three circles of cleaning solution (a classic Mickey) before the final cleansing.

Walt Disney World's Hidden Mickeys

Or they may leave three wet Mickey Mouse circles or other Disney character images on the pavement after mopping! Mickey even decorates manhole covers, survey markers, and utility covers in the ground, as you've probably already found out for yourself on some of the scavenger hunts. In the evenings, you may encounter Mickey spotlight images on the pavement or on outside walls near WDW attractions.

Enjoy all these Mickeys as you explore WDW. And if you want to take some home with you, rest assured that you can always find "Hidden" Mickeys on souvenir mugs, merchandise bags and boxes, T-shirts, and Christmas tree ornaments sold in the Disney World shops. So even when you're far away from WDW, you can continue to enjoy Hidden Mickeys.

Note: There are usually some especially good Hidden Mickeys on souvenir mugs—tiny and hard to spot. The mug designs change periodically, and every time Disney unveils a new design, the Hidden Mickeys change.

Chapter 9

My Favorite Hidden Mickeys

• • • • • •

In this book, I've described over 1,130 Hidden Mickeys at Walt Disney World. I enjoy every one of them, but the following are extra special to me. They're special because of their uniqueness, their deep camouflage (which makes them especially hard to find), or the "Eureka!" response they elicit when I spot them—or any combination of the above. Here then are my Top Ten Hidden Mickeys and, not far behind, Ten Honorable Mentions. I apologize to you if your favorite Hidden Mickey is not (yet) on the lists below.

My Top Ten

1. Once-a-Year Mickey. **Under the Sea – Journey of The Little Mermaid**, Fantasyland, Magic Kingdom. Each year around noon on Mickey Mouse's birthday (November 18), sunlight shines through holes in the rock to form a classic Mickey on the wall of the inside entrance queue. Stay alert because Mickey might show up here at other times of the year! (Chap. 2, Clue 100)

2. Fern Mickey. **The Garden Grill restaurant**, The Land, Epcot. This Mickey hides behind a fern in the big mural inside the restaurant. When I outline this Mickey (a Cast Member often helps me by handing me a broom to reach it and then highlighting it with a flashlight), I have witnessed folks in the restaurant smile and shout, "I see him! Look, there's Mickey!" (Chap. 3, Clue 103)

3. Star Wars. **Millennium Falcon: Smugglers Run**, Star Wars: Galaxy's Edge, Disney's Hollywood Studios. A tiny model of the Millennium Falcon hidden on the real Millennium Falcon starship. Awesome Hidden Image—Han Solo would be proud! (Chap. 4, Clue 33)

4. Jafar Rock. ***Gorilla Falls Exploration Trail***, Africa, Disney's Animal Kingdom. This three-dimensional head of Jafar is one of the most remarkable sculpted characters you'll see anywhere on Disney property. (Chap. 5, Clue 57)

5. Steamboat Willie Mickey. ***Under the Sea - Journey of The Little Mermaid***, Fantasyland, Magic Kingdom. The Imagineers sculpted Mickey in his Steamboat Willie persona on a series of large rocks at the exit of the attraction. It's a tour de force in the world of Hidden Mickeys! (Chap. 2, Clue 110)

6. Roof Mickey. ***Disney's Contemporary Resort***. Sitting on the edge of the roof of a backstage building next to the Contemporary Resort, this playful Mickey welcomes you to the Magic Kingdom. When you're on the monorail, show this Mickey to fellow travelers so they can join in the fun! (Chap. 6, Clue 230)

7. Mickey in cement. Near **Astro Orbiter**, Tomorrowland, Magic Kingdom. A classic Mickey, lightly traced in cement, is growing more faint with time. Hard to find, but worth the effort! (Chap. 2, Clue 149)

8. Beam Mickey. ***Disney's Boulder Ridge Villas***. Mickey peeks out of a hole in an overhead beam in the *Villas lobby*. Outstanding effect! Most folks don't even know he's up there, hiding! (Chap. 6, Clue 192)

Chapter 9: My Favorite Hidden Mickeys

9. Grim Reaper Mickey. **Haunted Mansion**, Liberty Square, Magic Kingdom. A classic, this wonderful Mickey image has survived refurbishments and seems even better and spookier than ever! (Chap. 2, Clue 87)

10. Purple Tile Mickey. **Disney's Polynesian Village Resort**. A classic Mickey in tile hides on the counter of the *Kona Island coffee and sushi bar*. This one's a real winner, especially when you get to point it out to folks who've never seen it. It's hiding in plain sight! (Chap. 6, Clue 207)

Ten Honorable Mentions

1. Silhouette Mickey. **Splash Mountain**, Frontierland, Magic Kingdom. Keep your eyes peeled for this fleeting image of Mickey's head and ears that appears for just a second. Don't blink! (Chap. 2, Clue 44)

2. 3-D Volcano Mickey. **Toy Story Mania!**, Toy Story Land, Disney's Hollywood Studios. While you're racking up points in the game, stay alert for this Hidden Mickey behind the target balloons. A convincing 3-D effect! (Chap. 4, Clue 48)

3. Sorcerer Mickey. At the rear of **Disney's Blizzard Beach**, Sorcerer Mickey is formed by stones jutting out from a bridge over *Cross Country Creek*. Very clever! (Chap. 7, Clue 9)

4. Globe Mickey. **Disney's Yacht Club Resort**. The lobby greeter will gladly give you hints if you have trouble spotting this great classic Mickey. It's faint and well-hidden! (Chap. 6, Clue 154)

5. Aquarium Rock Mickey. **The Seas with Nemo & Friends**, World Nature, Epcot. At the bottom of the aquarium lies one (or more) classic Mickeys formed of rocks. Cast Members (and guest divers) do a great job of maintaining these images. (Chap. 3, Clue 110)

6. Moniker Mickey. **Sunset Boulevard**, Disney's Hollywood Studios. Stamped in the cement sidewalk are references to the year Mickey was "born," 1928, and his very first name, "Mortimer." A cool homage to the Main Mouse! (Chap. 4, Clue 139)

7. Vine Mickey. **Disney's Animal Kingdom Lodge**. This green side-profile Mickey hides on the vine-covered column outside the rear lobby doors. Well-camouflaged and hard to find, but fun to spot. (Chap. 6, Clue 7)

8. Mickey in the Street. **Main Street, U.S.A.**, Magic Kingdom. A properly proportioned classic Mickey is impressed in the side street, and countless folks walk over it, unaware. Don't tread on Mickey! (Chap. 2, Clue 186)

9. Bioluminescent Mickey. **Avatar Flight of Passage**, Pandora - The World of Avatar, Disney's Animal Kingdom. Appearing several times along the entrance queue and once on the ride, this unearthly classic Mickey invites us to experience a lush, foreign world that amazes our senses. (Chap. 5, Clues 1, 2, and 5)

10. Solar Mickey. **Near Disney's Yacht Club**. Mickey generates energy for us at his *solar panel farm*. Not visible from the ground, you can admire the image from the air or with Google Earth (28° 24" N, 81° 45" W). (Chap. 7, Clue 73)

Chapter 10

Don't Stop Now!

Hidden Mickey mania is contagious. The benign pastime of searching out Hidden Mickeys has escalated into a bona fide vacation mission for many Walt Disney World fans. I'm proud to include myself among them. Searching for images of the Main Mouse can enhance a solo trip to the parks or a vacation for the entire family. Little ones delight in spotting and greeting Mickey Mouse characters in the parks and restaurants. As children grow, the Hidden Mickey game is a natural evolution of their fondness for the Mouse.

Join the search! With alert eyes and mind, you can spot Hidden Mickey classics and new Hidden Mickeys just waiting to be found. Even beginners have happened upon a new, unreported Hidden Mickey or two. As new attractions open and older ones get refurbished, new Hidden Mickeys await discovery.

It may be just my imagination, but I swear that every time I visit Walt Disney World, I spot a Hidden Mickey up in the clouds, watching over his domain! Do you think the Imagineers might actually have some influence on the atmosphere over Walt Disney World?

The Disney entertainment phenomenon is unique in many ways, and Hidden Mickey mania is one manifestation of Disney's universal appeal. Join in the fun! Maybe I'll see you at Walt Disney World, marveling (like me) at these Hidden Gems. They're waiting patiently for you to discover them.

Acknowledgements

No Hidden Mickey hunter works alone. While I've discovered many of the Hidden Mickeys in this book on my own—and personally verified every one of them—finding Hidden Mickeys is an ongoing group effort. I am indebted to the following Hidden Mickey seekers for alerting me to a number of Hidden Mickeys I might otherwise have missed. Thanks to each and every one of you for putting me on the track of one or more of these WDW treasures and, in some cases, also helping me to verify them. Extra special thanks to *Sharon Dale* for spotting over 240 Hidden Mickeys and to *Jesse Kline* for finding over 100 of these elusive gems!

Names in bold have spotted 10 or more. Visit my website, www.HiddenMickeyGuy.com, to enjoy newly discovered Hidden Mickeys.

Candi A., Maxine A., Nancy A., Frank Abbamonte, Scott Abney, Alex Abrahamzon, Debbie Acres, Jonah Adams, Kaitlyn Rae Adams, Ron Adams, Sarah Adams, The Adornettos, **Nancy Ahlsen,** Holly Ahronheim, Michael Akers, Lindsey Albrecht, Sabaheta Alek-Finkelman, James Algatt, Katie Allen, Matt Allgaier, Anthony Almeyda, Jordan Altug, Brianna Alvarez, Eric and Danielle Ambielli, Cathy Ames, John Ames, Jonah Amundsen, Mariah Amundsen, Amy Amyot, Alex Anderson, Chelsea Anderson, Michelle Anderson, Robert Anderson, AJ Angeline, Debbie Anschuetz, Robert Anschuetz, Sarah Anzjon, Kristin Archibald, Brittany Arentz, Elena Argaluza, Debbie Armstrong, Jason and Tammy and Lily Armstrong, Stanley Arnold, Jennifer Ashley, Mark and Dean Ashwaite, Michelle Astuti, Tacey Atkinson, **Attractions Magazine,** Chloe Augustine, Barb B., Dan B., Devon B., Ian B., Jason B., Jessica B., Andrew Babb, Ryan Bachman, Priscilla Baer, Sarah Bagwell, Tony and Matthew and Caroline and Stephanie Banzer, Salina Barbosa, Angie Barclay and kids, Mark Barnes, Sarah Barnes

Acknowledgements

and son, Daniel Barrach, Mario Barrozo, Corey Barrett, Gracen Barrett, Steven Madison Barrett, Vickie Barrett, Chris Barry, Diana Barry, Diane Barry, Samantha Barry, Anthony Bartiromo, Nicholas Bartoli, Johnny Bartolomeo, Fred Bastien, **James Baublitz,** Sarah Baywell, Penny and Jeff Beam, Eric Beaulieu, Adam Beauregard, Mike Beckerman, Brittany and Craig Bedelyon, Jonathan Beer, Faye Bedford, The Beesinger Family, Leila Beikmohamadi, **April Beisser,** Heather Beland, **Annmarie and David and Josh and Rick Benavidez,** Rich Benneau, Lauren Benson, Steve and Colleen and Michaela and Amanda Benson, The Benson Family, Richard Bent, Clark Benton, Jeffrey Berg, Patti Berg, Bryan and Stacy and Jenna and Barry Berger, Jason Berrang, Terry Berringer, David Berry, **David and Celia Berset,** Jenny Bess, Kristen Bevacqua, Tom Binder, Andy Birkett, Murray Bishop, Roberta Blackburn, Mark Blackie, **Erin Blackwell,** Trevor Blair, Louis Blanco, Isabel and Jeff Blank, **Nancy Blevins**, Edward Bliss, Fred Block, Laurie and Rebecca Bloodworth, The Bodmann Family, Jennifer Bogdan, **Tyler and Brandie Bolton,** Rich Bonneau, Michael Bonnett, Jr., Kevin Booton, Storie Borgman, Katie Borland, Craig Boudreaux, Jim Bougor, Ed Bouligny, Alicia Bourne, Wendy Bowen, The Bowles Family, Holly Bowling, Elizabeth Bowman, Alex Bowman, Nicole Bowman, Brooke Boyd, Donna Brackin, Alan Brainard, Shane Braisdell, Brent Brandon, Tina Brannen, Leyla Brborich, Todd Breakey, David Breede, Matthew Brennan, J. Bridge, Christine Bristow, Erin Broadbent, Patrick Broaddus, Ryan Brock, Colin Brooks, **Larry E. and Tanya Brooks,** Stuart Brooks, Daniel Brookwell, Stephen Brookwell, Chrissy Brown, Jaye Brown, Jeff Brown, Karen Brown and daughter, Peter Brown, Roberta Brown, The Brown Family, Emily Brubaker, John and Susan P. Bruederle, Paul Brune and family, Gabriella and Thierry and Matthieu Bruxelle, Erica Bryant, The Buaas Family, Cheryl Buchanan, Matt Buchanan and son, Justin Bucks, Earl

Burbridge, Liesa Buren, Nancy Burke, Lisa Burleson, Todd Busby, Jon Bushee, Brett Butcher, Ruth Butler and daughter, Giovanni C., Shari C., Kimberly Cabral, Villa Cadlle, Bret Caldwell, **Peter Caldwell,** Kerri Callahan, Sarah Callanan, Abigail Campbell, Anne Campbell, David Campbell, Lisa Campbell, Rob and Annabel Campbell, Michael-Lindsay-Alex and Hailey Campe, Craig Canady, Jason Cannons, Todd Carballo, Stan Carder, Chris Carlson, Cedric Caron, Deborah Carpenter, Gary Carr, James Carraher, K. A. Carter, Kacey Cassette, Robbie Castro, Lily Caswell, Jade and Dominic Cavalco, Alexis Cavileer, Mary Anne Ceci, Christina Cella, Kelly Challand, **Jessica Champoux**, Austin Chanu, J. Chappa, Julie Chappa, Chloe Charette, Jim Cheslin, Catherine Chiarello, Nikki Christensen, Dana Christos, Alyssa Ciaccio, Vito Ciaccio, Andrew Ciampi, Michael Ciampi, Samantha Ciampi, AnneMarie L. Clanton and family, Jay Andy Clark, Matt Clarke, Matthew Clemons, Malcolm Cleveland, John Clover, Lizzie Cochran, Alexa Cohen, Serena Anne Cohen, Zach Cohen, Rob Coile and daughter, Elizabeth Coler, John Coliton, Kent Collins, **Mary Jo Collins,** Michael Collins, William and Colleen Colmenares, Jason Colpitts, Eleanor Coltman, Greg Conlin, Joey Connors, Jeffrey Contompasis, Lindsay Contreras, Timmy Coogan, Ian Cordle, Cheryl Costello, Colleen Costello, Calvin Cotanche, Bill Cote, Sherrie Cotton, Angela Coutavas, Sara Cox, Karen Crabtree, David Craig, Allison Crawford, George Crippen, Rob Croskery, Lydia and Michael Cross, Catherine Crouch, Gary Cruise, Halley Crum, Denise and Tyler and Ashley Cruz, Kasie Culp, Erica Culver, Nancy Curl, Brian Currier, Traci Curth, Aiden D., Curtis D., Katie D., Nick D., Tyler Daganzo, Marie and Bruce Daigneault, Alicia Dakins, **Sharon and Chloe Dale,** John Anthony D' Alotto, Christina Dorce and brother, Jim Darling, Christopher Dash, Frankie DaSilva, Alex Davessar, David Davies, Shannon DeAraujo, Anthony Dearman, Alexander de Armas, Bob Decker, Keenan DeFrisco, Amy Degenstein,

Acknowledgements

Dwayne Degler, Michele DeGrace, Pam De Guzman and daughter, Bethany and Christine Delaurentis, Robert Delgado, Sarah Del Grande, Steph Del Grande, Dottie Del Signore, Mike Demopoulos, Jacob DePriest, Michael DeRose, Stephen DeSanto, Marcel Despres, Rich DeTeresa, Wanda Deveau, **Tim and Karen Devine,** Dania Dewese, Sondra Dewey, James Dezern, The DiBenedetto Family, Cara Di Cicco, Jennifer Dickey, Mary DiEuliis, The Digon Family, Doug Dillard, James and Jennifer DiMaggio, Suzannah DiMarzio, Max Dinan, Sam Dinan, Mark Dingman, Mario DiPlacido, Alexander Disney, Karen Dodson, Calvin Dolsay, Gina Dorkins, Marcus Dorothy, Michael Doucette, Jim Doyle, Sarah Dozert, Kelsey Draves, Dave Drumheller, Dave Drylie, Laura Dubberly, Jim Dufek, Angelica Dufer, James Duggan, Joey Duggan, Tom Durr, Abby Dwyer, Alex Dwyer, Ian Dwyer, Robert E., Jamillia Ear, John Early, Joy and Abigail Eats, Jason Ebels, Linda Eckwerth, Susan Edgington, The Familie Edmondson, Erik Edstrom, Seth Edward, Nicholas Elardo, M. Eldred, Amber Ellis, Karen Ellis, John Emmert, Eric England, Lillie England, Ben English, David and Elizabeth Epley, Kelly and Kimberly Erickson, Michael Ethridge, Nick Exley, Larissa F., Eric Fabian, Alyson Fair, Nick Falco, Adam Fanjoy, Ken Fanti, Marcos Faria, Parker Faria, Ashley Fayett, Ronald and Gianna Fazio, Joshua and Krystina Fears, Gracie and Jamie Fenton, Alan and Craig Fergus, Ronald Ferraco, Kathy Fetters, Dom Fiandra, Kenney Fichter, Jim Finley, John Finley, Elaine Finnigan, Ashley Rae Fischer, Matthew Flaherty, Dennis Flath, Michelle Flege, Kendra Fleming, Chelsey Flood, Sharon Flood, Jessica Flowers, Anthony Flynn, Dave Flynn, Stephanie Foley, Taylor Fong, Carlos Font, Melissa and Jacob Forbes, Mario Forcellati, Eldon J. Forcey, Chet Ford, Terry Foreacre, Joseph Fortenbaugh, Mark Fowle, Joe Franceschino, Sr. and Joe and Diane Franceschino, Gianna Francis, Jessica and Brent Fraser, Debbie Frazier, Eden Frazier, Matt Freeman, Connie Freese, Jordyn

Freiermuth, T.J. Frey, Eli Fried, Devon Friedman, Rachel Friedman, Rebecca Friedman, Ryan and Fairen Frisinger, Chip Froelich, Jake Fruci, Anna and April and Anthony Fuchs, Diane Furtado, Shane G., Aiden Gaddis, Eric Gagnon, Jackie Gailey, Mandy Gainey and family, Michelle Gala, **Jason Gall,** Jack Gallaher, Dave Gallant, Chrystine Gallegos, Jake Galloway, Justine Gamale, Traci Garber, Traci Gardellis, Brad Garfinkel, Marilyn Garfinkel, Scott Garland, Gunnar Garner, Tony Garon, Melissa Garrigus, Kristen Gartrell, Terry and Julia Garvey, Ryan Gatewood, Christy Gattis, Adam Geaneas, Anthony Gentile, Austin George, Cole Gershkovich, Rick Giancarlo, Pauline Gibson, Kaela and Ryan and Jake Gilbert, Ethan Giles, Owen Gilley, Alana Girard, Grayson Girard, **James Girard**, Julian Girard, Lincoln Girard, Chris Glass, Ryan Glynn, **Tyler Glynn,** Chase Goeser, Mark Goldhaber, Nathan Goley, Jeremiah Good, Ty Goode, Andrew Goodwill, Jack Goodwill, June Goodwill, William Goodwill, Vanessa Gordon, Trevor Goren, James and Edward Goring, Alyssa Gormish, Ryan Goukler, The Groebner Children, Josh Graham, Michele Gramm, Jeff and Joyce Grant, Stacy and Gavin Grasley, Todd Grasley, Tim Grassey, Dani Gray, Jim Greenhouse, Mark Greenwald, Rick Gregg, Adam Gregorich, Bill Griffin, George Griffin, Robert Grohman, Werner Grundlingh, Louis C. Guidry, Lorri Gumanow, Amanda Gunn, Elizabeth Gutman, Ryan Gutzat, Chris and Cindy H., Christine H., Cindy H., Rick Haas, Daniel Hadden, Evan Hade, The Hade Family, Brandi Hall, Byron Hall, Gracie and Dana Hall, Lydia Hall, Melanie Hall, Michael Halverson, Mike Hamilton, Shannon Hamilton, Jennifer Hammond, Theresa Hamway, James Hansen, Jake Hardin, Elsa Harding, Donna Hardter, Ray Harkness, Ed Harriger, Stephen Harris, Alan Harrison, Beth Harrison, **Stephanie Harrison,** Brian Harshberger, Grant Hart and brother, David Hartzell, Bernice Hasher, Laura and Ross Haston, Bryan Hauser, Mike Hawkins, Tara Hawley, Abbi Hawthorne, Debbie

Acknowledgements

Hayden, Colin Healy, Sean Heard, Ryan Hecht, Mary Heidenberg, Kurt Heinecke, Haley Heintz, Claudia and Ralph Hemsley, Carrie Henderson, Sean Hendrix, Brian Henry, Denise Hernandez, Liz Hernandez, Otto Hernandez, Louise Herrick, **Iris and Zachary Herron,** Nathaniel Hershberger, Amanda Hertel, Jennifer Hess, Ricky Hett, Tobias Heyn, Meredith Hiatt, Beth Higginbotham, Aaron Hill, Jamie Lee Hindes, Jim Hines, Joan Hinkle, Mark Hitt, Jay Hobson, Matt Hochberg, Rick Hoefinghoff, Ed Hoffman, Paul Hoffman, Denise Hoffmann, sdmt Hogan, Chip Holland, Vivian Holland, Matt Holley, Michael Hollingsworth, Joyce Holroyd, Melanie Holtsman, Jamie Holz, Craig Hood, Deonna Hores, Jenny Horn, Jasmine Horning, Evelyn Horton, Noah Howard, Patrick Howard, Kim Howe, Jonathan Hoyle, Erik Hubbard, Josh Hudson, Keith Hudson, Tony Hudson, Emily and Lynette Huey, Elton Hughes, Brennan Huizinga, Amy Hunt, William Huntley, Kaitlyn Husak, Cameron Hutt, The Huwar and Fabanich Family, **Bill and Donna ladonisi,** Ed Igoe, Dawn and Megan Ilsley, The Ilsley Family, Alex Inman, Andy Inserra, Mike Ireland, Sarah Ireland, Amanda lseminger, Joel Isom, James Ivers, Ashley Izzo, Andy Jackson, Graham Jackson, Mark Jackson, Mike Jackson, Scott Jackson and niece, Carley Jagel, Andy Jasinski, Mark Jeffries, Angela Jenkins, Cristin Jenkins, Troy Jewell, Eli and America Jimenez, Tammy Jimenez, Chris Johnson, Jessica Johnson, KJ Johnson, Kenneth Johnson, Rayanne Johnson, Trisha Johnson, Samantha and John and Brian Jonckheere, Brecken Jones, Laura Jones, The Jones Family, Tim Jones, Wendy Jones, Michael Jowett, Michelle June, Benjamin K., Julie K., Maha Kaissi, Michael Kania, Gary Kaplow, Jon Karlowa, Debbie Karnes, Ray Kastner, Constance Katsafanas, Kathy Katsafanas, William Katzer, Kristin Kaylor, Dan Kearns, Brent William Kee, Aaron and Evan Keller, Gayle Keller, Jennifer Keller, Robert Keller, Declan Kelly, Devin Kelly, Jim Kelly, Steven Kempa, Melanie Kemper, The Kemper

Family, Deb Kendall, Jasmine Kennedy, John Kessel, Brian Keys, Abhilasha Khetan, Daniel J. Kielsmeier, Heather Killough-Walden, Sam Kimport, Bonnie King, James King, Chris Kirchein, Rachel Kirk, Max Kirkpatrick, Maggie Kirkwood, Rochelle Klay, Aaron Klein, Cheryl Klein, Hilary Klein, Patty Klein, Patty and Patrick and Adam and Megan Klein, Paul and Michelle Klein, Mitchell Michini Klepac, **Jesse and Jordan Kline,** Jordan Kline, Sarah Kline, Steve Knapp, Kelsey and Jessica Knee, Benjamin Knobloch, John Koerber, Deb Koma, Gloria Konsler, Rich Kordalski, Shirley Kordalski, Jack Koss, Jack and John and Christine Koss, Wendy Kraemer, Amy Krauss, Monte Kremin, Tim Kress, Chris Kretzman, Austin Kruckmeyer, Troy Kubes, Ed Kulzer, Ali and Jennifer Kurtz, Matthew Kushner, Jackie Kushnier, Katie Kushnier, Brenden L., Nathan L., Mikey Laing, **Leah Lakatosh,** Brian Lake, Joshua Lake, Paul Lalli, Dyan Lally, Kim Lamb, Stephen Landkamer, Anne Langlotz, Brian Lanier, Ramsay Lanier, Meris Larkins, **Bev and Scott and Dick Larson,** Tim Larson, Richard Lathrop, Allison Laudage, Rebecca Lawler, Julie Lawrence, Daniel Lawson, Jeff Lawson, Lea Ann Lavy, Dr. E. Kye Layton, Melanie LeBlanc, Russell LeBlanc, Will LeBlanc, Jake Lehneis, Joshua Lehrer, Becca Leipzig, Meghan and Chris Lemmo, Justin Lemonds, Kathryn Leonard, Lisa Leonard, Jennifer Leone, AJ Leong, Brian Leong, Linda Lesar, Angie Leslie, Jessica Levenson, **Justin Lewicki,** Billy Lewis, Bradley Lewis, Luke Licygiewicz, Taricia Lightfoot, Kyle Lighting, The Lindberg Family, Beth Lindemann, Chuck Lionberger, Jeffrey Lipack, Jenn Lisack, Elaine Litten, Louise Lloyd, Sara Lodgen, C. Loesch, Bryan Long, Christie Long, Kristen Long, J. Scott Lopes, Jamie Lopez, **Marc and Josiah Lorenzo,** Emily Lounds, Matthew Lounds, **Jeff Love,** Stephen Lovelette, John Lovett, Kent and Pam Low, Ashley Lowe, Nick Lowman, Sam Loynes, The Luckner Family, Ash Lux, Jack Lynch, Jennifer Lynch, Jim Lyon, Will Lyon, Linda Mac, Sharon Machuga (and Mei Li),

Acknowledgements

Alexander Mack, Chris Macri, Michelle MacVane, Keri Madeira, Cholle Madere, Dusty Madere, Hope Madere, Karen Madere, Mason Madere, Shane Madere, Andy Madsen, Beci Mahnken, Rich and Vanessa Maigue, John Majcherek, Austin Malone, Michael Manall, Salvatore Manente, Katherine Manetta, Sharla Manglass, Brent Manley, Brett Manley, Adam Manno, Kristy Mantarro, Frank Marando, Lindsay Marcus, Jeff Margheim, Alisha Markle, Michael Marla, Connor and Jessica Marley, Vanessa Marquez, John and Stephanie Marshall, Drake Martin, Jeffrey Martin, John N. Martin, Jr., Breanne Martine, Brian Martsolf, Ginny Massoni, Jake Massoni, James Massoni, Brooke Matinides, Pam May, Rocky May, Aaron Mayer, Erin Maynard, Allison and Andy Mayo, Amy Mazzela, Greg Mazzella, Kelly McAdams, Isaiah McAllister, Aurora McBride, Kevin McCarey, Alexander McClintick, Griffin McCreary, The McCully Family, Mark McCurry, Chris McDaniel, Matthew and William McDaniel, Fawn and Holden McDonald, Mark McDonald, Chris McDonnell, Dawson McFarlin, Steve McGee, Meradith McGee-Hale (and Carter), Jessica McGilvary, Sarah McGovern, Saffron McGregor, Cameron McGuire, Rick McHugh, Billy and Zoe McInerney, Andrea McKenna, Carrie McLaren, Ryan – Rachel - Samantha and Robert McMillan, **Donna McMurrey,** Allissa McNair, Michala McNair, JerriAnne and Susan McPherson, Jill Meadows, Doug Means, Mark Medley, Joseph Mehr, **Matt Mellarkey,** Andrew Melville, Amy Mentz, Brian Mentz, Erin Merrill, **Jeremy Metz**, Tammy Metz, Sharon Meyer, Kim Michaux, **Bill and Kari Middeke,** Anthony Miele, H. Mildonian, Bill Miles, Toni-Lynn Miles, William Miles, Julie Millan, Alexis Miller, Geoff Miller, Herb Miller, Krista and Maeve Miller, Rich Miller, Todd and Jennifer and Sean Miller, Stephen and Brianna Millevoi, Patti Minden, David Mitchell, Jager Mitchell, Sandy Modesitt, Aruna Mohan, Perry Molinoff, Kelly Monaghan, Claire Monahan, Lou Mongello, Michele Moody, Jennifer Moon,

Joy Mooney, David Moore, Rick Moore, Sharon Moore, Ron Moorhouse, Marc Moran, Denise Morelli, Mickey Morgan, The Moriarty Family, Rick Morin, Patti Lei Morris, Joseph Moschinger, Phil Motto, Scott Mueller, The Muklewicz Family, Ed Muller, Christina Muller, Carla Mullin, Brodie Mumphrey, Baseer Muqri, Lori Murch, Christine Murphy, Marty Murray and son, Brenda N., L. Naizer, Lindsey Naizer, Kurt Nank, Hannah and Ed Naughton, Anthony and Kristin Neglia, Leslie Nelson, **Michael Nemeroff,** Brayson Nesbitt, Mandy Newby, Jeff Newcomb, Mary Newell, Amy Newfield, Victoria Newhuis, Benjamin and Aden Newman, Devon Newport, Debbie Newton, Kortnie Marie Nieves, Darrin Nilsson, Joe Nixon, Ashley Nolf, Dennis Nordling, Annette Nuenke, Cheryl Nutter, Andrew and Matthew Nypower, Denise O., Andrew O'Brien, Erin O'Brien, George O'Brien, Scott O'Donnell, Eileen Knight Ogle, Steve Okeefe, Jeff Oldham, David Oliver, Mitch Oliver, Giovanni Oliveras, Beth Olliges, Kim Olsen, Bob Ondercik, Bobby Ondercik, Rita Ondercik, Sheri Ondercik, Susie Ondercik, A. O'Neill, Sarah and Jaime and Jim Opaleski, Lisa O'Reilly, Nicole O'Reilly, Gwen Orilio, Justin Orilio, Rodrigo and Alejandro and Rogelio Orta, Katie Ortynsky, Greg Ostravich, Ryan Ott, Joy Ousterout, The Outra Family, Denise Owen, Annette Owens, Charles Owens, Jake Owens, Annie P., Curtis P., Dom P., Josh P., Kristin P., Melissa P., Glenn and Vickie Pacheco, Bill Padonisi, Andrew Painter, Doreen Pakidis, Brad and Brittany Paliswat, Jessica Paneral, Ryan Paolo, Benoit Paquin, Nancy Paris, Caleb Parry, Laura Pasquali, Tom Pasquali, Calley Pate, Bob and Maryellen Paton, Chad and Megan Paton Evans, Sam and Lucy and Kimberly Paton Vegter, Alex Patrick, Brian Patterson, Drew Patterson, Kyla and Jen Patton, Lori Payne, Denise Peczinka, Jonathan Peczinka, Tawny L. Peedin, Glenn Peeters, Natalie Pence, Liz Penland and daughter, **Maya Perez, Octavio Perez, Suzanne Perez,** Todd Perlmutter, Matt Perkins, Mitch Pernal,

Acknowledgements

Caleb Perry, Jenny Perry, John Perry III, John Perry IV, Christine Peruski, Mark Petar, Sheila Peter, Kristina Peterson, Lucy Peterson, Tony and Kara Peterson, Steve Petty, Patrick Phelan, Melanie and Tessa Pickett, Martin Pierce, Victoria Pike, Ray Pilgrim, Brooke Pimental, Linda Pinto, Sara Pirraglia, Tony Pirrelli, Susan Pitts, Linda Pizzuro, Amanda Plante, Cynthia Platt and family, Brian Policano, Krista Porter, Roberta Powers, Al Prete, Karen and Grace Price, Katherine Price, Kirby Price, Nathan Price, Walt Prindle, Hayden ProntoHussey, Caleb Pryor, Matt Pucci, Wendy Pugh-Hummel, Todd Pushman, Erica R., Tessa R., Tim Rachuba, Deb Ragno, Richard Rando, Nicholas Ranger, Kolding Rasmussen, Chris Rathsack, Brendan Ratner, Carol Ray, Sharon Reedy, Stacy Reedy, James Reen, Derrick Rees, Amber Reeves, Davis Reeves, Len Reeves, Lynne Reilly, Johnny and Jyle Reis, Michael Remy, Kathy Riccardi, Chris Ricci, Nik Ricci, Mikey Ricco, Richie Rich, Linda L. Richards, Bob Richmond, D. Richmond, Richard Rick, Chuck and Sharon Ridgely, Sarah Ridgway-Rees, Brian Rigsby, Ron Riley, Antonio Riquelme, Jose Riquelme, Rob and Kathy Risavy, Bryan Rivera, Shawn Robertson, Joy E. Robertson-Finley, Andy and Jay and Angel Robey, Joseph Robinson, Lauren Robinson, Lawrence Robinson, Lawrence Robson, S. Rodriguez, Lauren Roeser-Nordling, Geoff Rogos, Marie Rogowski, Terry Rohrer, Robyn Romine, Daniel Root, Nick Rosa, Clara Rosadas, Kimberly Rosati, Emily Rose, Jackie and Matt Roseboom, Nancy Rosenberg, Trent Routien, Teresa Rovery, Timothy Rowe, Mitch Rozetar, Robert Rubano, Kathy Rubin, Chris Rudolph, James Rudolph, Jim Rudolph, Annmarie Rumford, Shauna Rupert-Sessions, Ed Russell, Christine Russo, Steve Russo, Callie S., Heather S., Ken S., Steve S., Tom S. and Terri, Robin Sackevich, I and Y Sakurada, Andy Salerno, Ashley Saliba, Anthony Salzano, Peter Samilenko, Sheila Sanders, Tami Sanker, Christina Santoro, Hannah Savage, Rachel Savage, Andrew Savers, Dee Dee Scarborough, Jackie Scheibis, Natalee and Lauren Schell, The Scheuher Family, John Schiaparelli, Stephanie Schiavoni, Josh Schickler, Matt Schimkus, Ashlea Schneider, Julie Schneider, **Sherrie Schoening,** Marc Schreiber, Ashley Schultz, Hank Schultz, Steve Schultz, Spencer Schweinfurth, Paschal and Di Sciarra, Bethany and **Michael Scibetta**, Carol Scopa, Mike Scopa, Jeri Scott, Keira Scott, Liam and Michelle ScribnerMacLean, Todd Seales, Jack Seidenberg, Steve Seifert, Patti Sena, David and Aubree Serkoch, Debbi Sessa, Trent Sexton, Khrys Sganga, Chris Shank, The Shank Family (Angela, Christopher, and Shane), Leslie Sharkey, John Sheehan, Randy Shelton, William Shelton, Isabella Shenberger, Yinan Shentu, Kristen and Bridget Sheridan, Susan Shirey, Bob Shoemaker, Richard Shore, Faith and Abby Short, Bret Shortell, Andy Shull, Bill and Kim Shultz, Stephanie Shultz, Scott Siblovin, Josh Siegel, Scott Sigouin, Deb Silhan, Tyler Silhan, Rick Simard, Stephen Simmons, Steve Simmons, James Simon, KJ Simpson, **Jimmy Sisson,** Alexander Sjursaether, Tom Skaine, Bridget Skallet, **The Skazick Family from the UK, Nick Skiles,** Luke Skinner, Katie Slater, Mike Sluss, Michael Smart, Byon Smiddy, Laurie Smiley and grandsons, Bonnie Smith, David Smith, Elaine Smith, Neil Smith, Rebecca Smith, Shannon E. Smith, Sharon Smith, John Snider, Michele Snoddy, Wesley Snyder, Bret Sohl, Owen Sokoloff and son, Stan Solo, Jack Sorensen, Benjamin Soto, Roy Souders, Zach Souders, Douglas Southworth, Kitty Spangler, Megan Spellman, Ryan Spellman, Erica Spencer, Steve Spevak, Michele Sponagle, Kailah Spratt, Roberta Stafira, Morgan Stair, Megan Stallings, Todd Standley, Rich - Diane - Andrew and James Stangle, Chris Stank, Michael and Emily Steele, Kevin Stein, Joshua Steiner, Nicholas Steinhoff, Lindsey Stephens, Sharon Stevenson, Lori Stewart, Mark Sties, Skip and Susan and Jack Stinson, Lyndsey Stoehrer, Heather Stone, **Jay Stonefield,** Kate Stough, Ben Stowell, Branson Strawderman,

Acknowledgements

William Strobel, Allen Stroud, The Suarez Family, **Cherie Sulko**, Darlene Sulko, Jill Sullivan, Chris and Cathy Sutherland, David Sutton, Dan Swain, Riley Swanson, Jeff Swearingen, Jordan and Kenya Swiss, Joey Sylvester, Kathy Szczerba, Brittani T., Jen T., Jenni Tackett, Alex Taday, Sharon Tamplain, Joe Tanzillo, Kenzie Tapia, Jared Tavernari, Jordan Taylor, Karen Taylor, Leanne Taylor, Vance Taylor, Len Testa, Samantha and Mikayla Tewksbury, Alayna Theunissen, Brian Thomas, Kimmie Thomas, Roni Thomas-Patterson, Patsy Thomasson and family, Brian Thompson, Jake Thompson, James Thompson, Laura Thompson, Thomas M. Thompson, Pamela Thor, Emily and Kate Thorington, Albert Thweatt, Carter Thweatt, Max Thweatt, Erin Tickno, Paige Tiffany, Susie Tilley, **Martha Tischler,** Kristy and Scott and Jim and Kim Todd, Debra Tolsma and Alex, Holly Tomashek, Frank Tonra, Frank Tonra Jr., Frank Tonra III, Jaxon Tonra, Keith Tonra, Mallory Tonra, The Tonras, Kevin Toomey, Donald Torr, Whitney Townsend, Christina Tozzi, Lauren and Steven Tracy, Kendra Trahan, **Scott Trask,** Nathan Trent, Jessica Trentacosta, Marcel Troost, Jay B. Trudgen, Beverley Tuck, Brandon Tucker, Ashley Kennedy Turner, Glenn Turner, Matthew and Emma Turrisi, Derek Tyler, Charles Tyner, Thomas Tyner, Colin Ulbrich, Karen Ullman, Terry Ulrich, Luke Urso, Melissa Uzzilia, Nicole V., Stephen Valente, Sandra Valgardson, Shivani Varma, Adrian Vasquez, Helen Vaterlaws-Whiteside, MaxEmanuel Vingerhoets, Aninka van Staden, Frank van Wijk, Mason Vaughan, Chris Vaughn, **Wayne and Angie Vaughn,** Tairyn Velie, Tracy Vesel, Jim Vignola, The Vitrano Family, Jared Voegele, Fred Vosecky, Christpher and Alisha Vozella, Joshua W., Kym W., Deven Wagenhoffer, Maureen Wahtera, Caio Wakamatsu, Harry Walker, Jeanne Walker, Lucille Walker, Amanda Wallace, Michael Walsh, The Walsh Family, Grace Walter, Christine Wang, Matthew Wang, Jonathan Ward, Rachel Ward, Sharon Ward, Kathy Warner, Sean-Paul Warnick,

Michael Waters, Christopher Watson, Matthew Watson, Mary Weaver, The Weaver Family, Andy Webb, Austin Weber, Dena Weber, Eric Weber, Rebecca Webster, Scott Weideman, Sarah Weinberg, Fred Weiner, Joshua Weiss, Cheri Weitkamp, Max Weitkamp, The Welch Family, Brett Weldon, Carrie Welf, Matt Wells, Jed Werner, Robert Wescovich, Michelle Wesolowski, Dustine West, James West, John Weyrich, Matthew Whalen, Craig Wheeler, John Wheeler, Kate Whiddon, Shona Whiddon, Jennah and Noah Whitcomb, **Alena White,** Jared White, Jeff Whitlock, Katarina Whitmarsh, Sharon Whitney, Patricia Whitson, Dylan Whittemore, Jack Widman, Andrew Wierzbicki and sister, Victoria A. Wieting, Jim Wiggins, Becky Williams, Carla Williams, Chris Williams, Jason Williams, Kevin Williams, Scott Williams, Shannon Williams, Susan Williams, Darrel and Alexis Williamson, Ida Williamson, Garrett Willis, Johnson Willis, Deb Wills, Amory Wilson, Debbie Wilson, Jeannette Winner, Sara Witt, Darren Wittko, Brian Wojtowicz, Chrissy Wooding, Barb Wooldridge, Harry Wootan, Marli Worden, Elizabeth Worth, Brook Wozniak, Kassidy and Cody Wright, Allison Wyatt, Jeanine Yamanaka, Lynn Yaw, Trevor Yeatts, Kevin Yee, Alexander Young, Callum Young, Heather Young, Jonathon Young, Robert and Mary Jo Young, Andrew Yturaldi, Alexandra Z., Adam Zaner, Meghann Zanotta, Eric Zech, Christianna Ziccardi, Lea Zich, Kristine Zolciak, Julie Zanolla, Catherine Zori,

AND

Aaron, Aimee, AJ, Al, Alan, Alanna, Alex, Alexis, Alison, Allie, Allison, Alpha, Alyssa, Amanda, Amber, Amelaia, Amelia, Amy, Andy, Anime Hockey grrl, Ann, Anonymous, Anubis316, Areyna, Ariana, Ariel, Ashton, Austin, azc, Barbara, Becky, Benjamin, Beth, Bill, Blair, Bob, Brad, Brad & Courtney, Brandon, Brandy, Brian, Brianne, Brooke, Bryan, Bryan@allaboutthemouse.com, Cailin, Caitlin, Caitlyn, Captain Mike,

Acknowledgements

Carlos, Caroline, Carolyn, Casey, Cassie, Catherine, Cathreine, Caylie, Charlene, Charles, Charlie, Charlotte, Cheryl, Chloe, Christopher, Christy, Cindy, Claire, Claudia, Cole, Colin, Colin-Kevin-Connor-Jodi-Nana and Pops, Colleen, Corey and mother-in-law, Courtney, Crispynoodle, C.T., Danielle, Darren, Dave, David, Debbie, Denise, Devon, Disney R&N, dloncub, Donna, Ear to There Tours, Eli, Eloy, Emily, Emma, Eric, Erik, Evan, Fernando, Foxx, Gage, Gen, Georgette, Georgia, Gilbert, Giorgio, Giovanni, glaslady, Gracie, Graffix, Grant, Greg, Hanah, Hannah, Heidi, Hidden Kid, Hidden Mickster, Hoffman, Holden, Holly, lmercado, Jackie, jade kitty, Jake, Jake of Lake Mary, Jamie, Janelle, Jared, Jason, Jason (TrendyMagic), JB, Jean, Jeanette, JE. D, Jennah, Jennifer, Jeremy, Jessica, JG, Jim, Jodi and Nana and Pops, Joe, John, Jonathan, Jordan, Joseph, Josh, JP and son, Julie, Justin, Jyl, Kaela, Kasre, Katie, Kelly, Kel ma, Ken, Kent, Keri, Kerri, Kevin, Kimberly, Kimmie, Kira, Kitzzy, Klara, Kristin, Kristy, Kyle, Laura, Laura and Joe, Lauren, Laurie, Lea, Lea Ann, Lia, Liam, Lisa, Liz, Luis, Luke, Lyinel, Lynn, Madison, Makenzie, Marc, Maria, Marissa, Mary Ann and daughter, Mason, Matt, matt@attractionsmagazine.com, Matthew, Maureen, Max, Megan, Melanie, Melissa, Memoree, Mia, Michael, Michelle, Mike, MOEMOE55, Nao, Natalie, Nick, Nickole, Nicole, Noah, O'Malley, onthegoinmco, Patti, Peter, Quinten, Rachel, Rich, Rick, Rikki, rjf1423, Robert, Roman, Ronald, Rumbanana, Sam, Samantha, Samantha Ann, Sarah, Scott, Sean, Shannon, Sharon, Sharon from Auburn, Sheri, Shinozuka, Skiyalater, Snickers, Someone, Sonali, Stacey, Stacy, Stephanie, Susan, Tami, Taricia, Taylor, TheTimTracker, Thomas, Tim, Tony, Toontownkid4, Trevor, Tricia, Triffyboo, Trina, Tyler, Vicki, Vickie, Victoria, Wall-E, Wendy, Wendy and her Stepmom, Winnie, Zach, and Zachary

Index to Mickey's Hiding Places

This Index includes only those rides, restaurants, hotels, and other places and attractions that harbor confirmed Hidden Mickeys. So, if the attraction you're looking for isn't included, Mickey isn't hiding there. Or if he is, I haven't spotted him yet.

Page numbers refer to the Clues.

The following abbreviations appear in this Index:

AK - Disney's Animal Kingdom
DS - Disney Springs
E - Epcot
HS - Disney's Hollywood Studios
MK - Magic Kingdom
R - Resort venue
WP - Water Park

A

AbracadaBar (R) 229
Adventureland (MK)
 bridge to the Hub 38
Affection Section (AK) 183
Alien Swirling Saucers (HS) 131
All-Star Resorts. See Disney's All-Star Resorts
Animal Kingdom Lodge (R) 216
 Kidani Village 218
Animation Courtyard (HS) 137
Ariel's Grotto (MK) 31, 34, 44
Art of Animation Resort 221
Artist Point restaurant (R) 234
Astro Orbiter, near (MK) 41
Avatar Flight of Passage (AK) 172
Awesome Planet (E) 95

Index

B

Backlot Express, The (HS) 139
Barnstormer, The (MK) 43
BaseLine Tap House (HS) 140
Bay Lake Tower, outside (R) 241
Be Our Guest Restaurant (MK) 27
Beach Club Resort 230
   Beach Club Solarium 230
   Beach Club Villas 231
   Beaches & Cream Soda Shop 231
Beauty and the Beast-Live on Stage (HS) 136
Big Thunder Mountain Railroad (MK) 30
Big Top Souvenirs (MK) 43
Blizzard Beach (WP) 284
BoardWalk Resort 229
Boma restaurant (R) 217
Boneyard, The (AK) 185
Bonjour Village Gifts (MK) 44
Buzz Lightyear's Space Ranger Spin (MK) 28

C

Caffe Italiano cart (MK) 46
California Grill restaurant (R) 240
Canada (E) 93
Cape May Cafe (R) 230
Caribbean Beach Resort 224
Carousel of Progress, Walt Disney's (MK) 40
Casey Jr. Splash 'N' Soak Station (MK) 43
Castle Couture shop (MK) 38
Celebration, Florida; near to 293
Chef Art Smith's Homecomin' (DS) 286
Chef Mickey's Restaurant (R) 240
Chester & Hester's Dinosaur Treasures (AK) 185
China (E) 89
Chinese Theater (HS) 137
Cirque du Soleil (DS) 287
Club Cool (E) 98
Columbia Harbour House (MK) 34
Conservation Station (AK) 179
Contemporary Resort 240
   Bay Lake Tower, outside 241
   monorail area 240
Coronado Springs Resort 220
   Dig Site pool area 220
   Gran Destino Tower 221
Cover Story store (HS) 142
Cretaceous Trail (AK) 185

Crystal Arts store, outside (MK) 45
Crystal Palace, The (MK) 45

D

DINOSAUR (AK) 176
Discovery Trading Company shop (AK) 186
Disney Junior Play & Dance! (HS) 136
Disney Springs Marketplace (DS)
    entrance to 288
    near the lake 291
Disney's All-Star Resorts 219
    Movies 220
    Music 219
    Sports 219
Disney's Candy Cauldron (DS) 287
Disney's Days of Christmas store (DS) 288
Disney's Fairytale Wedding Pavilion (R) 238
Disney's Pin Traders store (DS) 290
DisneyStyle Store (DS) 288
Disney's Wonderful World of Memories (DS) 288
Dockside Diner (HS) 141
Dumbo the Flying Elephant (MK), near 43

E

Emporium store (MK) 45
    near 45
Enchanted Tales with Belle (MK) 41, 44
Entrance/exit areas
    Disney's Hollywood Studios 142
    Disney's Animal Kingdom 187
    Disney Springs Marketplace 288
    Magic Kingdom 24
Enzo's Hideaway (DS) 286
Epcot, near 292
Erin McKenna's Bakery NYC, near (DS) 286
ESPN Wide World of Sports 284
Expedition Everest (AK) 173

F

Fairytale Garden (MK) 42
Fantasia Gardens 292
Fantasmic! (HS) 142
Fantasyland Train Station, exit area (MK) 42
Ferryboats
    from MK to TTC 24
Festival of the Lion King (AK) 178

Index

50's Prime Time Cafe (HS) 138
Finding Nemo: The Big Blue... and Beyond! (AK) 178
Flame Tree Barbecue restaurant (AK) 186
Fort Wilderness Resort 232, 284
Fossil Fun Games area (AK) 186
France (E) 93
Frontier Trading Post (MK) 45
Frontierland Shootin' Arcade (MK) 33
Frozen Ever After (E) 85

G

Garden Grill Restaurant (E) 95
Gaston's Statue (MK) 44
Germany (E) 90
Ghirardelli Soda Fountain & Chocolate Shop (DS) 291
Golden Oak sign 284
Golf courses
   Magnolia 284
   Miniature - See Miniature golf courses
Goofy's Candy Co. (DS) 289
Gorilla Falls Exploration Trail (AK) 178
Gran Fiesta Tour Starring the Three Caballeros (E) 88
Grand Floridian Resort & Spa 238
   Convention Center entrance 240
Guardians of the Galaxy: Cosmic Rewind (E) 84
Guidemap, Disney's Hollywood Studios (HS) 142

H

Harambe Fruit Market (AK) 183
Haunted Mansion (MK) 33
Hollywood Boulevard area (HS) 141
   intersection with Sunset Boulevard (HS) 141
Hollywood Brown Derby, The (HS) 137
Hollywood & Vine restaurant (HS) 138
House of Blues Restaurant & Bar (DS) 287

I

lmageWorks (E) 98
Impressions de France (E) 93
Indiana Jones Epic Stunt Spectacular! (HS) 138
Interstate 4, near Celebration, Florida 293
Island Mercantile shop (AK) 186
Italy (E) 90
"it's a small world" (MK) 37
It's Tough to be a Bug! (AK) 176

J

Japan (E) 91
Jiko restaurant (R) 217
Journey Into Imagination with Figment (E) 97
Jungle Cruise (MK) 31

K

Kali River Rapids (AK) 176
Karamell-Küche shop (E) 90
Keystone Clothiers, behind (HS) 141
Katsura Grill (E) 89
Kilimanjaro Safaris (AK) 175

L

Le Cellier Steakhouse (E) 93
Legends of Hollywood store ((HS) 138
L'Esprit de la Provence shop (E) 93
Liberty Square Riverboat, at entrance (MK) 33
Liberty Tree Tavern (MK) 44
Living with the Land (E) 93

M

Magic Carpets of Aladdin (MK) near 38
Magic Kingdom Park, near 293
Magnolia Golf Course 284
Maharajah Jungle Trek (AK) 177
Main Street Confectionery (MK) 46
Main Street Train Station (MK) 24, 46
Main Street Trolley (MK) 46
Main Street, U.S.A. (MK) 45
Mama Melrose's Ristorante Italiano (HS) 140
Many Adventures of Winnie the Pooh (MK) 25
Map, Disney's Hollywood Studios (HS) 142
Mara restaurant, The (R) 217
Maria and Enzo's restaurant (DS) 286
Market Merchants, The (HS) 129
Marketplace Carousel (DS) 289
Martha's Vineyard (R) 230
Merchant of Venus shop (MK) 40
Mexico (E) 88
Mickey & Minnie's Runaway Railway (HS) 126, 137
Mickey's Meet 'N' Greet (MK) 41
Mickey's of Hollywood (HS) 142
Mickey's PhilharMagic (MK) 39
Millennium Falcon: Smugglers Run (HS) 129

Index

Miniature Golf Courses 291
    Fantasia Gardens 292
    Winter Summerland 292
Mission: SPACE (E) 86
Mitsukoshi store (E) 92
Monsters, Inc. Laugh Floor (MK) 41
Morimoto Asia restaurant (DS) 286
Morocco (E) 92
Muppet*Vision 3D (HS) 134

N

Na'vi River Journey (AK) 172
Norway (E) 89

O

Old Key West Resort 225
Once Upon a Toy (DS) 289
Outpost between China & Germany (E) 89

P

Pandora, walkways (AK) 173, 184
Pecos Bill Tall Tale Inn and Cafe (MK) 45
Pete's Silly Sideshow (MK) 43
Peter Pan's Flight (MK) 30
    near to 37
Pinocchio Village Haus (MK) 37
Pirates of the Caribbean (MK) 32
Pizzafari restaurant (AK) 184
Polynesian Village Resort 237
Pop Century Resort 222
Port Orleans Resort - French Quarter 226
Port Orleans Resort - Riverside 226
Princess Fairytale Hall (MK) 39

R

Rainforest Cafe (DS) 289
Rainforest Cafe entrance sign in park (AK) 187
Red Carpet Dreams, Meet Disney Stars (HS) 136
Remy's Ratatouille Adventure (E) 84
Restaurantosaurus (AK) 185
Riverside Depot shop (AK) 186
Riviera Resort 224
Rock 'n' Roller Coaster Starring Aerosmith (HS) 131
Rosie's All-American Cafe (HS) 138

S

San Angel Inn Restaurante (E) 88, 89
Sanaa restaurant (R) 218
Saratoga Springs Resort & Spa 227
Sassagoula River Cruise ferry (DS, R) 289
Sci-Fi Dine-In Theater Restaurant (HS) 139
Seven Dwarfs Mine Train (MK) 25
Shades of Green Resort 242
Sid Cahuenga's One-of-a-Kind (HS) 142
Sir Mickey's Store (MK) 38
Slinky Dog Dash (HS) 130
Soarin' Around the World (E) 85
Solar Panel Farm, near Epcot 292
Space Mountain (MK) 26
Spaceship Earth (E) 98
Splash Mountain (MK) 29
Splitsville Luxury Lanes (DS) 287
Stage 1 Company Store (HS) 140
Star Tours - The Adventures Continue (HS) 134
Star Wars Launch Bay and BB-8 (HS) 136
Starbucks (DS) 287
Storybook Circus area (MK) 42
Studios Guidemap (HS) 142
Sunset Boulevard (HS) 138, 141

T

Tamu Tamu Refreshments (AK) 183
"Tangled" Tower restroom area (MK) 37
Territory Lounge (R) 234
Test Track (E) 85
The American Adventure (E) 90
   show 91
Theater in the Wild (AK) 178
The Barnstormer (MK) 43
The Boneyard (AK) 185
The Crystal Palace (MK) 45
The Garden Grill Restaurant (E) 95
The Hollywood Brown Derby (HS) 137
The Land (E) 93-96
   entrance area 95
   sign for 96
The Market Merchants (HS) 129
The Seas with Nemo & Friends (E) 96
The Tree of Life (AK) 184, 186
The Trolley Car Cafe (HS) 141
Tomorrowland "Cool Scanner" Station (MK) 40
Tomorrowland Speedway (MK) 26

Index

Tomorrowland Trans Auth PeopleMover (MK) 39
Tom Sawyer Island (MK) 31
Tony's Town Square Restaurant (MK) 46
Tortuga Tavern (MK) 45
Tower of Terror, The Twilight Zone (HS) 133
Town Square Plaza (MK) 46
Town Square Theater (MK) 41
Toy Story Mania! (HS) 130
Trail's End Restaurant (R) 233
Trattoria al Forno restaurant (R) 229
Tree of Life, The (AK) 184, 186
Tren-D store (DS) 290
T-REX restaurant (DS) 291
TriceraTop Spin (AK) 185
Turtle Talk With Crush (E) 87
Tusker House Restaurant (AK) 183
Typhoon Lagoon (WP) 285
    en route to 285

U

Under the Sea~Jour of The Little Mermaid (MK) 34
United Kingdom (E) 93

V

Village Traders Shop (E) 89
Vista Boulevard (R) 284
Voyage of The Little Mermaid (HS) 135
    outside, above entrance 137

W

Walt Disney Presents (HS) 136
Walt Disney's Enchanted Tiki Room (MK) 38
Wandering Reindeer shop, The (E) 89
WDW Casting Center 291
WDW Railroad (MK)
    Fantasyland Train Station exit 42
Wedding Pavilion, Disney's Fairytale (R) 238
Whispering Canyon Cafe (R) 234
Wide World of Sports, ESPN 284
Wilderness Lodge 233
    Boulder Ridge Villas 235
Wildlife Express Train station (AK) 183
Winter Summerland 292
Woody's Lunch Box (HS) 137
World of Disney store (DS) 291

Y

Yacht Club Resort 231
Yachtsman Steakhouse (R) 231